The Business Marketing Course
Managing in Complex Networks

Second Edition

David Ford
Lars-Erik Gadde
Håkan Håkansson
Ivan Snehota

John Wiley & Sons, Ltd

Th   ourse

Other Wiley Editorial Offices

John Wiley & Sons Inc., 111 River Street, Hoboken, NJ 07030, USA

Jossey-Bass, 989 Market Street, San Francisco, CA 94103-1741, USA

Wiley-VCH Verlag GmbH, Boschstr. 12, D-69469 Weinheim, Germany

John Wiley & Sons Australia Ltd, 42 McDougall Street, Milton, Queensland 4064, Australia

John Wiley & Sons (Asia) Pte Ltd, 2 Clementi Loop #02-01, Jin Xing Distripark, Singapore 129809

John Wiley & Sons Canada Ltd, 6045 Freemont Blvd, Mississauga, ONT, Canada, L5R 4J3

Wiley also publishes its books in a variety of electronic formats. Some content that appears in
print may not be available in electronic books.

Library of Congress Cataloging-in-Publication Data

Ford, David, 1944-
The business marketing course : managing in complex networks/David Ford ... [et al.]. – 2nd ed.
    p. cm.
    ISBN-13: 978-0-470-03450-7
    ISBN-10: 0-470-03450-5
    1. Marketing.   2. Marketing–Management.   3. Business
    networks–Management.   I. Title.
   HF5415.F566 2006
   658 8–dc22   2006016571

British Library Cataloguing in Publication Data

A catalogue record for this book is available from the British Library

ISBN-13: 978-0-470-03450-7
ISBN-10: 0-470-03450-5

Typeset in 10/12 pt Goudy by Thomson Digital
Printed and bound in Great Britain by Bell & Bain, Glasgow
This book is printed on acid-free paper responsibly manufactured from sustainable forestry in
which at least two trees are planted for each one used for paper production.

The IMP (Industrial Marketing and Purchasing) Group was formed in 1976 by researchers from five European countries. The group's first work was a large-scale comparative study of industrial marketing and purchasing across Europe. Results from this study were published by John Wiley in 1982, edited by Håkan Håkansson, under the title *International Industrial Marketing and Purchasing: An Interaction Approach*. The group's "interaction approach" is based on the importance for both researchers and managers of understanding the interaction between active buyers and sellers in continuing business relationships. The group has since carried out a large number of studies into business relationships and the wider networks in which they operate. This work is published in numerous books and articles. A selection of this work can be seen in *Understanding Business Marketing and Purchasing* (3rd edition), edited by David Ford (International Thomson, 2001). The second edition of *Managing Business Relationships*, also by David Ford and a team of IMP authors, was published in 2003 by John Wiley & Sons, Ltd. This book encapsulates the teaching, research, consulting and writing experience of the IMP Group. The group hosts an international conference in September of each year which attracts a large number of researchers working in the areas of business marketing, purchasing and inter-company networks. The group publishes an on-line journal, *IMP Journal*. This together with other output from the group and its conferences can be found at impgroup.org.

The authors wish to dedicate this book to our good friend Peter Turnbull and to all members of the IMP Group.

CONTENTS

Notes on the Authors

David Ford is Professor of Marketing at the University of Bath UK.

Lars-Erik Gadde is Professor of Industrial Marketing at the Chalmers University of Technology, Gothenburg, Sweden.

Håkan Håkansson is Professor of Industrial Marketing at BI, the Nordic School of Management, Oslo, Norway.

Ivan Snehota is Professor of Marketing at the University of Lugano, Switzerland.

PREFACE TO THE SECOND EDITION

Welcome to the second edition of *The Business Marketing Course*. When we produced the first edition in 2002, we said that the book was intended to provide the basis for a course on business marketing for students on undergraduate or MBA courses. We also hoped that it will be useful for managers wishing to understand what happens in business markets and to improve their skills in analysis and strategy development. The book appears to have been quite successful and so we were pleased when the publishers asked for a second edition that would include "some changes and upgrades". We started with this intention, but we finished up by rewriting the whole book. This means that either our thinking has moved on somewhat in the last few years or that the first edition wasn't very good!

The book is still firmly based on the ideas of the IMP (Industrial Marketing and Purchasing) Group. We have also still tried to avoid producing a long, heavy, expensive "textbook" that students taking a relatively short option in business marketing would be unlikely to buy. Or if they did buy it, they would be unlikely to read it. Therefore, the book consists of just ten chapters that deal with what we believe are the critical issues that students need to understand. These chapters correspond approximately to the ten or twelve sessions of a typical elective course in Business Marketing.

Second, and more importantly, we have tried to write a book for students based on our view of the reality of business marketing. We believe that business marketing is not just something that a supplier does to its customers. It is something that happens between a supplier and each of its customers, as they search for and find each other, meet and negotiate, assess each other, make deals, develop offerings, deliver them, monitor their use, develop them further, and so on.

Both supplier and customer are actively involved in this interaction. Both of them have problems that they try to solve by dealing with each other. This interaction takes place in a relationship between the customer and supplier that may last for many years. Some of these relationships will be vital to either or both of the companies involved. Others will be just one of many hundreds or thousands that make up the company's portfolio. But whatever their size or importance, each of these customers has to be understood and each of these relationships has to be managed.

We believe that managing customer relationships is the critical task of the business marketer and this book concentrates on describing this task.

We have tried in this edition to help readers to understand the complex business networks in which business marketing and purchasing takes place. The first two chapters of the book try to explain what business networks are all about; how networks vary; and how business marketers can analyse them and find their position in them and use this analysis as a basis for marketing strategy.

In Chapter 3 we build on this network analysis to show how a business marketer can examine individual supplier–customer relationships and relationship portfolios. Chapter 4 examines the technological basis of business relationships and explains how marketers can make sense of the technological position of their customers and of their own company as a basis for their relationships with their customers. In Chapter 5 we look at business customers in more detail. We explore the problems they face, the choices open to them and the strategies that different customers are likely to adopt in their supplier relationships.

Armed with this understanding of technologies, networks and customers, Chapter 6 shows the reader how customer relationships can be managed. Chapter 7 explains how a business supplier solves its customers' problems through a complex offering consisting of a number of elements such as product, service, delivery and advice. We also examine the important issue of adaptations to the marketer's offering to cope with individual customer requirements. We then use these ideas of offerings and adaptations to investigate how business marketers can work effectively with others in their company to actually implement their offerings for customers. Chapter 9 provides a thorough coverage of the issues that business marketers face in taking pricing decisions. Finally, in Chapter 10 we bring together many of the ideas that we have developed in the book to examine the issue of overall business and marketing strategy.

We have also included an assignment at the end of each chapter that we would use in our classes for either discussion or assessed work. We hope that these assignments will be useful to instructors and interesting to students.

Four authors have been involved in producing this second edition. But of course, we are aware that no-one can ever really claim that their ideas are their own. We have worked together and with others in the IMP Group for many years and so we are sure that what little we do know about business marketing is largely held in common, rather than being ours alone. We are particularly grateful to those who worked with us on the first edition: Thomas Ritter, Pete Naude, Steve Brown and Pierre Berthon. We have used much of their thinking in this book. We are also very grateful for the research and ideas of many others, including our students, who have also contributed greatly to this book and to the continuing work of the IMP Group.

We have enjoyed writing this book. We all hope that readers will also gain as much from it as we have.

David Ford
University of Bath
March 2006

The Idea of Business Networks

Introduction

We are all consumers. We all experience how companies try to persuade us to shop in their stores, eat in their restaurants or buy their brands of chocolate bars, insurance policies or cars. We are familiar with the way that these companies package together a combination of product and service in the hope that they will meet our requirements. We spend time reading their brochures or looking in their shop windows. We compare prices and try to judge the relative value of offerings from different companies, before parting with our money. We see their advertising that is designed to excite our curiosity or make us identify with the people and the style of life that they portray. We are fascinated by the technological innovations of these companies. We comment to each other about their products and services and about their skills in bringing them to us. We are all "experts" in consumer marketing.

But each purchase that *we* make from a supplier is only possible because of a vast array of activities by many different *companies*. Unlike consumer marketing, these activities are likely to be invisible to us. But it is through them that products and services are designed, developed, produced, bought, sold, delivered and combined to make up the offerings that are finally marketed to us. This book is about those activities and in particular, about how marketing takes place *between* the companies that are involved. This is business marketing and it has many similarities with the consumer marketing that we experience every day:

- Both consumer and business marketing are parts of a single process that leads to a purchase by a final consumer.
- Both require marketers to understand the problems and motivations of their customers.
- Both require companies to develop and tailor their own skills and resources *and those of other suppliers* in order to satisfy their customers' requirements.
- Both involve companies trying to influence the behaviour of actual and potential customers.
- And finally, both consumer and business marketers are oriented towards making profit for themselves.

But we will see in this book that business marketing is also different from consumer marketing in a number of ways. These differences are because of the particular problems faced by business customers and their suppliers and because of the ways in which they try to solve those problems. Most students of marketing take up jobs in business marketing and so need to understand its special characteristics. Business marketing is more complex than consumer marketing in many ways and so it can be more challenging for those who work in it or study it. But an understanding of business marketing can also help students to a better appreciation of realities of market behaviour and marketing in general.

A Network Approach to Business Marketing

The main task of this chapter is to provide an overview of what is involved in business marketing. To provide this overview, we will take a *network approach*.

A network approach means that we won't start by looking at what happens *inside* a marketing company and examining *its* problems or the ways *it* should plan or how *it* should find customers to buy its offerings. Instead, we will start by looking *outside* the company at the surrounding *network* of other companies in which all businesses are enmeshed. It is within this network that a marketing company will find its customers, its competitors, its own suppliers and those companies with which it will have to cooperate. A business marketer has to understand the dynamics of this network if she is to develop successful strategy within it.

A business marketer needs to analyse the particular problems that face the different companies in the network. The marketer also needs to know what resources they have and what they are trying to do with their businesses. This analysis of the surrounding companies combined with an assessment of the marketing company's own resources (that we will deal with in Chapters 3 and 4) will enable the marketer to work out what are the opportunities and constraints within which he can build a strategy for his own company.

Some of the things that go wrong in business marketing

We can contrast a network approach with three other approaches that are common in business marketing, but which cause problems for the companies that take them, as follows:

- **The sales approach:** Many business companies look at the business world simply as a set of people that may be persuaded to buy their products. Many of these companies invest heavily in their sales efforts. But this approach is based on what the *marketer* wants. It can lead to a distorted view of the world of business that makes it difficult for the marketer to understand the *real problems* of the companies in the network, much less to address those problems.
- **The market approach:** This occurs when the marketer sees the business world as a homogeneous "market" or market segment that is made up of similar customers with identical requirements and which can be marketed to in a standardized way. This approach is derived from ideas of the "marketing mix" used in consumer marketing. The market approach involves building a market offering based on the "right" combination

of product characteristics, promotion, price and distribution to appeal to a market as a whole. But business customers don't all have the same problems and don't all want to address them in the same way. The market approach ignores the diversity and complexity of the business world and the importance and uniqueness of individual customers and their problems.

- **The single purchase approach:** This approach occurs when the marketer thinks that success in her job involves "winning" as many individual, discrete orders from different customers as possible. The single purchase approach is also quite common. It is based on attempts that have been made over many years to analyse and categorize what happens in a single sale or purchase. But as we will see, business customers don't just make a series of individual, unrelated purchases. Instead, they build up *relationships* with their suppliers as a way of solving their current and developing problems. The single purchase approach ignores this. It is based on a dangerous misunderstanding of how business customers and their suppliers interact with each other over time and how they each try to solve their particular problems.

Using a network approach in this book will also give us an idea of the scale and complexity of the world of business. It will help us to see that business marketing requires a clear understanding of the specific problems of individual companies in that network and that success can only be based on helping at least some of them to solve, or at least to cope with, some of those problems. Our analysis will also show us that business marketing is not just a set of easily learned techniques that can be applied in a mechanical fashion. Instead, we will see that business marketing is a long-term activity and that it involves working *with* our customers, but also *with* our suppliers and sometimes even *with* our competitors to solve their problems and ours. We will also see that business marketing involves sometimes working *against* some of these others, or working *through* them or *in spite* of them.

Understanding Business Networks

The idea of business networks is rather hard to encapsulate in a few sentences, so we will start the process of analysis by looking at the scale and complexity of networks, as follows.

The scale of business networks

The ultimate destination of all marketing activity is the final consumer: you and I. So, you and I are important parts of the network that brings goods and services to us. But according to the most recent US Commercial Census:

- Consumers in the USA bought around $10.4 trillion of goods and services in 2002. These purchases were made from over 1.1 million retail outlets and direct marketers. These are also in the network. These 1.1 million outlets bought the things that they sold to consumers from business marketing companies.

- 350,000 manufacturers also bought products and services from business marketers. They worked on these products and sold the resulting output to other manufacturers, distributors and retailers.
- There are also 710,000 construction companies in the USA that buy materials and equipment that they use to build houses and commercial buildings that they sell to consumers and business.
- 199,000 transportation companies in the US also buy materials and equipment from business marketers and use these to provide services to business and consumers.
- In total there are 5.7 million business customers in the US. These businesses made sales of over $22 trillion in 2002.

All of these businesses are in the network.

We can also get an idea of the scale of business activity in the network that is invisible to us as consumers, if we look at the rapidly growing area of e-commerce. In 2003, 94% of the total volume of e-commerce in the USA was carried out by *business marketers selling to business customers.*

All of the businesses we have referred to and all of the businesses in the world are *related* to each other either directly or indirectly. Even if they are not customers and suppliers to each other, they may share suppliers or customers or buy or sell things that are then bought and added to by others. If this is not the case, then at least the changes that take place in and between these other companies will affect them in some way at some time.

The business network is huge. It is clear that if we wish to make sense of what is happening around a particular business, we will have to *carefully* limit the area that we look at and that we say comprises *a* network.

Obviously there is no clearly defined line that we could draw round a network and what we include and what we look at will depend on what we are concerned with. For example, if we are concerned with issues to do with logistics around a new airport then we may include the following in our network: logistics service providers and their customers; freight and passenger airlines; warehousing companies; the airport operators etc. In contrast, if we are concerned with examining security issues at the same airport, we may still include some of these companies in the network that we examine. But we are also likely to include the police, the army and terrorist groups in the network we examine.

The complexity of business networks

The importance of restricting ourselves to the analysis of a *particular* business network is confirmed when we realize the scale, complexity and diversity of business customers, suppliers, institutions, influencers as well as the range of their problems and potential solutions. This complexity adds to our difficulty in making sense of a network. Some aspects of the complexity surrounding customers are listed in Figure 1.1 and discussed below.

Products and problems

We may be interested in the customers and suppliers for a particular product. But even if we can define the characteristics of the product, it is still not easy to say *what* it is that

NONE OF THE FOLLOWING ISSUES ABOUT BUSINESS
CUSTOMERS ARE FIXED AND EACH MAY BE DIFFICULT
TO DETERMINE BY A BUSINESS MARKETER:

- WHAT CUSTOMERS BUY
- WHO SAYS WHAT THEY SHOULD BUY
- WHY THEY BUY IT
- WHAT THEY BUY TOGETHER WITH IT
- HOW THEY BUY IT
- WHO BUYS IT
- WHO USES IT
- WHO PAYS FOR IT
- WHAT THEY DO WITH IT
- HOW MUCH THEY UNDERSTAND IT
- WHAT ELSE THEY COULD BUY INSTEAD
- WHO ELSE THEY COULD BUY FROM

Figure 1.1   The complex world of business customers.

a customer is buying. This is illustrated by one of the best-known sayings in marketing: "There is no market for drills, but there is a huge market for holes".[1]

Customers don't buy products or services; they buy what these things will do for them, or more accurately, they buy things in order to solve their particular problems.

Although there are problems that many companies have in common, the total number of problems is greater than the number of companies in the network. For example, almost all companies have problems that involve data and computation. As follows:

- A small business may have problems keeping its accounts up to date, but may also need to save the time of the people that run the business.
- In contrast, a chemical company may have the problem of how to handle a large increase in demand from its customers, without having to make major capital investment.

---

[1] This saying is from Peter Drucker (1990) The Emerging Theory of Manufacturing, *Harvard Business Review*, May–June, 94–102. "Why were 1 million quarter inch drills sold last year in the US? Was it because people needed quarter inch drills? No they needed quarter inch holes".

- An insurance company may have a problem in recruiting skilled staff to make sales to its customers.
- A developing country may have terrible problems with its education system.

The small business customer may think of buying a single personal computer to automate its office. It will also need software to operate the PC. If it is computer-literate, it may buy a package from a website or if not, it may seek the advice of a local computer store that will also deliver and commission the computer and train the staff.

The chemical company may also find a way of coping with its production problems that involves PCs. But it probably won't choose or "buy" them. Instead they will come as part of an integrated process control system sold to them by a systems integrator. In this case the choice of PCs will be made by the system provider that has designed the operating system.

The insurance company may seek to solve its problem by buying hundreds of PCs to operate a new sales management software system. This company will probably have its own IT system and may buy PCs directly from a manufacturer, or have them supplied by the company that supplies the software for its sales management system. Alternatively, it may decide that the problems of running a large in-house sales force are too great and the cost is too high. In this case, it may seek to solve its problem by disposing of its staff and subcontracting its sales activity to independent insurance agents. If this happens, it will be trying to solve its problems by *not* buying any PCs! But, instead, it may also negotiate a group deal with a PC supplier so that the independent insurance agents that it tries to recruit can buy PCs at a discount.

The developing country may wish to revolutionize its education system by providing every child with a PC. But it will only buy the PCs after taking advice from consultants and if they cost less than $100 each. No such PCs exist at the moment. But a number of companies and research institutes are working together trying to design a $100 computer that will be simple and perhaps "wind-up" rather than be battery-operated. If and when $100 computers can be produced and sold to the developing country, they may actually be paid for as part of an aid package from the country that designed them. They will probably be made in another developing country by a company owned by a multinational. If the new PCs are successful, they won't just be sold to developing countries, but will probably radically alter the number and the way that PCs are bought by others. The introduction of these PCs may also alter the way that many other electronic devices are made, priced, sold, bought and used.

If we are interested in what is happening in the purchase, sales and development of PCs then all the companies and influencers that we have mentioned will be in the network that we will need to examine. We will also see that it is not just the customers in the network that are diverse. So too are the suppliers. If we continue with our computing example, we see that many different types of supplier companies are in the network. These include companies that make PCs and market them direct to customers, and companies that design PCs, market them under their own brand, but have them made by others. There will also be people that supply advice and those that supply hardware and software that they buy from others. There will be some companies that develop software, either for general use or for specific applications. There will also be companies that integrate hardware and software from a variety of sources and design and install a package to cope with particular or complex customer problems. Some of the complexities of suppliers that we may find in a business network are illustrated in Figure 1.2 and in Box 1.1.

- MANY COMPETING SUPPLIERS ALSO COOPERATE WITH EACH OTHER TO DEVELOP AND DELIVER THEIR OFFERINGS *TOGETHER.*

- SOME MANUFACTURERS BUY PRODUCTS FROM AND SELL PRODUCTS TO THEIR "COMPETITORS".

- MANY "MANUFACTURERS" DON'T MAKE ANYTHING, BUT BUY EVERYTHING THEY SELL FROM OTHER SUPPLIERS.

- SOME OF THESE COMPANIES DESIGN THEIR PRODUCTS; SOME BUY THE DESIGN FROM OTHERS. MANY MANUFACTURERS HAVE NO DESIGN SKILLS AND MAKE TO THE DESIGN OF THEIR CUSTOMERS.

- SOME COMPANIES SUPPLY THE DESIGN FOR PRODUCTS TO THEIR CUSTOMERS. THESE CUSTOMERS THEN MAKE PRODUCTS TO THAT DESIGN AND SELL TO THEIR OWN CUSTOMERS.

- MANY RETAILERS DESIGN THE PRODUCTS THEY SELL, SPECIFY HOW THEY SHOULD BE MADE AND THE WORKING CONDITIONS OF THE STAFF IN THEIR SUPPLIERS.

- MANY MANUFACTURERS WILL SUPPLY DIRECTLY TO END CONSUMERS, AS WELL AS SELLING TO WHOLESALERS OR RETAILERS.

- MANY RETAILERS SELL PRODUCTS UNDER THEIR OWN BRAND-NAME AND DESIGN AND ARRANGE PRODUCTION. THEY ARE "MANUFACTURERS WITHOUT FACTORIES".

- MANY COMPANIES ACT AS AGENTS FOR MAJOR CUSTOMERS AND FIND, SELECT AND MANAGE SUPPLIES FOR THEM FROM MANUFACTURERS.

- SOME COMPANIES DO NOT SELL PRODUCTS TO CUSTOMERS, BUT INSTEAD PROVIDE SERVICES BASED ON THOSE PRODUCTS.

- SOME CUSTOMERS BECOME COMPETITORS OF THEIR SUPPLIERS BY SELLING PRODUCTS THAT THEY HAVE BOUGHT FROM THEM TO OTHER CUSTOMERS.

Figure 1.2 The complex world of the business marketer.

> ### Box 1.1   Interdependencies in Complex Networks
>
> Octel Network Services is a firm in Dallas that operates more than one million electronic voice "mailboxes". One of its major clients is EDS. EDS, in turn, has a $3.2 billion contract to run the computer and telecoms networks of Xerox. This deal involves 1,700 employees of Xerox transferring to EDS. Xerox itself provides invoicing and billing services for Motorola, which in turn designs and makes parts of Octel's voice-messaging systems and thus the circle is completed![2]
>
> In March 2000 lightning struck a computer-chip making factory in New Mexico, USA, owned by the Dutch firm, Philips. It started a small fire that only lasted about 10 minutes. But it caused havoc in the super-clean environment required for chip making. The Swedish mobile-phone company Ericsson was a customer of that factory and was unable to find an alternative source of supply. Ericsson went on to report a loss of over $2 billion in its mobile phone business that year. This loss left it as an also-ran in a business in which it had once been a leader.[3]

These illustrations of the complexity of networks provide an insight into their nature. A business network consists of many companies, each with their own problems and resources that are somehow linked together in order to solve those problems and to exploit those resources.

If we want to understand business and business marketing we cannot confine ourselves to our obvious customers, or our obvious competitors. Change, opportunities and threats can and will arise from throughout the network and marketers are likely to be the only people in a business company that are able to examine and understand these.

A Small Numbers Game

We started to talk about a business network by thinking of over 5 million companies in one country. But of course most of these 5 million companies will buy goods and services made or sold in other countries and many of them will probably sell to other countries themselves. This seems to stretch the network further and further. But despite the scale and complexity of the business world, business (and consumer) marketing is often a small numbers game. For example, if you listen to discussions between managers involved in marketing personal care products, such as hair colourants etc, it becomes clear that they are preoccupied with a very small number of extremely important customers, who happen to be retailers. Unless the consumer marketers' products are well displayed

---

[2] S Brown, R Lamming, J Bessant and P Jones (2000) *Strategic Operations Management*, Oxford, Butterworth-Heinemann.

[3] *Economist*, October 29 2005, p 83.

on the shelves of these few large retail chains, the marketing company cannot achieve sales, irrespective of the features of their products or their skills in advertising or promotion. In this way, consumer marketing is very similar to business marketing. A business marketer may have thousands or maybe hundreds of actual or potential customers, but perhaps only a very few that really matter in terms of their sales potential or their impact on other customers. An illustration of the importance of major retailers is given in Box 1.2.

Box 1.2   The Importance of Major Customers: Carphone Warehouse and the Pink Razr

The Motorola Razr mobile phone was available in black and silver colour. In September 2005, a manager at Carphone Warehouse, an important phone retailer noticed that there was a huge *male* bias in sales of this phone. So he asked Motorola to make 250,000 *pink* Razrs exclusively for Carphone Warehouse. The order was worth £40 million and this was followed by another large order. Over 600,000 pink phones were sold by this one retailer across Europe by the end of January 2006.

Each company in a network will have many suppliers. But again if we look closely at these we will see that only a few of them are really of major importance. Globalization has not simply led to a multiplication of suppliers and customers. Mergers, acquisitions, strategic retreats and bankruptcies have led to high concentration in many product areas. For example, over half of the world's food containers are produced by Owens-Illinois, 90% of the world's demand for some key electronics components is supplied by Intel. Lynn has pointed to the dangers of the overdependence on few suppliers and few locations that exists in many business networks today.[4] For example, one casualty of a pandemic would be the system that supplies the US with medical respiratory masks!

Thus, an important and seemingly inescapable characteristic of business networks and of marketing within them is that companies are often strongly *interdependent* on each other as customer or supplier. When a customer finds a supplier that either can or is prepared to invest time and effort to solve one of its major problems it is likely to stay with that supplier and invest its own time and money in making their *relationship* work effectively. Similarly, when a supplier finds a customer that is an actual or potential source of revenue, profit, or new technology then it is likely to invest in that relationship. Business relationships and the interdependencies on which they are based are the key ingredients of a network. Throughout this book we will be examining these relationships that are often complex and long-term.

---

[4] Barry Lynn (2005) *End of the Line: The Rise and Coming Fall of the Global Corporation*, New York, Doubleday.

We will see that the core task of business marketing (and purchasing) is the finding, developing and managing of these critical business relationships within the complex network that surrounds them.

Dynamic Networks

Business networks are not stable. They are constantly evolving as technology develops, as old problems are solved and new ones emerge and as those companies find new ways to deal with them with new counterparts (see Figure 1.3). We can isolate some of the major dynamics within business networks under three main headings: dynamics of companies; dynamics of relationships; dynamics of networks:

Dynamics of companies

Many of the changes in business marketing stem from the dynamics of companies themselves. It is no exaggeration to say that the nature of the business enterprise is changing. The business world is moving away from large integrated companies that carry out many or most of the activities needed to bring offerings to end-customers. This move occurs because companies are unable to sustain the level of investment necessary to be up-to-date in all of the skills, technologies and activities that are necessary to produce and deliver

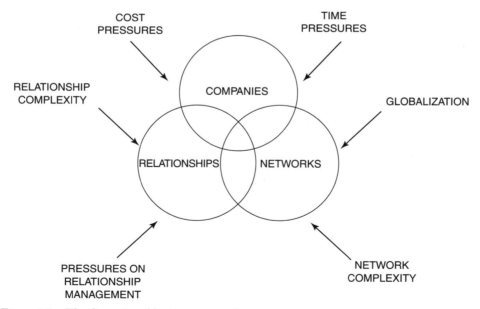

Figure 1.3 The dynamics of business networks.

offerings to their customers. Instead, we increasingly see that companies concentrate their investment and their activities on only a few activities which they believe to be core or in which they can excel. They then rely on suppliers to provide more of the products and services for them that are needed to complete their offerings. At the same time we see the emergence of new companies that operate within this model and which achieve growth and flexibility with only very limited investment by exploiting the specialized skills of others.[5] These changes mean that business marketers are now required to provide much more comprehensive offerings. These offerings often involve suppliers in taking over important elements of the business of their customers.[6]

Companies face increased competition from many new sources. This has meant that companies are extremely concerned to lower both the purchase price that they pay for an offering and the total lifetime costs of using the offering. They are also keen to reduce the staff costs of their purchasing departments and the wider costs of their operations. This leads them to reduce the total number of their suppliers and to require some suppliers to take on the role of managing others (we will look at how Toyota has tried to achieve this in Chapter 2). The pressure from their customers to lower prices forces suppliers to lower their own costs and this then affects other suppliers throughout the network. It may also prompt some suppliers to take on activities previously carried out by others and this increases the pressures on them. Cost pressures may also lead some customers to sacrifice the benefits they have gained through long-term relationships with some suppliers and switch to others to obtain some short-term price reductions.

The speed of technological change means that companies have less time in which to develop new products, introduce them to customers and gain a return on their investment before those products become obsolete and unsaleable. Some electronics companies speak about "six-month markets" whilst those in the fashion business have to operate on a six-week cycle. Sometimes companies try to solve this problem by working closely with a small number of suppliers. Other times, companies abandon previously important relationships and search widely for a quicker, perhaps cheaper, but perhaps less optimal, standard solution to many of their problems.

The dynamics of relationships

Business relationships have generally become more complex. This is because the technological intensity of offerings and the high cost of technological development mean that companies have to concentrate on fewer of the technologies which they need to produce their own offerings. They are then dependent on suppliers to do more for them and their expectations of suppliers have increased. For example, it is common for suppliers

---

[5] For example, Keen footwear has grown from start-up to a sales volume of $300 million in three years. Keen uses independent freelance designers and has all its shoes produced in China. Keen employs around 40 people. See Chapter 2.

[6] For example, the Australian airline Qantas is currently considering contracting out the entire maintenance function for its aircraft.

to provide a package of product and service. They may also guarantee the extent to which that offering can be used and the cost savings it will achieve, and agree to buy the offering back at a fixed price at the end of its life. Frequently, customers require their suppliers to carry the risks involved in developing an offering, so that the supplier can only recoup this investment if the customer's own offering is successful. The increasing technological intensity of offerings also means that suppliers are dependent on their customers to cooperate in the development of their offerings and more people from different functional areas are likely to be involved in the relationship. A most extreme example of this in one of our studies was a relationship in which 600 people in the customer were in regular, significant contact with 200 people in the supplier.[7] Relationships have also become more complex because information technology can now integrate the operations of supplier and customer more closely and reduce their *combined* cost base. Examples include inter-company CAD/CAM systems; inter-organizational information systems, inter-company Enterprise Resource Planning Systems etc.

The increased complexity of business relationships adds to the problems of the business marketer and his customer in coordinating all of the interactions between them. For example, the purchasing manager at a large mechanical engineering company admitted that he had been in his job for a whole year before he found out that two large meetings were held annually at which the technicians from his own firm met with those from a supplier and discussed technical issues. They had not seen any reason to tell the purchasing manager about the meetings as they thought that, "no commercial issues were discussed"![8] Relationship complexity also means that the traditional role of the business salesperson is being reduced in many cases. This is because there are now far more ways for customers and suppliers to communicate with each other. But it is also because many salespeople have neither the technological knowledge nor the organizational power to undertake a major role in some relationships. It is far more likely to be other, more highly technically skilled staff that negotiate the details of an offering and how it needs to be adapted to a customer's requirements. Sales and even marketing people are reduced to a service function in many companies, where they smooth any ruffled feathers and keep a relationship on track, rather than being responsible for frontline selling or relationship management.

Many business customers are also aware of the issues of relationship management and network issues and have devoted considerable efforts to developing their own processes of supplier and relationship assessment.[9] This places increasing pressure on business marketers to develop their own strategies if they are not to become passive players in the portfolio management processes of their customers.

Finally, business marketers increasingly have to manage relationships with a number of different companies who are involved in a project for a particular customer. For example,

[7]Håkan Håkansson and Lars-Erik Gadde (1992) *Professional Purchasing*, London, Routledge.

[8]Håkan Håkansson and Lars-Erik Gadde (1992) *Professional Purchasing*, London, Routledge.

[9]R Lamming, P Cousins and D Notman (1996) Beyond Vendor Assessment: Relationship Assessment Programs, *European Journal of Purchasing and Supply Management*, vol 2, no 4, 173–181. P Cousins (2000) Supply Base Rationalisation: Myth or Reality, *European Journal of Purchasing and Supply Management*, vol 3, no 4, 199–207.

the sale of a traffic congestion charging scheme for a city would involve liaison between: the producers of the smart cards for drivers to use; the producers of the chips that hold data on the cards; the software company that programmes the chips; the maker of the road-side card-readers; the providers of the customer billing services; the overall system operator, and the city itself, as final customer.

Dynamics of networks

Although the idea of business networks as a way of understanding business marketing is relatively recent, major changes are occurring in networks themselves which affect business marketing. Two of the most significant are as follows.

Globalisation: The globalisation of networks means that business marketers are now subject to competitive pressures from a much wider range of companies, each of which has rapid access to similar technologies. It also means that the development and implementation of offerings can now take place on a global basis using facilities in many different countries. For example, GE Capital Services opened India's first international call centre in the mid 1990s. It now employs more than 5,000 people there on jobs ranging from collecting money from delinquent credit-card users to data-mining. Similarly, it has been estimated that a typical Western bank could outsource 17–24% of its cost base to India, reducing its cost to income ratio by 6–9% and in many cases doubling its profits.[10]

Secondly, all of these changes in companies, relationships and networks that we have discussed are possible because companies have access to much greater information on the world around them. This information and the changes to which it leads can mean that companies are simultaneously drawn closer together and at the same time have both a requirement and the opportunity to look outside their existing relationships. Both phenomena are occurring simultaneously and increase complexity, leading to change and instability in companies, relationships and networks.

Conclusions

This introductory chapter has emphasized the complexity of the world in which business marketers must operate. Our emphasis on this complexity at the beginning of this book is deliberate: business marketers must strive to understand the complexity of the network that surrounds them and work within it, rather than adopt a more deceptively simple approach. We have outlined three of these simpler and more traditional approaches to business marketing: the Sales Approach, the Market Approach and the Single Purchase Approach and pointed to some of the problems that these may cause the marketer. In succeeding chapters we will build on the Network Approach and discover some of the ways to analyse business networks and then move towards ways in which companies can operate effectively within them.

[10] *Economist*, May 5, 2001.

Further Reading

Håkan Håkansson, Debbie Harrison and Alexandre Waluszewski, eds (2004) *Rethinking Marketing*, Chichester, John Wiley & Sons, Ltd.

IM Kirzner (1996) *The Meaning of the Market Process*, London, Routledge.

WW Powell (1990) Neither Market nor Hierarchy, *Research in Organisational Behavior*, vol 12, 295–336.

JD Lewis (1995) *The Connected Corporation: How Leading Companies Win through Customer–Supplier Relationships*. New York, Free Press.

B Uzzi (1997) Social Structure and Competition in Inter-Firm Networks: The Paradox of Embeddedness, *Administrative Science Quarterly*, vol 42, no 1, 35–67.

Assignment for Chapter 1: The Wallace Company

The Wallace Company's business consists almost entirely of design, manufacture and sale of specialized equipment that is used by other companies to produce plastic products.

The Wallace Company has approximately 65 customers. No single customer accounts for more than 15% of sales, but the 10 largest customers account for about 75% of total sales volume. Direct export business amounts to about 2.5% of total sales.

The company maintains a research and development department designed to meet the specialized needs of the plastics industry in the development and improvement of plastics equipment. Because of the close integration of Wallace's products and customers, the Sales Manager and one Salesperson handle all sales through personal contact.

The company has never done any advertising because it is the opinion of the Chairman that "advertising is unnecessary" as the company manufactures to order and within the specifications of customers in a highly specialized field. He believes that it is more advisable to invest in additional research and development any amount which might otherwise be set aside for advertising. At a meeting of his Directors he stated:

> The total number of potential customers we have does not exceed 200. We are already selling to 65 of these, and I believe that if we can improve some aspects of our equipment, we shall be able to get our machinery into at least another 30 plants. As a result, I see no reasons for changing the present sales policy. The success of Wallace depends upon whether or not the research and development departments can keep ahead of our competitors.

The Sales Manager, however, believes that the company should begin an advertising programme. His reasoning is based on an analysis of his own and the Salesperson's time. This analysis showed:

- 35% of their time was spent with customers and prospects.
- 58% of their time was devoted to travelling and awaiting interviews.
- 12% of their time was taken up with reports, office work and the like.

Deducting Saturdays, Sundays, Holidays and a three-week vacation period, there were 214 working days per year. On the basis of an eight-hour day, the Salesperson had 1,712 hours of working time per year. With 200 accounts on which to call, they were able to devote an average of only 4.5 hours with each company, twice a year. The Sales Manager also indicated that there was an average of four persons in each company who had to be contacted.

As a result, he felt that he was not making the most effective use of his productive ability because he was devoting too much of his time to the dozen-and-one chores which could be more economically performed by advertising. In order to emphasize the importance of this, he broke down the sales function into six basic steps:

1. Making contact
2. Arousing interest
3. Stimulating preference
4. Making a specific proposal
5. Closing the order
6. Keeping the customer sold

He then analysed each step as follows:

1. Making contact. Salespersons can make a few contacts each day; advertising can make thousands of contacts each day.
2. Arousing interest. Salespersons can arouse interest in a few prospects each day. Advertising can interest all our potential prospects.
3. Stimulating preference. Salesmen can create preference in one place at one time. Advertising can be everywhere at once creating preference.
4. Making a specific proposal and
5. Closing the order. These are the steps that, in our business, the Salesperson, and he alone, can do best.
6. Keeping the customer sold. This can be done more effectively by advertising, because key men in industry change jobs, titles and location at the rate of 50% per year, in normal times.

Using advertising to do steps 1, 2, 3 and 6 will free the Salesperson's time from these jobs, enabling him to concentrate on steps 4 and 5. In this way, a Salesperson can do a more effective job of performing the two steps for which he is best equipped.

Questions

Examine the business situation facing Wallace. How typical is it?

What problems could you suggest that would make a potential customer approach Wallace?

Discuss the two points of view stated in the case. Advise the Chairman on the ways in which you think he should allocate his resources between R&D, Advertising, etc.

ANALYSING BUSINESS NETWORKS

2

Aims of this Chapter

- To explain the variations in different types of business networks.
- To present a framework for analysing networks.
- To explain the substance of individual business relationships and to show how these are related to each other in a wider network structure.

Introduction

Chapter 1 introduced the idea of a network approach to business marketing and highlighted some of the characteristics of business networks as well as their dynamics. In this chapter we will introduce ways for the business marketer to analyse business networks and examine where and how individual relationships fit within the network.[1]

In the previous chapter we explained that a business marketer is likely to have far fewer customers than a consumer marketer. Some customers may be relatively unimportant to the marketer, but others may be responsible for a large share of her total business and be vital to the success of her company. We also explained that the transactions between a business supplier and its customers are not isolated events that are unrelated to each other. Instead, each of these transactions takes place in a relationship and each is related to the previous experience of the companies and to what they plan for the future. Rather than meeting as strangers, the companies tend to know each other quite well and may adapt different aspects of their offerings and operations to suit each other's requirements.

[1] A comprehensive review of ideas on business networks is provided in Geoff Easton (1992) Industrial Networks: A Review, in Bjorn Axelsson and Geoff Easton, *Industrial Networks: A New View of Reality*, London, Routledge, pp 3–27.

In Chapter 1 we emphasized that finding, developing and managing relationships with customers is at the core of business marketing. A business marketing company will also have relationships with its own suppliers. These suppliers are critical as what they supply is likely to be an important constituent of the offering that the marketer has to sell to its customers. Each of the company's suppliers will also have relationships with their suppliers and with their other customers. Each of its customers will have relationships with other suppliers and with their own customers. All these relationships are affected by the others and are intertwined in a network. This network is the arena in which the business marketer must operate. The relationships in the network enable the company to grow and develop, but they are also a constraint on that development and may restrict its activities.

We start the chapter by examining three networks to illustrate some of the issues that are involved in their analysis. Following from this we build a set of tools for network analysis. The chapter is based on the idea that if we want to understand the situation of a business marketing company and its opportunities then we have to examine how it is related to other companies. Rather than being a free agent able to develop and implement their strategy alone, each is dependent on others in order to act and each has to react to or accommodate the aims and strategies of others. In other words, the basic assumption of network thinking is that, "no business is an island".[2]

The growing technological intensity of companies' offerings and the rising costs of technological development have led companies to specialize in fewer of the skills needed to satisfy the requirements of their end-customers. This has increased the *interdependencies* between component producers, assemblers, distributors, service and logistics suppliers, and others. At the same time, problems in managing relationships and the interconnections between them have led to a greater interest in networks by business people.

A Range of Networks

We have already made it clear that the network that we will want to analyse will be determined by the particular issues that we are concerned with. Three of the most distinctive examples of this particularity are when we are concerned with: how companies are supplied with the offerings that they require; how offerings are distributed; and how new offerings are developed. We will examine these three different examples of networks in turn, as follows.

Supplier networks

Figure 2.1 illustrates what a network might look like if we needed to examine how a major customer was supplied. This particular network is viewed from the perspective of Toyota.

[2] Håkan Håkansson and Ivan Snehota (1990) No Business is an Island: The Network Concept of Business Strategy, *Scandinavian Journal of Management*, vol 14, no 3, 177–200.

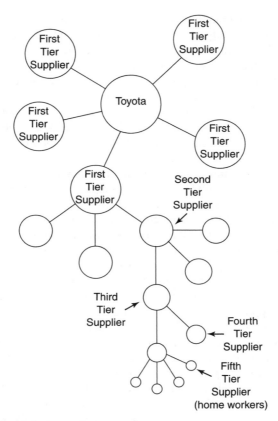

Figure 2.1 Toyota's supply network.

Source: Reprinted from D Blenkhorn and AH Noori (1999) What it Takes to Supply Japanese OEMs, *Industrial Marketing Management*, vol 19, no 1. Copyright 1999 with permission from Elsevier.

The network evolved over a long period of time, largely because Toyota would not be able to work with all of the 50,000 suppliers that it needs to contribute to its own offerings. So instead, Toyota chose to work closely with a small number of "system-suppliers", which were willing and able to take on this role. Each of these system-suppliers is responsible for both the design and the production of a certain part of the final car. In turn, each system-supplier has a restricted number of suppliers, in the second tier that deliver parts of the system to it. In the third tier are suppliers that deliver standardized, non-adapted components to lower-level suppliers and to other companies elsewhere in the wider network (not shown here). The example illustrates several significant features of networks:

- **Indirect relationships:** These allow a customer in a network to be systematically related to a large number of suppliers, in this case over 50,000, even though it only has direct contacts with a small number of them. Because its suppliers are all working in the same way, the network branches out to allow a customer access to a wide range of suppliers both geographically and technologically. It can achieve this with just a few well-developed relationships. However, the existence of a structure of relationships is not enough. Toyota has to be sure that even the relationships in which it is not directly involved are working effectively. This has taken Toyota several decades to achieve.

- **Coordination between relationships:** For the network to work well from the perspective of the large customer, the development of that customer's relationships with its immediate suppliers must be coordinated with those suppliers' own relationships with others. It is only when the relationships all work well together that they will create substantial value for the customer.

- **Influence of large companies:** The example demonstrates that a large company can have a very significant role in the overall development of a network. A large company can combine different relationships with each other in a productive way, provided that it is prepared to understand the perspectives of others in the network, to invest in relationship development and take a long-term strategic viewpoint.

- **Problems with a single perspective:** Despite the influence that a large company can have on a network, it is important to stress that a network drawn from the perspective of a single company can never capture the total situation. The network in Figure 2.1 is described from Toyota's point of view. If we described the network from the perspective of a system supplier, it would have been quite different and would have included different customers and suppliers. The picture of a network changes depending on our starting point and there are as many networks as there are starting points. Even more importantly, the network isn't owned and can never be completely controlled by one company. It only exists at a particular point in time because all of the companies accept their position and their relationships. But each will have problems and the network will constantly change as each tries to deal with these problems. Finally, it is common for customers to try to manage the interdependencies in a network by considering them as part of their own linear "supply-chain". But the idea of having its own supply-chain is likely to restrict a company's view of the reality of the network surrounding it. More importantly, the idea of its own supply-chain may allow a company to fall into the dangerous trap of imagining that the company's relationships only exist for its own benefit!

Distribution networks

Figure 2.2 illustrates the way that a network would look if we were interested in distribution issues for a particular company. The figure describes the distribution of computers from the perspective of a large supplying company: IBM. The figure shows the different ways that computers can reach IBM's customers in Italy. This network shows a number of different features, when compared with the one that was drawn to analyse supply issues:

- **Variety of companies:** Figure 2.2 shows a variety of different types of companies that appear to be performing more or less the same activity – selling computers to customers. The companies vary in their size, technical capabilities and competencies. They also vary in the ways that they relate to IBM and their other suppliers and

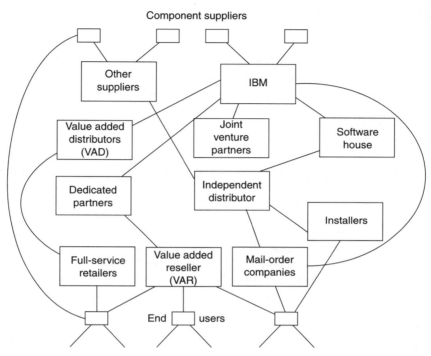

Component suppliers

Figure 2.2   IBM's distribution network.

Source: D Ford (ed) (2001) *Understanding Business Markets and Purchasing*, London, Thomson Learning.

in the ways that they service their own customers. These companies have evolved to provide different solutions to a variety of customer problems. All these problems centre on computing, but they require offerings consisting of different combinations of product, service, delivery and advice and that are sold at different prices. IBM would be unable to provide this range of different offerings to a large number of end-customers. But the variety of companies in the network enables IBM and other suppliers to have their own offerings combined with the distributors' different skills to produce a wide range of problem solutions for end-users. But having to deal with such a variety of companies also causes difficulties for a supplier such as IBM: it will have to select the ones it wishes to work more or less closely with and provide each of them with a variety of offerings to suit their particular problems and requirements.

• **Variety of relationships:** Not only will the supplier in this network have to provide a range of offerings, but it will also have to manage a range of different relationships with its distributors. This variety of relationships is needed because the distributors are different themselves, because they require different things from their suppliers and have different relationships with their customers.

- **Difficulties of control:** This network shows how difficult it is even for a very large company to determine who takes part in a network and how they should relate to each other. This may appear to contradict one of the conclusions about the first network that we discussed. But although a single company has some discretion in a network, it certainly is not the only one trying to influence its development. The evolution of a network is the outcome of all of these efforts, rather than the dictates of any one company.

Product development network

The network in Figure 2.3 was drawn by an MBA student who was investigating product development for a mobile-phone service-provider. The network shows a number of different features when compared with the two previous networks:

- **Range of companies:** This network appears to be bigger and more complex than those we drew in the previous diagrams. This is only because the analyst has chosen to look much wider than when examining the *apparently* narrower issues of distribution or product supply. The diagram shows that in order to understand product/service development it is necessary to examine the requirements, resources and intentions of many different types of organization.
- **Complex offerings:** The corporate or personal customer for mobile telephony does not buy a simple product or service. Instead, both require a complex offering of product, service, advice, delivery and price that is sometimes adapted to their individual requirements. Different elements of the offering will be provided by different companies and the development of new offerings will require the skills, resources and involvement of many of these.
- **Non-business members of the network:** The use of mobile telephony requires the development of industry-wide standards of technology and operation and controls over the way that individual companies work. Standards bodies, regulating authorities and government departments are often involved in technological innovation and must be included in the network.
- **Innovation:** Figure 2.3 illustrates three important aspects of business innovation that we will discuss further in Chapter 4. Firstly, innovation almost always involves more than one company. Secondly, innovation always involves more than one technology. Usually, a newly developed technology has to be combined with already existing technologies in order to make it useful. Thirdly, technological innovation that affects companies can arise from many sources, both from "inside" the network that we have examined or, if the analyst has taken too narrow a perspective, from "outside" that network.
- **Coordination:** The network in Figure 2.3 highlights the problems for a single company seeking product development or technological innovation. No company can achieve innovation alone and so the process of innovation in business networks is likely to involve a combination of cooperation, conflict, leadership, coercion and reward between many

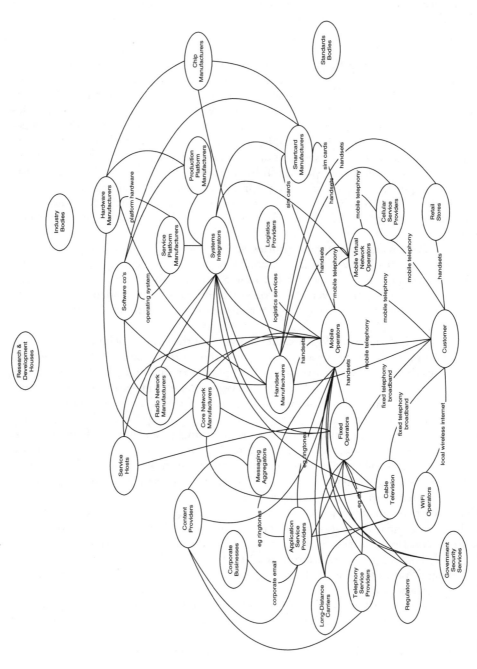

Figure 2.3 A product development network.

companies. If innovation does occur then it is likely to affect many more companies than those directly involved, both "inside" and "outside" the network that has been analysed.

The features we have identified in the three examples can be summarized as follows.

In order to examine a network we need to choose a focal point, for example, a particular company. We can then examine the network from this perspective. As soon as we change this focal point, then we will see a new set of relationships and companies and the network will be different. It is useful to examine a network from the perspective of different companies. For example, it is often instructive for a marketer to examine a network from the perspective of a major customer or one of that customer's customers. By examining a network carefully, a creative marketer can achieve a realistic understanding of her own position in the minds of customers and suppliers. She can also start to understand the dynamics of the network and even help the company to work to change the network by seeing the potential interdependencies that others have overlooked.

A network provides both opportunities and restrictions for any company, but no one company controls the network. A company may try to design its own network, as Toyota has done, but it may find out that others are also trying to influence the network in such a way that even the strongest companies have to adapt. IBM, Toyota and the companies in the product development network have all learned this through experience.

The existence of a network does not alter the fact that the key task of business marketing (and purchasing) is to manage each single relationship of their company. It is through its relationships that a company learns and adapts to the surrounding network. It is through them that a company exploits and develops its own abilities and gains access to those of others. It is also through relationships that a company can influence different companies elsewhere in the network.

A network structure means that it is possible for a single company to influence a large number of other companies, even if it has a limited number of direct relationships. It also means that the company can be influenced by a large number of companies. It is not unusual to find examples of companies trying to systematically relate to companies up to three tiers away, such as Toyota in the example above.

Each company in a network establishes connections between its different relationships. A company's relationships with its suppliers, when combined with its own resources, contribute to the offerings that form the basis of its relationships with its customers. The company's relationships with all its customers also contribute to the development and fulfilment of those offerings and form the basis of its relationships with its suppliers.

There is a danger when drawing a network from the perspective of a single company, that the company may believe that it is more important to others than it actually is and that it can control the network more than it actually can.

The value of a network analysis can be seen in the example in Box 2.1.

Box 2.1   How Things can go Wrong for a Company in a Network

"Lender"[3] became a major player in the HLTV business – high-loans-to-value. HLTV loans are secured on the equity that consumers have in the value of their homes, just like normal loans. But the difference is that HLTV companies will lend up to 125% of that equity. This means that the loans provide less security to the lender than more conventional ones and hence they are often referred to as "sub-prime". The HLTV market had grown rapidly in the United States and Lender accounted for a large share of this market.

Lender can be viewed as a conventional consumer marketing company. It makes loans through retail channels, including its own "loan shops" and via commercial banks that act as distributors for its loan products. Its marketing employs mail-shots and television advertising, fronted by a well-known and trusted personality. However, another view of Lender's business is shown in the network diagram in Figure 2.4. This network diagram also helps to explain the severe difficulties that the company hit in 1998, despite its marketing success.

Lender describes its business as follows: "Lender originates, services, securitizes and sells consumer receivables". In other words, Lender originates loans from its consumers and sells them to other companies in the network. In fact, consumers are at least as much its producers as its customers. Lender does not have access itself to a large volume of low-interest, long-term funds that it would need if it were to hold its loans on its balance sheet until they matured. So it uses securitization to bring together seemingly unrelated actors in the network – those investors that have money to lend and those consumers who are "credit-challenged". In return, Lender receives revenue from consumers for initial charges on the loans and it also receives a margin from the financial institutions. As well as investment banks and institutional investors, the network also includes rating agencies, the media and government regulators. Each brings its specialized resources in the form of expertise and finance:

- Institutional investors, such as insurance companies and pension providers buy a set of risk and return characteristics when they buy a security and the price depends on their perception of risk.
- Investment banks act between borrowers and lenders in the network. They will only buy securities that investors wish to purchase so that they are not left with costly assets they cannot sell.
- Rating agencies play both a direct and an indirect role within the network. Before Lender can securitize any loans, regulators such as the SEC (Securities and Exchange Commission) require them to obtain a rating from one of four private rating agencies. Indirectly the agencies try to bring shape and order to the evolving network.

[3] The name of the company has been changed. This case was developed from the work of an under-graduate project group at the University of Bath.

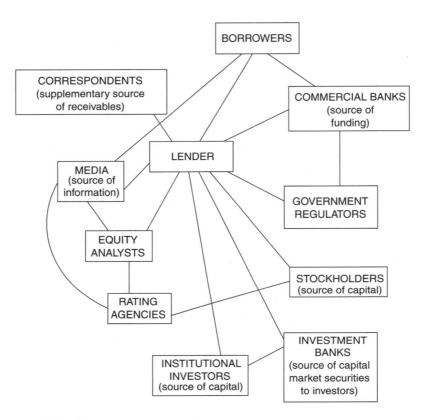

Figure 2.4   The high-loans-to-value network.

How it went wrong for Lender

Lender was a marketing success. Demand was strong and Lender was able to create and develop relationships with "quality" consumers, ie those likely to pay their debts. However, the increasing volume of lower-quality loans generated by their competitors increased concerns about HLTV business within the network among the media, regulators, rating agencies and investors.

Then the Asian financial crises broke in 1998 and Russia defaulted on its debt. The attitudes to risk of US investors changed immediately and they flocked to the safety of US Treasury Bonds. Investors in Lender's securities required ever-higher rates of return and new securitizations became more difficult or impossible. A number of Lender's competitors went bankrupt and this caused investors to retreat further. Lender's share price fell sharply and it was forced to put itself up for sale and seek massive financial restructuring.

Lender had a wide portfolio of relationships with a number of investors and investment banks and produced a torrent of general press releases to explain its activities. But, unlike some other companies, it had not developed strong relationships with individual investors, who would take a long-term view of their relationship when investment conditions deteriorated. Nor was it adept at communicating its current situation and plans within its relationships. One journalist expressed this as follows:

[Lender] has not been hobbled by rising delinquencies, loan losses ... or fraudulent accounting ... rather, [Lender] seems to have been dragged down by surrounding ... forces, botched communication with analysts and investors and a whirlwind of rumours.

This case shows how a company's activities can only be understood by looking at the wider network. Lender was a successful consumer marketing company, but this is only one part of the network and it is closely related to all the other things that happen in it. Lender had an unclear view of its position in the network and it failed to appreciate the dynamics of the network. Nor had Lender developed the relationships that it needed to build its position. It built its business on the basis of a static view of an unstable network.

Analysing a Single Relationship in a Network

We now need to provide some building blocks to enable us to examine business networks and to cope with some of their complexity. We will start this process by looking at a way to analyse the *content* of a single relationship in a network.[4] We will use three dimensions for this content analysis: Activity Links, Resource Ties and Actor Bonds, as follows.

Activity links

A business relationship is likely to systematically link together some of the activities that are performed in a supplier and a customer, as follows:

- The relationship may link the basic service or production activities of the companies. One example of these links is when a supplier of electrical cable cuts cable to the exact lengths required by a shipbuilder, rather than simply supplying a single roll of cable that the customer would have to cut for itself. Another example is when a supplier overhauls a customer's equipment on site, rather than the customer having to return the equipment to the supplier's depot.
- A relationship may also link activities that facilitate or control a production process. A common example of this is when a supplier and customer coordinate their activities so that components are provided on a "just-in-time" basis, thereby reducing inventories at both the supplier and the customer.

[4] This section is developed from Håkan Håkansson and Ivan Snehota (eds) (1995) *Developing Relationships in Business Networks*, London, Routledge.

- A relationship may also link logistics or design between the two companies, such as when a software supplier links the development of its software to the design of its services by an insurance company.

A business marketer faces the important question of which activities to link with its customers. This decision will depend on the nature of the customer's problem and the customer's view of the value of the relationship, as well as the supplier's own strategy for that relationship. For example, a customer may see its problem as the need to reduce its overall operational costs, rather than simply to buy suitable products or services. In this case a supplier that is prepared to invest in developing complex activity links may be suitable for it. But a similar approach by the supplier is unlikely to be successful where a customer is unwilling to commit itself to the costs and dependence on a single supplier that would be involved. In this case a more limited linking of activities between the companies is likely to be more appropriate. Another question facing the business marketer concerns how the linking should be done. This will involve the marketer working closely with his own operating staff. These are also likely to be interacting with the customer. Marketers and operating staff, working together, will need to relate the levels of investment that are required in a relationship and their likely pay-offs to an overall strategy for that relationship.

The activity links between two companies will not exist, nor will they have developed in isolation. Instead, these links will be influenced by others between companies across the network. They will form part of a wider activity structure and this structure is illustrated for five companies in Figure 2.5.

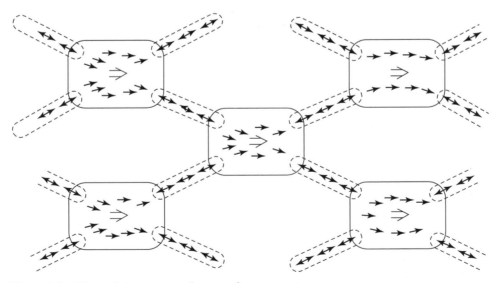

Figure 2.5   The activity structure between five companies.

Source: H Håkansson and I Snehota (1992) *Developing Business Relationships in Industrial Networks*, London, Thomson Learning.

Resource ties

A relationship can also tie together resources from both of the companies, as shown in Figure 2.6. It may be the physical facilities of the two companies that are tied together, such as when a pipeline connects an oil refinery owned by one company to a petrochemical plant operated by another. But more commonly, it is the knowledge resources of the two companies that are adapted to each other. One example of this is when a telecoms company operates a dedicated call-centre for a retailer. Another example of tying knowledge resources is when a component supplier uses its development resources to develop new parts for one of its automotive customers.

The process of systematically tying some of the resources of the two companies in a relationship to each other has an important effect on the resources themselves. As those resources become more developed to meet the requirements of one relationship, they are likely to become less suitable for use in others. This effect has important implications for business marketers, because it means that resource investment decisions or even ways of thinking about technical or operating issues for one customer can reduce the marketer's ability to relate effectively to others. Resource ties can develop gradually and unconsciously as problems are solved within a relationship and this process can reduce the flexibility of both companies. In contrast, when resources are tied together between companies in new ways then innovation often occurs. This can lead to the development of offerings with wide application in other relationships. The conflicting effects of resource ties in reducing the flexibility of companies or in generating innovation with possibly widespread application emphasize the

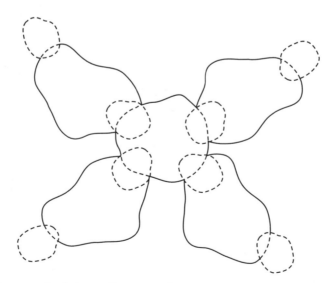

Figure 2.6   Resource ties between five companies.

Source: H Håkansson and I Snehota (1992) *Developing Business Relationships in Industrial Networks*, London, Thomson Learning.

importance for the business marketer of examining or *auditing* each of her important relationships. We will deal fully with the process of relationship audit in Chapter 6.

Actor bonds

A business relationship is built by people and will always have a social dimension. People in the two companies get to know each other and the interactions between them are important in developing trust between the companies, which is necessary for the relationship to develop. The sentiments, attitudes, norms and values of the people involved will be affected by the way that a relationship evolves and the two companies become part of a single social system. The social dimensions of a relationship comprise the actor bonds that exist between the two companies. These bonds are a central part of the identity of a company and affect the way that it works with other companies. Figure 2.7 shows a schematic illustration of the actor bonds between individuals in five companies.

A relationship connects situations that are separated from each other by time. The current situation of a relationship is built on what has occurred in the past and it forms the basis of what will happen in the future. By managing relationships in a conscious way, the business marketer is taking advantage of history. But the marketer must also be aware of the role and importance of the bonds between individuals in the development of a relationship and the attitudes and expectations of those who are involved in it. These bonds have great importance in problem-solving and reassurance between companies. They can

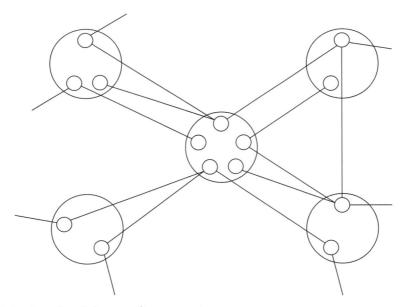

Figure 2.7   Actor bonds between five companies.

Source: H Håkansson and I Snehota (1992) *Developing Business Relationships in Industrial Networks*, London, Thomson Learning.

also be dangerous in those situations where individuals put their personal requirements or their personal relationships before the requirements of their own company.

Characterizing relationships

It is possible for a marketer to investigate the content of different relationships in a network by interviews with those involved and by analysis of offerings, facilities and routines. In this way, the marketer is able to build a picture of the links, ties and bonds in those relationships. An example of this is provided in Figure 2.8 for a single customer and three of its largest suppliers. The volume of transactions within each relationship is indicated by the diameter of the circles. Figure 2.8 illustrates a number of differences between the three relationships, as follows:

- **Relationship 3:** This is the largest relationship in terms of volume and consists mainly of actor bonds. It is described by the customer's purchasing manager as very positive: "There are never any problems with this supplier." But despite good interpersonal relationships the companies have done little to integrate their activities or to make resource investments in their relationship.
- **Relationship 1:** The customer considers that this relationship with the smallest supplier is much more difficult to handle. Actor bonds are relatively undeveloped. There has recently been a major conflict with this supplier about how to exploit some of the technical developments that have been made within the relationship.
- **Relationship 2:** This relationship is different from the other two as it includes more resource ties, but without strong activity links. An example of this would be in the case of a supplier of equipment or a supplier of design or development services. Here the design of

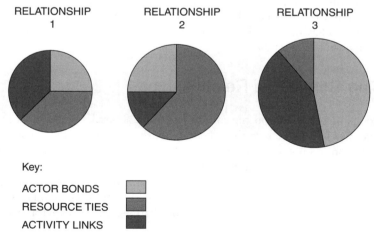

Figure 2.8   The substance of three relationships.

Source: H Håkansson and I Snehota (1992) *Developing Business Relationships in Industrial Networks*, London, Thomson Learning.

the offering itself is critical, but this can often be carried out without strong links between the supplier and customer. Such relationships are often quite easy to handle because they can be isolated from other aspects of the two companies' operations using a dedicated project group. However, the resource ties in this relationship may lead to problems in the companies' other relationships. This is because those resources may have affected either or both of the companies' resources, making them less suitable for use elsewhere.

A comparison of these three relationships illustrates a number of important points for the business marketer:

- There will always be significant differences between a supplier's relationships with different customers, even if each is well developed and mature. Relationships are not single-dimensional and the business marketer needs to analyse them multidimensionally. The content of a relationship is the outcome of a number of factors including: the strategies of the two companies; the characteristics of the network; the problems and resources of the two companies; and the way that the relationship itself has evolved. Differences in the content of a relationship will affect the relationship management task for the marketer.
- The absence of conflicts or difficulties in a relationship is not necessarily a good sign. It can also be an indication that nothing much is happening and there is insufficient interaction taking place. All relationships where there is a lot happening will have difficulties and conflicts. These difficulties also give supplier and customer the opportunity to learn more about each other. Conflicts that are handled well by the marketer can contribute to the development of a relationship.
- Marketing companies often have relationships in which they have worked hard to build actor bonds with a customer. However, they may not have worked so hard to build activity links and resource ties. Relationships that are heavily based on actor bonds are probably not fulfilling their potential, because the value of a relationship is directly related to the links and ties between the companies. Also, "nice and friendly" relationships that are built solely on actor bonds are much easier to break than those with strong activity links and resource ties.

Analysing Connected Relationships

The two companies in a relationship cannot just think about developing that relationship by itself, but must also relate it to the other relationships they have. Managing and developing a relationship is not an isolated activity, but just one piece in a larger puzzle that we call a network. A business marketer responsible for developing a single relationship must consequently look at that relationship in this wider context. We can examine this context along three dimensions that build on those we have used to examine a single relationship. The three are the activity pattern, resource constellation and web of actors, as follows.

Activity pattern

Figure 2.9 shows an activity pattern involving a supplier and a customer and some of their other relationships. The activities that the supplier and customer perform in relation to

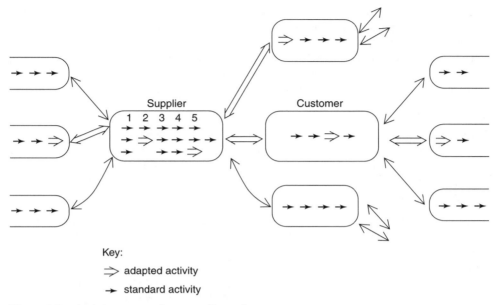

Key:

$\Rightarrow$ adapted activity

$\rightarrow$ standard activity

Figure 2.9 Activity pattern for a supplier and customer.

each other synchronize the two companies' operations. But all their other relationships provide restrictions and opportunities for these activities. Production, service provision, logistics, administration, design can all be moved, redesigned or connected to each other in different ways *and in different relationships*, on both the supplier's and the customer's side. The activity pattern is not fixed and changes within it may involve some companies taking on activities previously carried out by others, either with their cooperation or against their wishes. For example, independent wholesalers have now disappeared from many networks and retailers are likely to source their products directly from manufacturers. More recently, grocery retailers in particular have insisted on buying products at "factory gate" prices. The retailers themselves are now responsible for all stages of distribution from factory to consumer. This move increases the proportion of the total value-added between production and consumption for which they are responsible. The activity pattern at any particular point in time is determined by interaction between all of the companies involved. This interaction between the companies determines the efficiency of the network as a whole as well as how it meets the different requirements of those involved.

Figure 2.9 might give the impression that it is possible to get a single, complete picture of the total activity pattern. However, this is not the case in most situations for two main reasons:

• The sheer number of different activities restricts the analysis. Each activity can be broken down into greater detail and each can be re-integrated into new larger activities. The complexity of the activity pattern surrounding any one company has increased enormously. This increase in the complexity of activity patterns has occurred because the cost of acquiring the skills and technologies to develop and implement offerings has increased dramatically. Companies now concentrate on fewer activities, in which they hope to excel. The activities that they previously carried out are spread among many other companies in the network with which they have relationships. Developments in information technology contribute to the coordination of this wider spread of activities.

• There is no clear boundary that can be drawn around an activity pattern. Every border or limitation must be arbitrary and will depend on the starting point and the subject of the analysis. For the activities in Figure 2.9 the pattern we have shown will probably only appear appropriate for those in the centre of the pattern. If the pattern were examined from the perspective of one of the peripheral activities, then another boundary, including other activities, would be necessary.

The impossibility of drawing a single complete picture of the total activity pattern may appear to be bad news for a business marketer. It does reinforce the need for the marketer to constantly re-examine relationships and patterns. But it also means that the marketer must be realistic in his expectations of analysis. This analysis must be carried out with the clear objective of looking at specific activities or problems, rather than attempting a global view. More positively, the complexity of activity patterns also demonstrates the enormous potential that exists in a network to change and to develop all existing patterns. There will never be a final and optimal pattern.

Resource constellation

The resources involved in a single relationship are also parts of a larger whole. The offerings of any single company depend on its own resources and those of other companies. A company's resources have no fixed value. The value of these resources will depend on how they are tied to the resources of other companies. Through interaction, the different resources are systematically related to each other, embedded in others' operations and developed in order to cope with the characteristics and requirements of different companies. For example, a supplier of logistics services may have its own distribution depots and vehicle fleet. These resources may evolve to accommodate the different requirements of large or small users, those that have their own central warehouses or those that have no facilities. Thus, the resource investments that have been made by the logistics supplier in its depot are based on the resources held by its customers. In turn the supplier's decisions will influence decisions made by its customers about their investment in their own facilities and distribution expertise and about their relationships with other logistics providers.

The resources in the evolving constellation will be complementary. But there will always be some contradictions, such as those customers that continue to invest in their own facilities while also using those of a contractor. Previous examples of resource combination illustrate its difficulties and complexities. Thus it took more than twenty years from the introduction of computers before they were combined with the keyboard, although this seems absolutely natural today. The keyboard itself has had the QWERTY design since the end of the nineteenth century. This design was related to the mechanical functioning of typewriters. The design was intended to make it impossible to type quickly, so that the typing levers did not become entangled with each other. Thus, an early resource combination still exists despite the fact that one part has been completely changed.

The importance of resource constellations means that business marketers must examine their existing offerings and the resources on which they are based in both their own company and in their customers. The marketer must ask at least three questions:

- What has influenced the development of the resource constellation: is it the product of history or determined by convenience in existing relationships?
- Can the resource constellation be developed to solve the problems of customers or suppliers more effectively?
- Can costs be reduced through new resource combinations with our customers, with their customers, with our suppliers or with our customers' other suppliers?

Web of actors

The companies in a network do not just consist of a set of resources that perform activities. These companies and the relationships between them are purposefully directed by many individuals. These individuals form a social structure and each has a view or a *network picture* of each other, both as individuals and as part of the total network.[5] The individuals in a web of actors act on the basis of their network picture and by doing so they bring the network to life. As in all social structures, there are elements of friendship, closeness, distance, antagonism, prejudice, and so on. The social structure of the network has many aspects: individuals may belong to professional associations; they may change their employment between companies in the same network; their companies may be connected through ownership or there may be strong cultural or operational links between them. These individuals try systematically to influence each other as their companies co-evolve. This process of individual influence is both an effect of the co-evolving relationships between companies in the network, but also an important influence on it.

The actor bonds in a network are closely related to the development of trust and commitment between individuals and their companies. Individuals gain from the efforts of others and learn from their experience of success and failure. The web of actors may also lead to the development of stereotypes or informal rules about what should and should not be done in the network. In these ways, actor bonds can inhibit change or mean that innovation in the network is more likely to come from those who are outside the web or who do not know the rules!

Like all aspects of a network, actor bonds are multidimensional. Companies and the individual actors within them relate to each other in many ways and for many reasons. Because of this complexity, it is meaningless for the business marketer to try to make an overall ranking or to use a single dimension to assess her interactions or relationships. Instead, the marketer must assess the value of every customer and supplier relationship

---

[5] For a discussion of network pictures see Ford et al. (2003) *Managing Business Relationships*, 2nd edition, Chichester, John Wiley & Sons, Ltd.

on particular dimensions. Thus, large-volume customers are likely to be significant as an important source of revenue. But, lower-volume customers may also be important. They may have special requirements and, because of the bonds between them, both companies can develop new skills to meet these requirements. Other customers may be valuable, even though there are few bonds between them and the supplier, because they contribute much more revenue than they cost. Business marketers must examine the nature and value of the bonds between their company and its customers and between others that surround it. These bonds to a large extent determine the pattern of resource allocation and the activities between companies. This is often in ways that may not make immediate economic sense, but have a strong logic in terms of trust, confidence, learning or reliability. In the same way the absence of these bonds can confound the development of relationships in the face of an apparently overwhelming technological or economic logic. We will examine the importance of managing a portfolio of different customer relationships in Chapter 6.

Patterns in a Network

We have now used the ideas of actors, activities and resources to examine the characteristics of a single relationship and to show how that relationship forms part of a wider network. We can also use these dimensions to show the overall patterns that exist in different networks and to point to their implications for the business marketer. Some networks are dominated by *activities*, some by particular *resources* and some by powerful companies or *actors* that are high on the priorities of all of the companies in the network:

- **Activity-centred patterns:** Some business networks are dominated by the existence of an extensive set of activities of either production or transportation. One example is the automotive industry, in which a large number of companies produce different parts of a finished car in a coordinated production system. Another example is the airline industry, where many different companies provide fuel, baggage handling, catering, air-traffic control, check-in, etc. The timing and synchronization of activities are a central issue for most of those involved in these networks and the networks are dominated by the search for efficiency gains. The numbers of items being produced means that a small improvement in one activity will produce a large total effect. Activity-centred patterns are increasing as companies are concentrating on performing fewer activities in-house and contracting out more to subcontractors. They require the business marketer to develop a clear picture of the interconnected activities around her and to work with a range of companies extending beyond her immediate customers and suppliers.
- **Resource-centred patterns:** Other networks are dominated by a large, fixed resource. Examples include the networks that surround petroleum production, mining, railway operation, utilities and many process industries. The capital costs of the resource will have to be met almost irrespective of output and this means that it is important to maximize its utilization. The characteristics of the resource and the way that it can be linked to other resources to improve utilization will be central aspects that form the network pattern. There are often large activity structures in this situation, involving

many companies because of the need to fully utilize the resource. Business marketers in this situation are often involved in complex analysis of fixed and variable costs and pricing decisions. We will examine the question of pricing in different cost situations in Chapter 9.

- **Actor-centred patterns:** Finally, there are networks where the pattern is dominated by a powerful company or actor. Examples include the fashion industry where companies such as Nike, Benetton and Marks & Spencer dominate a network of material suppliers, garment makers and designers. Other examples are in insurance and other services. The reasons for this dominance can be functional, such as the importance of large volumes in order to operate as in banks and insurance companies. But it can also be due to government influence or the power of a brand or for historical reasons. Business marketers in actor-centred networks are often involved in asymmetric relationships with powerful customers. They face important decisions about the dependence on a single large customer, the effects of this customer's requirements on the resources that they can afford to develop and the ways in which they can seek to reduce their dependence.

None of these three types of content are exclusive and it is possible to find some elements of each in most networks but one type usually dominates in each case and affects the pattern of the network and the way in which all companies and all marketers must operate.

Positions in a Network

So far in this chapter we have developed a number of concepts that will help us to understand and describe the network of relationships in which a business marketer operates. In this final section we will bring these together to make sense of a single company's position in the network and to introduce some ideas on the role of the business marketer.

A network is a special organizational form that relates companies to each other in a particular structure based on their relationships with others. Each company in a network has a unique *position* in relation to all the others:

A company's network position is defined by the characteristics of the company's relationships and the benefits and obligations that arise from them.

The tasks facing a business marketer will depend on his company's position in the network and we can illustrate this by looking at the system suppliers in our earlier example of Toyota. Marketers in a system supplier have to manage a complex direct relationship with Toyota, through which they are obliged to supply a major part of a vehicle. But the success of the system supplier's relationship with Toyota will depend on the system supplier's relationships with its suppliers in the second and third tiers of the network. Toyota expects them to use these relationships to provide it with access to the skills and resources of other suppliers without it having to manage the relationship itself. In turn, the second and third tier suppliers expect the system supplier to provide them with access to a major customer. This access is of course conditional on the system supplier maintaining its relationship with Toyota. The system supplier's position provides them with the benefit of being able to strongly influence the operations, revenues and prices of their suppliers. Also, because of their access to the wider network and their integration and development skills, they are much more important to Toyota than a second tier supplier of a single commodity, with which they have no direct contact. The system supplier may also have important relationships with other customers. These relationships may involve less integration between the supplier and its customers. These other relationships may involve lower costs for the supplier or require different levels of technological development.

An assessment of network position is an important basis for the business marketer to achieve change in that position. For example, a system supplier to Toyota may choose to invest in a wider range of relationships with its suppliers to strengthen and increase the scale of its relationship with Toyota. Alternatively, it may try to develop relationships with other major customers, perhaps in other countries. Other companies in the network will simultaneously be examining their own position in the network. For example, a second or third tier supplier may decide to invest in the technological resources to design its own dedicated offerings so that it can build *direct* relationships with other major customers. Similarly, Toyota could seek to change its position by establishing direct relationships with a number of current second tier suppliers to increase its flexibility and reduce dependence on a few system suppliers. All these changes would require the companies concerned to build relationships, all would involve the acquisition of resources or technologies and all would affect the current relationships and positions of many companies in the network, whether directly involved or not. Thus a business marketer has to be conscious of the network position of his company. He must be aware of all its customer and supplier relationships and more or less involved in maintaining, developing or changing each of them. His job is far more complex than simply trying to make sales to its customer.

Conclusions

This chapter has introduced some of the complexities of business marketing. Business marketing is not just about developing good offerings and selling them well. It is not just about developing and managing many different relationships over time and taking difficult decisions about resource allocation between them. All of these are important but the activities of a business marketer take place within the wider context of a network. The network affects each relationship in the same way that each relationship affects the transactions that take place within it. It is vital for the business marketer to be aware of the surrounding network. This is so that he can consider the effects on a customer relationship of that customer's relationship with its other suppliers and its own customers, as well as those between the marketer and its other customers and its suppliers. Even more importantly, a company's network position determines the opportunities and restrictions that it faces. A realistic understanding of these is an essential preliminary to developing and changing that network position. Analysing network position, deciding and achieving change are the essence of business marketing strategy.

A relationship is more complex than a single transaction and a network is more complex than a single relationship. There is always a temptation for the marketer to deal at the simplest level and try to make short-term sales at the expense of a longer-term relationship or to concentrate within a single relationship and ignore the wider influences on that relationship. Similarly, there is often a tendency for the marketer to try to build the inter-personal bonds between his own company and the customer as a basis for a relationship and to neglect the development of time-consuming, costly, but potentially more durable, activity links and resource ties between the companies.

Further Reading

Wroe Alderson (1965) *Market Behavior and Executive Action*, Homewood, IL, Irwin.

RM Axelrod (1984) *The Evolution of Cooperation*, New York, Basic Books.

Bjorn Axelsson and Geoff Easton (1992) *Industrial Networks: A New View of Reality*, London, Routledge.

Wim Biemans (1992) *Managing Innovation within Networks*, London, Routledge.

David Ford (ed) (2001) *Understanding Business Marketing and Purchasing*, London, International Thomson, especially readings 3.1–3.9.

Håkan Håkansson and Ivan Snehota (eds) (1995) *Developing Relationships in Business Networks*, London, Routledge.

Håkan Håkansson and Ivan Snehota (1990) No Business is an Island: The Network Concept of Business Strategy, *Scandinavian Journal of Management*, vol 14, no 3, 177–200.

Assignment for Chapter 2

Choose a particular company in which you are interested or with which you have experi-ence. Draw a diagram of the network surrounding the company. The diagram should in-clude the company's major or significant suppliers, customers and competitors, and those, such as regulatory bodies, that influence its activities. Think carefully of the company's wider competitors.

Provide a description of the situation of the network using the concepts that we have discussed in this chapter. Examine the dynamics of the network that you have drawn and point to the possible changes that may occur. You should draw parallels between this net-work and those of others with similar characteristics.

CUSTOMERS AND SUPPLIERS: INTERACTION IN THE NETWORK

3

Aims of this Chapter

- To examine the ways that business customers make purchases and to point to the similarities and differences between business and consumer purchases.
- To analyse customer problems as the driving force behind purchases.
- To explain the elements of a business marketer's offering.
- To analyse customer and supplier uncertainties and abilities as a basis for the interactions between the two companies.

Introduction

In the previous chapter we examined the nature of business networks. The network provides the arena within which business marketing and purchasing take place and within which the business marketer must operate. In this chapter we will concentrate on understanding what happens within and between business suppliers and their customers as they *interact* within the context of a business network. It is important to bear in mind some of the points we have already tried to emphasize before reading this chapter:

- The companies in a business network are interdependent with each other. None of them are entirely free to act on their own. Companies need each other and the processes that occur in business networks are those of *interaction* rather than those of independent action.
- Business marketers and business purchasers face very similar tasks. Both must interact with counterparts in other companies. Both are concerned with problem-solving in their own company and in their counterpart. Both depend on staff in other functional areas in order to carry out their work. Both are responsible for finding, building and managing business relationships.

- It is important for the business marketer to see the world through the eyes of her customers and to understand their problems. This is necessary to avoid the danger of considering customers simply as people who may be persuaded to buy her products or to solve the problems of her own company.
- Because of the importance of "getting inside the heads" of customers and finding out how they see the world, we will start our analysis by looking at some aspects of how and why customers buy. Because of the experience that we all have as consumers, we will build this analysis around the similarities and differences and between the ways that consumers and businesses buy.

Similarities and Differences between Business and Consumer Purchases

There are some clear similarities between the ways that a company and individual consumers make important purchases:

- Neither business nor consumer purchases are isolated events. Both businesses and consumers will be affected by their previous experience with different suppliers and brands and both will consider any possible future purchases of similar products.
- Both business customers and consumers will need reassurance if there are aspects of the purchase that they can't assess for themselves. Both will seek advice from specialists, colleagues, trusted suppliers or friends if the purchase is difficult or complex.
- Both will agonize over some issues that they think are important, but disregard others that they may not know about. They may also both agonize over some issues that will subsequently turn out not to have been important at all!
- Both will make some of these issues explicit in their discussions with suppliers, but others will be only implicit in the discussions and hence much harder for a marketer to identify.
- Both will make many simple, repetitive purchases with little or no re-evaluation of the offering or supplier.
- Both will make purchases when their main concern is to minimize the amount of time that is involved in the purchase process.

But if we look closer, there also seem to be some differences between this business purchase and many consumer purchases. For example:

- **A number of people are likely to be involved in a business purchase:** These may be from different levels in the customer's hierarchy and from a number of functional areas, such as operations, finance, marketing or purchasing. Each function will have its own concerns about a particular purchase: operations managers are likely to be concerned with how reliable the purchase will be in use; marketing people may be preoccupied with how the purchase will add to the performance of the company's own offerings; while purchasing or finance staff may be very concerned with how expensive the purchase will be. Some of the people in the company may provide information on likely suppliers to their colleagues, some may evaluate different offerings or suppliers, others may fix the maximum price that the company is prepared to pay. Some may advise on what should be bought, while others take decisions based on that advice. The business marketer must identify who is involved in the purchase, where they are located, what are their particular problems and how can he reach and influence them.[1] A business purchase is likely to be more complex than a consumer purchase. But we should also remember that many important consumer purchases, such as a new car or even a pair of shoes, that are apparently made by a single person are actually often influenced by others, such as friends, family or peer group.

- **A single business purchase may take a long time from the moment when the issue is first raised till final delivery and use of an offering:** How long a business purchase takes will depend on many factors, such as the complexity of the customer's requirements; the importance or value of the purchase to the customer; the number of different interest-groups involved in the purchase; the level of their knowledge; and the help and advice that a supplier may provide. All of these factors would be important for a company buying a major business operating software. It would also be important in the purchase of a gas-fired power station by a company that had previously only used coal or when an airline was thinking of outsourcing its aircraft maintenance to a contractor for the first time. In contrast many other business purchases are for low-value, high-use operating supplies and minor products or services, such as computer peripherals, car-rental or transport services. Many of these purchases will be made instantly by computer as required and often from a previously approved supplier, unless there has been a particular problem with that supplier.

  Important consumer purchases can also take a long time, such as when someone decides to change their car. It may be a couple of years from when the consumer first thinks that their current car is getting past its best to the time when they actually own a new one.

- **The people involved in a business purchase are professional:** Trained individuals with the job title of "buyer" are often involved in making business purchases, sometimes alone and sometimes with others. But in a major purchase, the potential *users* of the purchase may be heavily involved in it and most concerned about what is bought and from whom. In this case the involvement of the purchasing manager may be limited to simply placing the order with the chosen supplier after other managers have decided what they want, even if he doesn't agree with them! In some cases there may be a formal procedure for making purchases, but in other cases it may be quite informal and it will be difficult for a marketer to see what is happening or who is involved.

  The difference between the skill and "professionalism" of business and consumer purchasers is not clear-cut. If a company is making a major purchase of something for

---

[1] Attempts to model both the process of business buyer behaviour and the involvement of different individuals and functions can be found in FE Webster and Y Wind (1972) A General Model of Organisational Buying Behaviour, *Journal of Marketing*, vol 36, no 2, 12–19, and Wesley Johnston and Thomas V Bonoma (1981) The Buying Center: Structure and Interaction Patterns, *Journal of Marketing*, vol 45, no 2, 143–56.

the first time then those involved may be rather intimidated by the process. They will be far less self-confident or "expert" than consumer buyers who are expert and experienced buyers of products that are important to them, such as when a keen cyclist buys a new bike.[2]

- **In many cases each business customer is individually important to a supplier and responsible for a significant proportion of its total sales:** Similarly, each supplier can be individually important to a customer. For example, if the customer is a large corporation then the loss of the account may be a disaster to the supplier. It would be a similar disaster for a customer to lose a supplier on which it has relied for an important part of its operations. An extreme case of dependence occurs in commercial aviation, where there are only two main suppliers of airliners and only a few dozen major customers.

  In contrast, other businesses have many customers that are *individually* unimportant. For example, Federal Express provides deliveries for thousands of businesses of all sizes. Federal Express may be much more important to each of these than they are to it. Nevertheless, Federal Express has to find ways to effectively manage its business with each of these customers because collectively they are certainly important to it. Many other business marketers have both a small number of large customers and a large number of small ones. For example, the major multinational engineering company, ABB has 100 customers that represent 60% of its total sales and 39,000 that account for the remaining 40%. This diversity of customers complicates the task facing the business marketer and we will examine this task in more detail in Chapter 6.

  Each individual consumer is usually relatively unimportant to a consumer marketer, individually. But a single supplier can be very important to a particular customer. For example, many people buy almost all of their food from a single supermarket or completely furnish their house from Ikea.

- **A business purchase or sale is not an isolated event:** Every transaction between business companies will be affected by the previous experience with each other of both the customer and the supplier. The experience gained during every one of their transactions will also influence the future dealings between the companies and with others. Many of these business relationships are complex. There is often frequent interaction and information-exchange between the two companies, involving a number of people from different functional areas on both sides. Business relationships are often long-term and require both customer and supplier to adapt a number of aspects of their activities. We have also seen when examining business networks that a single business relationship doesn't exist in isolation, but affects and is affected by others in the surrounding network.

Consumers also have continuing relationships with supermarkets, fashion stores and producers of everything from cars to coffee. Just like business customers, when consumers need to make a recurrent purchase then they are likely to go to the supplier

---

[2] For a model of the stages in the business buying process and how they vary in different circumstances, see Patrick Robinson, Charles Faris and Yoram Wind (1967) *Industrial Buying and Creative Marketing*, Boston, Allyn & Bacon, and Richard N Cardozo (1983) Modelling Organisational Buying Behaviour as a Sequence of Decisions, *Industrial Marketing Management*, vol 12, 75–81.

with which they have a good relationship. Consumer marketers try to cultivate these relationships using the techniques of "Relationship Marketing".[3] However, the interactions between consumers and their suppliers are likely to be *one-way*, from supplier to customer by impersonal media such as mail-shots. Consumer marketers are also much less likely to make adaptations to suit particular consumers. Although recently many of them have tried to develop the idea of "mass-customization" to more closely tailor their offerings to customer requirements.

Interacting in Relationships

We have emphasized that the companies in business networks are interdependent.[4] They are tied together by their relationships. Sometimes a relationship may be built for a single major purchase or sale, such as an important piece of capital equipment. In other cases a relationship may last for many years, growing or declining in importance to the participants as their problems change and their other relationships evolve.

Purchases and sales take place within relationships and the selection, development and managing of these relationships is the core task of business marketing. Each customer relationship has to be managed for the advantage of both customer and supplier, or it will not survive. Each customer relationship has to contribute towards problem-solving for both the customer and supplier. Each relationship has to capitalize on the respective skills, resources and technologies of both of the companies. Each relationship has to fit within the network positions of the two companies and their other relationships. Each relationship has to fit within the wider strategies and objectives of the two companies.

But the marketer can't manage customer relationships alone. She has neither the necessary knowledge of the customer's problems nor skills in solving them and she is also likely to be rather selfish in her dealings. This is business after all! More importantly, the marketer's customers are likely to think that, actually, it is *they* that are managing *their* supplier relationships. But a business relationship can't be managed by the customer alone,

---

[3] For a description of ideas on Relationship Marketing see Kristian Moller and Aino Halinen-Kaila (2000) Relationship Marketing, Its Roots and Direction, *Journal of Marketing Management*, vol 16, nos 1–3, 29–54; JN Sheth and A Parvatiyar (1995) Relationship Marketing in Consumer Markets: Antecedents and Consequences, *Journal of the Academy of Marketing Science*, vol 23, no 4, 255–71; Francis Buttle (1996) *Relationship Marketing: Theory and Practice*, London, Paul Chapman; and E Gummesson (1999) *Total Relationship Marketing*, Oxford, Butterworth-Heinemann.

[4] According to Mckinsey and Co, "globalization, specialization and new technologies are making interactions far more pervasive in developed economies. Currently, jobs that involve participating in interactions rather than extracting raw materials or making finished goods account for more than 80% of all employment in the United States. And jobs involving the most complex type of interactions, those requiring employees to analyze information, grapple with ambiguity, and solve problems make up the fastest-growing segment" (The Next Revolution in Interactions, Bradford C Johnson, James M Manyika and Lareina A Yee, *The McKinsey Quarterly*, December 9 2005).

for exactly the same reasons.[5] In fact, a business relationship between two companies is something like a marriage between two people in at least the following ways:

- Firstly, neither a marriage nor a business relationship can be directed by one of participants alone. Both customer and supplier will be concerned to gain their advantage from it, but both will be aware that this can only be achieved with the agreement, or at least the acceptance, of the other company. In Chapter 5 we will look in detail at how customers try to manage their relationships with suppliers and use them to solve their problems. Each business relationship is likely to be a complex mixture of cooperation, conflict, selfishness and selflessness, mutual benefit, coercion, persuasion, trust and deceit, taking and giving, benign and wilful neglect, good management and mismanagement.
- Secondly, what will happen in a business relationship and in a marriage cannot be foretold or planned by either of the participants involved in it. A marriage and a business relationship each acquires its own dynamic as each of the involved parties tries to understand it, contribute to it, enjoy and gain advantages from it and each tries to reconcile it to the pressures of other relationships and the other demands on them.
- Thirdly, both business relationships and marriages can decline, become inert, be superseded by other relationships or fail completely. This can be because of the inexperience, selfishness or unwillingness to make commitments of either of the parties involved.
- Fourthly, neither a business relationship nor a marriage suddenly comes into being. Both go through a process of development from first meeting, to finding out about each other, to making commitments towards each other and changing habits of life to accommodate the other party. We will explore this process of development in more detail to see if it provides insights into how a relationship can be more effectively managed.

However, the analogy between a marriage and a business relationship falls down if we try to extend it too far. This is for no other reason than that both of the companies involved will have many other, perhaps hundreds of relationships at the same time and each has to be managed effectively.[6]

Therefore it is more accurate to suggest that the task of the business marketer is to manage her company's customer relationships *with* that customer. We refer to this process as *interaction*. Interaction is at the heart of business marketing and purchasing and largely distinguishes it from consumer marketing. Interaction recognizes that neither customer nor supplier is free to act independently either in a single relationship or in the network as a whole. Each company is interdependent with others in its relationships and business marketing has to work within the opportunities and constraints of these interdependencies.

---

[5] However, inspection of much of the literature on Purchasing Management, and so-called CRM, Customer Relationship Management, shows that it is based on the idea that one or other of the companies involved can and should manage relationships.
[6] Well perhaps we should say that the analogy doesn't apply in most cases!

Interaction and interdependence are varying but critical elements of *each* of a company's customer relationships: whether that relationship is individually critical to a company's survival; whether it represents a major part of the company's total sales or purchases or is only one of thousands of similar relationships; whether it is friendly or antagonistic, close or distant, complex or simple.

The importance of customer relationships and of the interaction within them has a number of implications for the way that we think about business marketing and purchasing:

- Paradoxically, business marketing is not about selling products, although that may be its ultimate aim. The unit of analysis for the business marketing manager should not be single purchases or sales, or projects or deals, or sales territory or market, but each *relationship* that forms part of her total *portfolio of relationships*.
- It is not possible to make sense of a single business purchase or sale by looking at it in isolation, but only within the context of the relationship of which it forms part. Each transaction both affects and is affected by that relationship.
- Business relationships are a company's primary assets. Without them it cannot buy, sell, produce or deliver products or services. The development of relationships requires investment of time, money and resources and *the marketer's task is to maximize his company's benefits from those relationship investments.*
- Business relationships develop, integrate and exploit the skills, resources and technologies of both the supplier and the customer. Relationships link the activities of the companies, tie their resources to each other and form bonds between individuals from each company.
- Business marketing involves many relationships, each having different actual and potential benefits to the supplier to each customer. Some relationships may be highly profitable, while others generate a high volume of business. Some may lead to new technological developments or provide access to other companies, others are individually unimportant, but together are a useful source of business. Together they constitute the company's *relationship portfolio* and we will examine the tasks of portfolio management in some detail in Chapter 6
- Business purchasing is a very similar activity to business marketing. Both are involved in interaction and the development of their relationship will be the outcome of that interaction. Both companies have to choose counterparts on the basis of both of their own resources and skills. Both often have to convince the other that they are a "good" customer or supplier and worthy of special attention or adaptation. They both have to develop their relationship with a supplier or customer and often have to train them. Both have to interact with them and try to manage and exploit them on the basis of their own interests *and* those of their counterpart.

The similarities between the activities of business marketers and business buyers emphasize a critical difference between much of business marketing and consumer marketing. Consumer marketing is a relatively one-sided activity carried out by an active seller, seeking a reaction from a passive buyer. But business marketing is a process of *interaction* between two active parties.

Are close relationships always a good idea?

We have placed business relationships at the centre of the activities of the business marketer. Because of their centrality, we may think that marketers should always seek to develop "better", "more friendly" or "closer" relationships or even "partnerships" with their customers. But the business marketer will not have sufficient resources to develop close relationships with all her customers and it may not be a good idea to do so even if it were possible. We can outline the issues involved in this choice from the marketer's perspective as follows:

- **The case for close relationships:** Close or *high-involvement* relationships between customers and suppliers enable each to learn about the other, to adapt to each other's requirements and to benefit fully from each other's skills and resources. A company in a close relationship may also have less uncertainty because it can plan on the basis of its knowledge of what it can expect from its counterpart. A close relationship also reduces the risks and costs that companies face if they constantly have to deal with new counterparts: "better the devil you know". Finally, the investment required to develop a relationship means that in many cases it is unlikely that companies will be able to make a return on their investment in it *in just one or a few transactions*. When high investment is required then a close relationship is more likely to provide a return on that investment in the longer term.
- **The case against close relationships:** In many cases neither customer nor supplier would benefit from investing heavily in learning from and adapting to their counterpart's requirements.[7] Instead customers may gain more from "shopping around" for some purchases among a number of suppliers with which it has only a distant relationship. The customer could then aim to restrict itself to simple or standardized requirements and buy them in a series of separate transactions to minimize the price it pays. But in order to do this, the customer would need to invest in its *own* knowledge of what to buy and how to use it to produce its own offerings. Similarly, a supplier may sell to a series of customers without adapting towards them or investing in a close relationship with them. A limited investment reduces a supplier's dependence on that relationship and lowers the risks that may arise by tailoring its operations closely to a particular customer's way of thinking. Limiting relationship investment also maximizes a supplier's freedom to deal with other customers. For example, well developed, long-term relationships benefited Japanese industry in the 1980s. But it has been suggested that they have prevented the rapid restructuring in Japan that has been such a feature of the recent high growth performance of United States industry. In the USA, more open, competitive supplier links are the norm.

Throughout this book we will argue that business marketers and their customers must constantly reassess their relationships and manage them as far as possible to achieve benefits for itself and the customer in line with their overall aims, rather than using any standard approach or formula for different relationships. We have already noted in Chapter 1 that changes in business networks and specifically the growth of the internet have introduced new

[7] Håkan Håkansson and Ivan Snehota (1988) The Burden of Relationships, in Pete Naude and Peter W Turnbull (eds), *Network Dynamics in International Marketing*, Oxford, Elsevier Science.

types of companies able to operate in quite innovative types of relationships. This has reinforced the need for marketers to be able to take a tailored approach to their relationships.

What and Why do Companies Buy?

The answer to the question of *what* companies buy is that they buy lots of things. Some of these are similar to those bought by consumers and some are different. For example, they buy cars, components, raw materials, nights in hotels, machinery, delivery and cleaning services, advertising, advice, accounting, insurance and toilet rolls.

But if we ask a manager *why* he has chosen a certain supplier for a particular purchase then the answers are likely to vary widely. A first response may be, "I want the best quality". If we probe deeper then the manager may say that he has chosen the "most trusted supplier", or the "most versatile service", "the highest performance", "highest specification", "longest-lasting", "most up-to-date", "most consistent", or that he wants "best value", "highest-technology" or simply "reassurance".

One manager may say that he always buys from the same supplier, because this particular purchase is important to him and he dare not risk a change. Another manager may use the same supplier each time because that particular purchase is *unimportant* and he doesn't want to take time to think about it. Another might say that what really counts is not how good a product is, but how convenient it is to get hold of it.

This variety of answers tells us quite a lot about business marketing:

- Different customers can buy the *same* physical product or service for quite different reasons.
- "Quality" can mean many different things to different customers in different circumstances and the term is meaningless unless carefully defined in each context.
- We cannot make sense of the reasons for a customer's purchase by describing the physical properties of *what* it bought, or by asking it *why* it made the purchase.

But we do need to make sense of why companies really buy if we are to be able to develop and provide something to satisfy their requirements. To do this we have to look behind what customers obviously buy and what they *say* that they are seeking. In doing this we will look more closely at some of the language and terms that we have already been using. Some of these terms and the connections between them are shown in Figure 3.1.

Problems

A customer's problems are the starting point for its purchases and so are at the centre of business marketing. These problems can arise for many reasons, but they all relate to two basic activities of customers, for which they will look to their suppliers for support:

- **Rationalization:** Problems of rationalization concern the customer's need to carry out its operations as efficiently and economically as possible. For example, one customer may have a problem with the high failure rate in the components that it produces.

Business purchases are driven by specific *problems*

Customers are seeking *solutions* to their problems

Solutions require an *offering* from a supplier

Offerings consist of a combination of:

products/services/advice and delivery

at a particular cost that will include but not

be limited to the price paid

The solution to customer problems may also require

Adaptation by the supplier

and

Effort and adaptation by the customer

Figure 3.1   Why do customers buy, what do they buy and what does it cost?

Similarly, a contract-cleaning company may face a problem with poor utilization of the time of its staff. Another problem could be the escalating costs of operating its depots faced by a distribution company.

- **Development:** Problems can also arise for *positive* reasons, such as when a company is developing its operations or its offerings. An example of a development problem could be when a company is developing an innovative domestic appliance and needs to fit sophisticated control systems that it is unable to supply for itself. Another would be if a company planned to extend its personal-loan business to a different country but did not have the skills to set up and manage a call-centre in that country. Purchasing departments in companies have become more important in development problems as companies have come to rely more on suppliers as an important resource for solving their problems.

Different people in a company will each have their own problems. For example, the operations department may have the problem of operating with a shortage of skilled labour, while the marketing department may have the problem of poor customer data. Customers will be aware of some of their problems, but others they won't recognize. They will only be able to address some problems and others they will simply ignore or have to live with. Often it is a supplier that leads a customer to recognize a problem and address it. Solutions of many problems are found within existing customer–supplier relationships.

Each customer can solve a single problem in a wide variety of ways. For example, a producer of complex testing equipment may have the problem of increasing production costs. Among the ways it could try to obtain a solution to this rationalization problem would be by:

- buying new production equipment;
- employing a consultant to advise it on its production methods;
- using the services of a design-house to change its products so that they are simpler to assemble;
- stopping making many or all of its components and buying them from suppliers;
- stopping production completely and having its products produced by a contract manufacturing company.

An accounting company may have a rationalization problem in meeting the more demanding requirements of its audit customers. Among the ways that it could try to solve this would be by:

- hiring new staff;
- establishing a relationship with a company with a strong auditing department and agreeing to transfer audit work to them in return for taking on some of the other company's financial consulting business;
- buying an auditing firm.

A construction company may have the development problem that its growth is restricted because of inadequate capital. Among the ways that it could seek to solve this problem would be by:

- building a strong relationship with a venture capital supplier in return for an equity stake in the business;
- taking out a conventional interest-bearing loan;
- reducing its capital requirements by selling and leasing-back some of its facilities.

An analysis of customer problems is illustrated in Box 3.1. Analysis of customer problems has a number of important lessons for the business marketer:

- Firstly, it highlights that many of the companies that are apparently its competitors because they make the same products may not be real competitors because they are in the business of solving *different* customer problems. For example, many companies produce innovative packaging. Not all compete with each other. Some concentrate on very high-volume, low-cost packages for products such as cigarettes. Others concentrate on producing stylish, high-cost, small-volume, frequently changing packaging for products such as cosmetics.

Box 3.1   Analysing Customer Problems

Deliverer Inc is a supplier of maintenance repair and operating supplies. Deliverer maintains an inventory of around 400,000 items used by manufacturing and service companies to facilitate their operations. It talked to many maintenance managers who were some of its more important customers and carried out an analysis of the sort of problems that these customers most frequently faced. This analysis produced the following list:

"A machine has broken down."
"I have to carry out a programme of planned maintenance."
"I'm responsible for making sure that the machines are safe."
"I have a multitude of different machines to maintain."
"I haven't got the skills to do all the jobs."
"We have very poor maintenance stock management."
"My budget is reducing all the time."
"I have fewer maintenance staff."

Deliverer then analysed some of these problems in more detail, as follows:

THE MACHINE HAS BROKEN DOWN

"I need to identify the right part."
"I need to know whether to mend it, buy the part, or take it from stock."
"I need to find sources for the product and I have to choose the right source."
"I need the right tools."
"I need instructions to do the job."

I HAVE FEWER MAINTENANCE STAFF

"I need to find temporary staff."
"We want to improve our productivity."
"We need simpler processes."
"We must reduce our nonproductive time."
"I must prioritize better."
"I want to outsource some activities."
"My staff and I need broader skills."
"We need more external support."

WE HAVE VERY POOR MAINTENANCE STOCK MANAGEMENT

"I need to make it easy – dump the problem."
"I need someone to analyse my stock and requirements."
"I need to reduce my stock value."
"I want better stock systems."

"I need ease of access to products."
"My suppliers need to provide consignment stocking."
"I require replenishment information."

I HAVE A MULTITUDE OF MACHINES TO MAINTAIN

"I need to schedule planned maintenance."
"I would like to rationalize my suppliers."
"I want to use a single source of supply."
"I'd like to dump the problem."

This analysis led the company to change its offering to its maintenance customers. It added a "part-finder" to enable customers to locate and buy difficult-to-find parts. It provided a free maintenance hot-line for enquiries. It provided dedicated stock of parts for major customers at their own premises. Finally, it established a separate planned maintenance company to take the problem away completely for some of its customers.

- Secondly, many companies that supply different products or services may actually be competitors because they solve the same problems. For example, producers of machinery have many customers that are also their competitors. This is because other customers may choose to solve their production problems by not buying equipment, but by having components made for them.
- Thirdly, all companies and all people have many problems at any one time. Some they recognize, some they have never thought of, and some they have coped with for many years. A major aspect of business (and consumer) marketing is to identify potential customer problems, to raise customer awareness of them and to seek innovative ways of solving them.

Products and services

Managers are naturally preoccupied with their products and services and with how their "quality" compares with those of the companies they see as competitors. But a concentration on products and services is a poor starting point for successful business marketing. This is for the following reasons:

- Products and services are simply what a marketing company supplies. *Customers are not interested in products or services themselves.* They are only interested in what products and services will actually *do* for them and the problems that they will solve. A business marketer must look behind his products or services to see the problems of their customers and what the marketer actually *does* to solve them. For example, only approximately 30% of the lifetime costs of operating a fork-lift truck are associated with the vehicle itself. 70% of costs are associated with the driver. So the main rationalization problems for a warehouse operator are likely to do with its staff costs, with damage to products in the warehouse, with faulty selection of items and with safety. One fork-lift truck producer has become aware of this and is starting assessment and training schemes for truck operators and managers and looking at innovative ways of charging customers for use of their trucks. But in doing this the company has problems with its own sales-force which still sees its task as to "sell" the technical performance of the fork-lift trucks. It may try to solve this problem by buying some sophisticated sales training.

- Secondly, products and services are difficult to separate from each other. Almost all "products" have some service elements associated with them, such as installation or after-sales service. In fact in some cases, service performance is more important than the specification of the physical product: "Your software is no use to me, unless I get on-site help if things go wrong". Similarly, almost all "services" have some physical products associated with them. The services of a freight-forwarder include provision of physical containers and space in a ship or aircraft. Some intangible services can be associated with considerable physical equipment. For example, when we have a car serviced we are not only buying a mechanic's time, but we are gaining the benefit of the garage's specialized tuning equipment. In contrast, some large-scale service providers, such as merchant banks or management consultants, use little equipment and little physical product is associated with their activities.

- Thirdly, products and services are often interchangeable in the mind of a customer. For example, a firm of lawyers faced with the problem of how to keep its offices clean could decide to clean them itself by buying the necessary *products*, in this case vacuum cleaners. Alternatively, the firm could buy the *services* of a contract cleaning organization. On a much larger scale, an airline can buy the engines (products) for a new fleet of airliners or it can rent "power-by-the-hour" from the engine manufacturer, who would be responsible for the maintenance of the engines (service).

- Finally, products and services are only part of what is required for successful business marketing. It is for this reason that throughout this book we refer to the marketer's *offering*. We will see why it is important for marketers to make the change in their language away from product or service to offering.

Offerings

A marketer's offering is her promise to a customer. It is a promise that she will deliver something that together with some changes or efforts of the customer will solve, or at least enable the customer to cope with, a particular problem. An offering can be defined as follows:

> A supplier's offering is a *package* consisting of different proportions of physical product, service, advice, delivery and the costs, including price that are involved in using it.

The multiple aspects of a supplier's offering strongly affect the business marketer's activities, as follows:

- A single supplier can provide a different offering for each of its customers, *even if all of those offerings include the same physical product or service.*

- Delivery is not simply how an offering is delivered. Delivery is about getting the rest of the offering to the right places at the right time and enabling the customer to take advantage of that offering throughout its life. Delivery is not just about the logistics involved in getting the offering to the customer. Delivery is an intrinsic part of an offering and often it is the most critical of the elements.
- The value of an offering can only be assessed in terms of how effective a solution it is for the problems of a specific customer.
- Business marketers can successfully compete with others, even when their products or services are *identical*, as we may find in so-called commodity markets. They can do this by differentiating *any* aspect of their offering to better solve the customers' particular problems, rather than simply cutting their price. For example, their offering may have better delivery, or may include advice on how to use the product more efficiently.
- Business marketers must appreciate that in many cases neither their physical product nor service nor delivery is the most important element of their offering for a customer. Often it is the supplier's *advice* on what type of offering the customer should choose, or on how it can use the offering, that is a vital part of customer choice. In other situations, it is the supplier's ability or willingness to *adapt* one or more elements of her offering that is important to the customer. In other situations it is the marketer's skills in providing, managing *and controlling the costs* of its offering or adaptation that are critical to business success.
- The importance of a supplier's delivery, advice and adaptation to meet a customer's particular problems means that marketers need to be extremely careful in using the word "quality". This is particularly the case because the term, quality, is often used to refer just to the product element of an offering, especially by those in operating or development departments. Often those who do talk about "quality products" consider that service, delivery, advice and adaptations are simply costs to the supplier that are to be reduced wherever possible. But because these elements are intrinsic to the offering and often of considerable importance to the customer, marketers cannot afford a generalized, product-based, specification-driven view of quality.
- Buying a supplier's offering will involve a range of costs for the customer, only one of which will be the purchase price they pay. Other costs for the customer may include those of integrating the offering and adapting other aspects of its operations to accommodate it. Other costs could also include the benefits from other offerings that it has given up or the loss of its relationship with other suppliers. It is just as important for the marketer to understand and manage these customer costs as it is to assemble her offering. We will examine the management of these costs and prices in Chapter 9.
- The marketer must appreciate that a supplier's offering is never produced by it alone. It will be developed, produced and delivered to the customer by the supplier and by many others in the network, including the supplier's suppliers and often the other suppliers of the customer. A supplier will *always* need to use the resources of these other companies in the surrounding network and combine them with its own skills and resources to produce an offering. In many cases around 70–80% of the costs of the supplier's offering are accounted for by purchases from others. These purchases can include everything from electricity from a utility company, to logistics or design services or critical components for its product or the provision of service, adaptation or advice to the customer.

- A supplier's offering is often not developed in isolation from its customers, but *interactively* in the relationship between them. The customer may have an important role in designing the product or service element, in carrying out or arranging for logistics and adaptations. Indeed it may be the customer that provides the advice element to the supplier for the offering that passes between them. Overall, the offering is an *outcome of the relationship between customer and supplier.*
- The importance of other companies, including the customer, in developing and delivering an offering means that it is important for the business marketer to build productive relationships with many other companies in the surrounding network, both customers and suppliers, to be able to provide current and future offerings.

Solutions

An offering is a supplier's *own* view of the package it has developed. A customer will have a different view of it and will only be concerned with how effective it is as *a solution* to its problems. We have already seen that there are many potential solutions to each business problem, including the offerings of many different suppliers. The successful business marketer is one who can:

- Examine and develop its own offerings *as solutions to customers' problems,* not in terms of its own abstract criteria of "quality" of product or service.
- Compare its offerings, through the eyes of the customers, with other potential solutions to specific problems *of whatever type and from whatever source.*
- Advise customers on the choice of available solutions. Of course, a business marketer also has to *sell* or convince the customer that her offering actually *is* a good solution to its problems. But in doing this, the marketer must be aware that her relationship with a particular customer will depend on the extent to which her offering actually provides a solution to a particular problem.
- Actually implement the offering that she has promised to the customer, at the promised time and location, with the promised performance and consistency. In other words, the promise of a marketer's offering is of no value to a customer, unless it is *implemented.*

The effectiveness of the solution that a customer receives depends on the characteristics of the offering and the supplier's skill in actually implementing it for the customer. But the effectiveness of that solution will also depend on the *customer's* skills. These customer skills have a number of aspects, including the clarity with which it can define and describe its problems and how able it is to build relationships with suppliers and to motivate them to supply it. In other words, how able is it to *sell* itself to potential suppliers as a good customer. Necessary customer skills also include those of working with the supplier to develop its offering and to ensure that it is implemented and the ability to integrate an offering with the offerings of other suppliers and with its own operations.

This means that the effectiveness of the solution that a customer receives will depend on the nature of the relationship between the supplier and customer, *irrespective of the technical quality of the supplier's offering.*

Customer Uncertainties

It is quite straightforward for a company to solve a problem by making a purchase when:

- it is sure of the precise solution that will best meet its needs;
- it has relationships with several suppliers, each with offerings that match those needs;
- it is sure that it will actually receive the solution that was promised by the supplier's offering at the time that was promised and when it is sure that the offering is the lowest price of any that are available.

But this ideal situation is unlikely to occur in practice and companies can face a number of *uncertainties* in their purchases, irrespective of the problems that those purchases are intended to solve. These uncertainties affect the requirements that customers have of their suppliers and it is vital for a business marketer to understand them.

Need uncertainty

Very often a customer finds it difficult to define its problem, or it may not know the best solution for that problem. In this case we say that the customer has *need uncertainty*. Need uncertainty will strongly affect the way a customer approaches suppliers and the purchase itself, as follows:

- Customers with need uncertainty are likely to take a long time over their purchase.
- There is likely to be intense interaction with potential suppliers.
- They may have to seek advice from suppliers as to *how* they can solve their problem and what they should buy.
- They are likely to favour "close" suppliers with whom they already have a relationship or those that they trust, because they have a strong brand or perhaps because they are local to the customer.
- They are likely to concentrate a large proportion of the supplies to solve a particular problem with a single supplier. In other words they are likely to "get into bed" with that supplier.

We can see a similar situation to this in our own behaviour as consumers when we are unfamiliar with a major purchase, such as when buying an MP3 player for the first time; or when we lack self-confidence, such as when buying an "important" article of clothing. In both cases the functionality of the brand and reputation are important and loyalty to previous, trusted suppliers is likely to be strong.

Market uncertainty

Instead of a few potential suppliers for a clearly defined offering, a customer will often face a wide variety of potential solutions to a particular problem. Alternatively they may find that the technology in the area is changing rapidly, so that new and different solutions are arising all the time. In this case the company will not have a relationship that will provide an obvious solution to its problem and we say that it has *market uncertainty*.

A customer with market uncertainty is likely to behave very differently from one with need uncertainty:

- They are likely to devote considerable efforts to scanning the available suppliers and the different potential solutions.
- They are unlikely to concentrate their purchases from a single supplier, because that would lock them into that supplier's technology. Instead, they are likely to develop relationships with a number of competing suppliers.

Again there is a parallel between business buying and our own consumer purchasing. When we are faced with a wide range or rapidly changing set of complex products we are also likely to spend time scanning potential offerings. We may use journals such as *What Hi-Fi?* or *What Computer?* as a way to cope with our market uncertainty.

A marketer faced with a potential customer with high need uncertainty will find it worthwhile to devote efforts to increase its share of the customer's purchases. But if that customer has high market uncertainty then those efforts are unlikely to be worthwhile because the customer will wish to avoid concentration and spread its purchases around.

Transaction uncertainty

On other occasions, a customer company making a major purchase may be quite sure about what is the right solution and about the available offerings from different suppliers. But, it may be uncertain about whether the supplier will effectively *implement* its offering, or fulfil its promise, on time, in the right place, with the right performance, at the promised price, or do any of these things consistently. In this case we say that the customer has *transaction uncertainty*. Transaction uncertainty may occur in many routine or noncritical purchases or where several suppliers have similar offerings. In this case the customer is likely to seek a solution involving the least cost and effort. Transaction uncertainty may also occur in many situations where implementation is critical. For example, the customer may require consistent on-time delivery of components to several different locations worldwide. Similarly, a customer may face an absolute time constraint in executing a management buy-out or acquisition and will be totally dependent on legal advisors to meet that schedule. Transaction uncertainty will strongly affect a customer's behaviour, as follows:

- The customer is likely to investigate the supplier carefully, check aspects of its operations and performance and monitor its deliveries.
- The customer may seek to develop the supplier and try to improve its abilities to satisfy the customer's requirements.
- Alternatively, the customer may try to minimize its dependence on any one supplier and "play the market", by buying on the most advantageous terms from a range of suppliers on a short-term basis.

The approach of developing a supplier would involve investment by the customer in building a relationship with the supplier and would be more likely to occur for major purchases. The alternative of "playing the market" would avoid the costs of relationship investment, but would limit the customer's purchases to widely available standardized offerings. This approach is more likely to be used for minor purchases where the problem involved was clearly defined. Sometimes a customer will try to be able to avoid high-involvement relationships with suppliers and reduce its transaction uncertainty for major problems by simplifying its requirements so that a standard solution would suffice.

What customer uncertainties mean for marketing management

The uncertainties that a customer feels when contemplating a purchase are affected by the relationships that it has with different potential suppliers. This means that it is possible for a business marketer to manipulate the uncertainties that customers feel. For example, a supplier may try to increase a customer's *need uncertainty* by emphasizing the complexity of the problems on which the purchase is based and the range of considerations that the customer needs to take into account in making a choice. Alternatively, the supplier may reduce that need uncertainty by simplifying the considerations it draws to the customer's attention.

Similarly, a supplier may try to increase a customer's *market uncertainty* by highlighting the variations between its own offerings and those of different suppliers. In contrast, it could reduce market uncertainty by talking about the similarity between the technical standards of the different offerings.

This supplier could then stress that, although the offerings of different suppliers were apparently very similar, it was important for the customer to be able to trust a supplier to live up to promises on delivery or price or to be consistent in its performance over time. The supplier could then contrast the record of different suppliers in these ways, thus increasing the customer's *transaction uncertainty*.

Supplier Abilities

Of course the reason that a supplier would try to manipulate a customer's uncertainties would be so that they related more closely to the abilities that it wishes to exploit in the relationship. These abilities are of two types:

- **Problem-solving ability:** This is a supplier's ability to design and assemble an offering that will provide a solution to a customer's problem. All elements of an offering may be important in solving the customer's problem, but the adaptation and advice elements are likely to be critical when the customer has need or market uncertainty and are uncertain about the best way to solve their problems, or unsure about the range or rate of change of the different offerings in the market.

Problem-solving ability may require a large investment to develop or adapt an offering to suit customers' requirements. Problem-solving ability will also involve other companies in addition to the marketer's own company. These will include its own suppliers that may also have to adapt their offerings to help the marketer's company to assemble a dedicated offering. The importance of advice and adaptations for problem-solving mean that the costs to the supplier's own operations and those of managing each of its relationships are likely to be high, perhaps even involving technical sales, applications engineers or relationship managers.[8] These costs are likely to be reflected in the price of the offering. Of course, those customers with more simple or standardized problems, or with low need or market uncertainty, will not be prepared to pay the high price demanded by the supplier skills that they do not value and they may seek other suppliers.

- **Transfer ability:** A supplier's transfer ability is particularly important to a customer with high transaction uncertainty. Transfer ability concerns how well a supplier can *fulfil* its promised offering by delivering the offering to the customer at the time, price and functionality that it was anticipating. Just like problem-solving ability, transfer ability is also likely to involve other companies, such as logistics operators or service companies that will be critical to successful fulfilment. In some cases such as that of many industrial distributors, transfer ability involves an emphasis on low costs, consistency of supply or conformity to the specification of a standardized offering. But in other cases the fulfilment of an offering may depend on highly developed and high-cost logistical operations. This is often the case with the supply of components to mass production customers, such as vehicle assembly, where the same component will have to be delivered to a number of plants in different countries around the world.[9]

Strategic choice in abilities

Companies can differentiate themselves from others by emphasizing either their problem-solving or their transfer abilities. A supplier with strong problem-solving abilities will be able to develop and tailor a sophisticated solution to complex or difficult problems or to help customers with considerable need or market uncertainties. But the investment that the supplier has to make in its problem-solving abilities may be at the expense of its transfer abilities. This may mean that its ability to actually implement its offering to its customers may be inconsistent, late or subject to cost over-runs. However, some customers may have considerable uncertainties about what their needs really are or about what is happening in the supply market. Others may want the supplier to provide a solution to a difficult or complex problem. In these cases, the customers may be prepared to accept these inadequacies in implementation.

Other suppliers may invest their resources in their transfer abilities. This may mean that their offerings may be undifferentiated when compared to those of other suppliers. However, their transfer ability may mean that they can fulfil their offering consistently on time, on budget, to specification and to a rigorous logistical schedule. This transfer ability may be of great value to customers with considerable transaction uncertainty.

---

[8] We will discuss the role of relationship management in general in Chapter 5.

[9] Many of the ideas of "lean production" with minimal inventories involve using suppliers with strong transfer abilities to be able to cope with the challenge of tightly timed, complex deliveries, perhaps to a number of locations and with "zero defects". For a discussion of these issues, see JP Womac, DT Jones and D Roos (1990) *The Machine that Changed the World*, New York, RA Rawston Assoc, and Richard Chase, Nicholas Aquilano and Robert Jacobs (2001) *Operations Management for Competitive Advantage*, New York, McGraw-Hill.

Business marketers have to accept the tradeoffs that are implicit in the two abilities and accept that they are unlikely to be able to compete with other suppliers that have made different tradeoffs for customers with different problems and different uncertainties.

The activities of a number of suppliers may seem to centre on a particular product or service and all the suppliers' offerings may seem to be similar to each other's. But customers will seek those suppliers whose problem-solving or transfer abilities most closely relate to their uncertainties. Similarly, suppliers will seek those customers whose requirements most closely match their own abilities. This adds to the complexity and variation that exists in business networks and to the tasks facing the business marketer.

The uncertainties of customers are not constant. It is likely that a customer facing a problem for the first time will experience both need and market uncertainty: in other words it will be unsure about what it should buy and what is happening among different suppliers and potential solutions. In this situation, customers are likely to value those suppliers with strong problem-solving abilities. However, as customer experience increases and the technologies involved in their offerings become more widely understood then both customer need and market uncertainties are likely to decline in importance. Instead, customers are more likely to be interested in suppliers with strong transfer abilities. This situation is likely to exist until the technologies involved in offerings change radically or the nature of customer problems shifts. Unless business marketers are constantly in touch with changing customer uncertainties their organization and their abilities are likely to become out of line with customer requirements.

Box 3.2 provides an interesting example of the relationship between two suppliers and a major customer that deals with customer problems and uncertainties.

Box 3.2   Dealing with Customer Problems and Uncertainties, Compuware and the City of Oslo[10]

The City of Oslo is the largest employer in Norway and has more than 43,000 employees. Thousands of people depend on the city to provide services such as welfare, social security, healthcare and childcare.

The City of Oslo had experienced downtime in its operating systems which could have life or death importance. It was a high priority for the City of Oslo to improve this downtime, particularly in applications running the childcare system. These applications were outsourced to a Datacentre with whom the City of Oslo had a well developed relationship. But despite investing considerable human and financial resources, the problem was not solved. Hence, the City of Oslo requested the Datacentre to contact Compuware in order to investigate Compuware's tools for monitoring applications and measuring end-user response times.

---

[10] This case is based on the research of postgraduate students: Laura Bevill, Lara Qatami and Anne Horn-Hanssen. See also, http://www.compuware.com/corporate/default.htm and http://www. compuware.no/, "kundereferanser".

Compuware's customers are large organizations within the bank, oil, telecom, and retail industries as well as data-centres. These customers typically have their own information technology (IT) departments that manage complex information systems. Compuware had no existing relationship with the City of Oslo at the time.

One of the most difficult elements of building an offering for any of Compuware's customers is to thoroughly understand the customer's problems. Owing to the complexity of different customer IT systems, it is not always possible to easily find the underlying reasons for a technical problem. Additionally, it is not enough to understand the customer's technical need, but also necessary to relate the technical need to the corresponding business problem. Unless the consequences of *not* solving a problem are identified, the customer and supplier may waste valuable technical resources on a problem that does not have significant impact on the business.

But in this case, the customer had a specific problem that was relatively easy to identify: the City of Oslo wanted to resolve the problem with the downtime on their applications at a reasonable cost and time, given the time and money that had already been spent trying to solve it. The Datacentre had the same objectives, as they had specified targets for uptime on these applications in their contract with the City of Oslo.

Compuware suggested a solution based on their software called "Vantage". Vantage is able to monitor applications from the perspective of the user. It is able to identify reasons why applications are slow or go down, and can suggest resolutions. The development of the offering falls into the category defined as "collaborative investigation" (Chapter 6) where neither of the companies can identify the reason or the possible solutions for a problem.

Also in this case, the City of Oslo had need uncertainty about the type of solution that could fix the problem. "Customers with need uncertainty are likely to favour 'close' suppliers – those that they trust, either because they have a strong brand or because they already have a relationship with them." Because the City of Oslo had not previously cooperated with Compuware and in order to manage the City of Oslo's need uncertainty, Compuware, the Datacentre and the City of Oslo agreed to initially work together on a small pilot project, for a fraction of the total price of a full contract. The project would use Compuware's tools, within a short period of time, to investigate the problems with the childcare application and deliver a report on its findings. With this method, the City of Oslo and the Datacentre would lower the risk of investing too much time and effort, before they were sure that the offering would help to solve their problems. At the same time, Compuware gained the opportunity to build a cooperative relationship with the Datacentre and the City of Oslo.

The City of Oslo was an important potential customer for Compuware, who had not worked closely with these types of public sector organizations before. There was a strong consensus within Compuware to support the offering with the necessary resources and investments.

The pilot project was successful. Several key problems had been identified and fixed and it was also possible to show the effects of the offering on the end-user response times. The Datacentre was also presented with a solution that solved their customer's problem. "The quality of an offering is a measure of the extent to which it actually solves a particular problem for a particular customer." The success of the pilot project initiated a long-term relationship between Compuware, the City of Oslo and the Datacentre.

"The problems of business companies are often complex and can rarely be solved simply by a physical product alone." It was not just the Vantage product that contributed to the success of this offering. The City of Oslo also valued other elements in the offering from Compuware: the commitment of technical resources, the involvement of management and the level of adaptation and advice offered to solve the problems during the pilot study.

The pilot project was a large adaptation of a typical Compuware Vantage offering. It was not usual to invest so much time and resources to sell this particular offering. But in this case it formed part of Compuware's long-term strategy to build a customer relationship with the City of Oslo. The City of Oslo is now one of Compuware's strongest customer reference stories worldwide.

Problems and Uncertainties for the Supplier

We have emphasized the similarities between business marketing and business purchasing. These similarities also apply to the problems and uncertainties of customers and suppliers and how they deal with them, as follows:

- Suppliers also rely on their customers for ways of solving their problems and meeting their requirements.
- Suppliers also have to assess the available customers and compare these to their particular problems and establish, develop, manage and exploit relationships to obtain solutions for them.
- Suppliers also face uncertainties in their relationships and customers may try to manipulate those uncertainties. Suppliers look to customers for ways of coping with their uncertainties.
- *Both* suppliers *and* customers have to balance their own short-term interests in a relationship against those of their counterparts and against the long-term interests of both of them.

Supplier problems

An important aspect of business marketing is for the marketer to assess her own company's problems and judge how different customers can provide a solution to some of them. For example, a supplier may have a cash-flow problem and rely on one particularly large customer to provide the volume of business to reduce this. This same supplier may consequently face a problem of low profitability because this major customer insists on very low prices. The supplier is likely to seek other customers with different requirements but that will be the source of higher-margin business. Another supplier may have a problem because some of its products are technologically out-of-date. It may rely on a particular customer to solve this problem with it. The customer may be willing to invest in the joint development with the supplier of an innovative solution to one of its problems. The supplier may then be able to use this development in its relationships with other customers.

Supplier uncertainties

Irrespective of its problems and just like its customers, a supplier will face uncertainties in its dealings with its customers. It is important for a business marketer to understand her own uncertainties as well as to know about those of her customers. It is also important for the marketer to think about how her customers may try to manipulate these uncertainties. A supplier's uncertainties have much in common with those of a customer and we can outline them as follows:

- **Capacity uncertainty:** Very often a supplier is uncertain about how much of a particular type of offering it is likely to be able to sell in any time period. This *capacity uncertainty* is likely to be high in those suppliers with high fixed costs of production or development, or those that are dominated by a small number of major customers. A supplier faced with this uncertainty is likely to try to form close relationships with a number of customers in order to provide some assurance of sales volume.
- **Application uncertainty:** Suppliers often face uncertainty about *how* the offerings that they are able to produce can be most effectively used by customers and which type of problems they can best solve. This *application uncertainty* is likely to be high when the offering is based on recent technological development or when it needs to be integrated into customers' operations in a complex way, or when the application is changing rapidly. The direction that a particular technology takes and where and how it is used may be difficult to determine. But these directions will have a profound effect on the problems that customers face and hence on what they require from suppliers. A supplier faced with high application uncertainty will need to develop effective mechanisms to scan how a wide range of different customers are currently applying and are likely to apply its offering in the future.
- **Transaction uncertainty:** This is a similar uncertainty to that faced by a customer. A supplier may doubt that the customer *actually* knows what it should be buying. The supplier may not trust the customer to *actually* take delivery of the volume it ordered, at the time asked for, or to pay the price that was agreed. Transaction uncertainty is likely to be high when the supplier undertakes considerable development or adaptation work on behalf of its customers or where demand for its offerings is concentrated in few customers. A supplier faced with high transaction uncertainty has a similar choice to that of a customer. It can either try to establish a close relationship with its customers to learn more about their requirements and likely behaviour, or it can seek to reduce its dependence on a small number of customers by broadening its portfolio.

What its own uncertainties mean for suppliers

In the same way that a supplier may try to manipulate the uncertainties of a customer, a customer may try to manipulate the uncertainties of a supplier. For example, a customer can increase the *capacity uncertainty* of a supplier by emphasizing the unpredictability of demand from other customers for the supplier's offering. This may make the supplier value this customer much more. In contrast, a customer may try to reduce a supplier's *application uncertainty* by simplifying the specification of its requirements. The customer may also try to increase a supplier's *transaction uncertainty* by pointing to the extent of company failures amongst users of this type of offering.

A customer also brings two types of abilities to its interactions with a supplier. These are as follows:

- **Demand ability:** A customer's demand ability enables it to advise the supplier of the type of offering it should produce and to offer the supplier the volume and type of demand that it requires. In this way the customer assists the supplier in assembling its *offering* and in this way will appear a valuable customer. A customer's demand ability would be important to a supplier with high capacity uncertainty and high application uncertainty. A customer might have demand ability because of its high-volume requirements, but it might also be because it understands how to construct a supplier's offering and to integrate it into its own operations. This ability is likely to be particularly important to a supplier that is new to an application; or to one that has recently developed an offering based on innovative technology for which the application may be uncertain; or where the supplier needs to recover high development costs. A supplier might have to "pay a price" for the customer's demand ability by extensive interaction with the customer, or by adapting to its requirements, or by granting the customer a low price.

- **Transfer ability:** In the same way that a supplier's transfer ability is about reliably making sure that the customer receives the promised offering, so a customer's transfer ability is about its reliability in providing the promised type and volume of orders and information to the supplier, or more generally in managing a relationship. A customer with strong transfer ability will be appealing to a supplier as it will be little "trouble". In other words by using its own transfer ability, the customer will require less of the supplier's transfer abilities.

The uncertainties and abilities of supplier and customer are illustrated diagrammatically in Figure 3.2.

Interchangeable abilities

Customers and suppliers share an interest in ensuring that mutually satisfactory transactions take place between them. Their discussions and disagreements are likely to concern which of them should do what and which should incur the sacrifices that are involved. The abilities of suppliers and customers are to some extent interchangeable in a relationship and both companies can benefit from this. For example, many retailer customers use their skills to make up for inadequacies of their suppliers. They often provide the design and specification for the offerings of suppliers, based on the knowledge that comes from their relationships with their own customers. They also mandate how they should be produced. Both of these are based on the customer's demand ability. They also take responsibility for inspecting produce on farms or clothing in factories to see that it meets their requirements

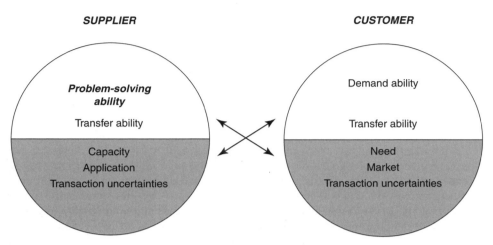

SUPPLIER

CUSTOMER

Figure 3.2 The uncertainties and abilities of customer and supplier.

and they control logistics to ensure timely delivery. This is based on the customer's transfer ability.

On the other hand, many suppliers design complete modules of a *customer's* final product, of which their components and those of others are part. This is based on their problem-solving skills. They might also carry out inspections of their own and others' components and supervise delivery of components directly to the place on the production line at which they are to be assembled, to ensure that no delays occur. This is based on their transfer skills.

This substitution of activities is only likely to occur in well developed, high-involvement relationships. We will examine the processes by which business marketers can develop their customer relationships in Chapter 6. We will see that the involvement of companies in business relationships can lead to a situation where it is difficult to separate the activities of buyer and seller from each other.

Conclusions

This chapter has introduced a number of concepts that will enable us to analyse, discuss and manage customer relationships. We have emphasized that it is customer problems that are at the heart of business marketing. Therefore the ability to understand customer problems is perhaps the most important asset that a business marketer can have. We have also seen that irrespective of the problem, a customer will approach suppliers with a number of uncertainties and these uncertainties will affect what it buys, how it buys and what it requires from a supplier. In both of the first two chapters of this book we have tried to explain that all companies in a network buy and sell and all face problems and uncertainties. This means that business marketers must also understand their own problems and uncertainties and how these should affect their interactions with customers and the offerings that they seek to provide.

In the following chapter, we will build on the central importance for the business marketer of understanding customer problems and use some of the tools that we have developed in this chapter to look closely at the actual problems that customers face and how they approach their solution.

Further Reading

David Ford, Lars Erik Gadde, Håkan Håkansson and Ivan Snehota (2003) *Managing Business Relationships*, 2nd edition, Chichester, John Wiley & Sons, Ltd.

David Ford (ed) (2002) *Understanding Business Marketing and Purchasing*, London, Thomson International.

David Ford and Håkan Håkansson (2005) The Idea of Interaction, *IMP Journal*, vol 1, no 1.

Håkan Håkansson and Ivan Snehota (1995) *Developing Relationships in Business Networks*, London, Routledge.

Michael Hammer and James Champy (1993) *Reengineering the Corporation*, New York, Harper Business Books.

Michael Hutt and Thomas Speh (2001) *Business Marketing Management*, Fort Worth, Dryden.

Wesley Johnston (1981) *Patterns in Industrial Buying Behaviour*, New York, Praeger.

Arch G Woodside and Niren Vyas (1987) *Industrial Purchasing Strategies*, Lexington, MA, Lexington Books.

Assignment for Chapter 3

You are Sheila Carmichael the marketing manager for Swift plc. Swift produces a range of general and customer-specific electronic components used by companies in a large number of different industries.

The following letter has just landed on your desk. You know that Jennings is a major customer. It manufactures a wide range of products used in the auto, aviation and construction industries and also sells products produced by other manufacturers. Its products are generally regarded as technically advanced and it has a strong new-product development department.

Before you reply, you want to think carefully about the issues that are raised. You realize that it won't be enough to simply apologize. You are also aware that there are now a number of similar suppliers to yourself that can offer a similar range of products and similar levels of product development resources and service. Your margins have been slipping and your sales growth has slowed. You have recently been thinking about the direction you should take the business.

Decide how you will deal with the letter and produce a clear plan for developing business with this customer. Explain how your approach to this customer will relate to wider issues of developing your business and your other relationships. Decide how you will approach Jennings with your plan and what you will say to him and when you will say it.

JENNINGS CONSTRUCTION

Sheila Carmichael,
Swift plc,
Baylis Road,
London SE22 7PB

Dear Sheila

I have worked in purchasing for fifteen years or so and I have always held Swift in high regard as a valuable and reliable supplier. To this end, when I joined Jennings as Purchasing Manager in 2002, I was keen to establish a formal purchasing agreement between our group of companies and your organization.

This initial agreement was reached with your Joan Smith and both parties soon began to reap the benefits of the deal. Joan subsequently moved on and Alan Coles took over as our account manager. During Alan's time looking after our account, we established good communications with regular quarterly review meetings. Unfortunately, following further reorganization at your company, Alan, like Joan, was moved on.

Our next account manager was David Jones, and it was from this point that we started experiencing problems and by the end of the year I was ready to prohibit any of our locations from using you. This was due mainly to David's threat to terminate our retrospective rebate agreement as he felt you were obtaining no additional business by providing this incentive. Having explained at length to David the structure of our business and the approach I suggested you should take, he reluctantly agreed to allow the scheme to continue.

I was next contacted by Philip Harris who advised me that he was our new account manager as Swift had again reorganized its sales-force. Philip was very positive about our agreement and we also had lengthy discussions about our proposed Visa card purchasing programme, but he did warn me that he didn't expect to be looking after our account for too long as he knew of yet another reorganization. I told him that this disappointed me and that I felt we were being treated badly by Swift and he promised to make sure things improved.

Towards the end of last year, I happened to meet your Sales Manager, Arnold Whitfield, who was talking at a conference I was attending. Arnold was doing a good job of telling us all how innovative and customer-focused Swift are. However, when I told him about our problems over lunch he was most disappointed and indeed shocked to hear of the service levels we were experiencing. He promised to make it a priority of his to look into the issues when he returned to the office and to report back. I am still waiting to hear from him nearly twelve months later.

Next, I received a phone call from a gentleman called Simon Brett who informed me that he had taken over as account manager. I explained my concerns to him and suggested methods that could be adopted by Swift to significantly increase the business they received from us. Simon accepted that all the changes were "unacceptable" and "disappointing" but he assured me that he was here to stay and things would improve. Needless to say, I was somewhat shocked when Christine James called in June to explain that she was our new account manager – our sixth in four years!

I think that there is a real difficulty with the manner in which Swift categorize customers and thus how they are serviced, i.e. account manager, local representative, telesales, etc. This seems to be done purely on their level of expenditure, ie those that spend above a certain amount get an account manager but those that spend little only receive telesales calls. While I can understand your logic for setting these procedures, I would expect there to be a degree of flexibility, or if you prefer: "customer focus". We have 18 manufacturing locations nationwide, ranging vastly in size and each one categorized by Swift depending upon their current spend levels, not their potential spend levels. Thus sites with a large potential are not being supplied by Swift because you are not prepared to have local representatives call them. I have suggested therefore, on several previous occasions, that selected Jennings sites receive an initial visit from a local representative. I am confident that this would generate considerable growth for Swift.

More importantly, you seem only interested in "shifting products" from you to us and totally disregard our problems. Business is tough for everyone these days!

Hopefully, the contents of this letter will serve as a reminder that we at Jennings Construction have the potential and desire to develop our relationship with Swift, but only if you are prepared to put some effort in yourselves. If you are not prepared to offer this commitment then I'm afraid it really is time for us to go our separate ways.

I await your reply with interest.

Yours sincerely

KN Townsend, Purchasing Manager

TECHNOLOGY, BUSINESS NETWORKS AND BUSINESS MARKETING

4

Aims of this Chapter

- To show how business marketing is inextricably linked to the technologies on which a company's offerings are based, as well as those of the company's suppliers and customers.
- To analyse different types of technology and provide a structure to help business marketers understand the technological strengths and weaknesses of their company.
- To describe how companies acquire, manage and exploit their technologies and the implications of these activities for business marketing.
- To examine the role and effects of technology in business networks and in individual relationships.

Introduction

Throughout this book we emphasize that business marketers and business buyers face similar tasks. Both of them are involved in solving problems for their own company and both of them achieve this by solving problems for each other. Customers face a huge range of potential problems, including those that come from expanding sales for its own offerings or declining margins on those offerings. A supplier's problems can be similarly diverse, including those associated with an ageing range of offerings or disorganization in its internal operations.

Business problem-solving takes place through interaction between companies within their relationships. Suppliers and customers are interdependent with each other in these relationships. In this chapter we examine what is perhaps the most important basis of that interdependence and the key to problem-solving for the business marketer and customer.

The basis of the interdependencies of the companies in a network is the respective technologies of those companies.[1] These technologies enable problem-solving to take place within business relationships. Hence, technologies are the basis of business marketing and purchasing. We will see in this chapter that technology, relationships and business problem-solving are closely intertwined, so that:

- a business relationship would have no value without the technologies of both of the companies that are involved in it; and
- a company's technologies would have no value without its relationships.

The Idea of Technology

A business relationship provides access for each company to the technologies of its counterparts. The technologies of both of the supplier and customer companies in a relationship are combined together in order to develop, implement, integrate and use the offerings of the supplier. Each customer combines the offerings of many suppliers in its own offering. This offering in turn contributes to the offerings of others in the network. Hence, the offerings of any one company in a network depend on its own technologies and those of numerous other companies. It wasn't always so.

When Henry Ford opened his Rouge River plant in Deerborn, Michigan, the plant made its own steel and glass. It forged springs, pressed sheet metal, cast cylinder blocks. It made tyres using rubber from Ford's plantations in Brazil and it despatched completed cars to customers on its own railroad.

To do this, Ford had to be able to design the cars and all the components within them. It also had to know how to make all of the components and assemble the finished vehicle. In other words it had to have all of the product technologies (to enable it to design things) and the process technologies (to enable it to make them).

Nowadays, fully integrated operations like Ford are rare. This is simply because it is too expensive and simply beyond the abilities of an individual company to keep up-to-date with all of the technologies it needs for its operations. For example, most cars are still built with sheet steel, but aesthetic and performance requirements mean that they are now designed with the aid of complex software. Car makers now have to incorporate computerized engine management systems, computer-controlled suspensions, climate control and devices to tell us if the tyres are flat, to navigate us to our destination and soothe us on our way with the music of our choice.

No car maker fully understands all of these things. It couldn't possibly keep up-to-speed with companies that specialize in software for vehicle design, or the suppliers of engine electronics, computerized suspensions, satellite navigation systems, audio equipment etc etc. Hence car assemblers and other companies depend more and more on their relationships with others to provide the *benefits* of the technologies that they need, but don't or can't have themselves. This dependence on the technologies of others means that business

[1] We will shortly define what we mean by technology in more detail. But for the moment, we can say that a technology is simply an ability to design or to make something.

relationships have become both more complex and more variable. For example, a company may choose to develop its own design skills in some areas that it regards as critical to the success of its offerings, but it may then buy products or services from another company *based on those designs*. The company may develop some other things that it needs jointly with a particular supplier, customer or even a competitor. It may then produce these for itself. It will buy others "off the shelf" from a company that supplies a number of competing customers. The joint development of technologies is illustrated by the case of Marks & Spencer in Box 4.1.

Box 4.1   Working with Suppliers in Developing Technology

The retailer Marks & Spencer has always operated in a way that is different from the conventional idea of a store that simply buys and resells. For example, Marks & Spencer was closely involved with one of its suppliers in developing cotton bed-sheets that don't crease, no matter how much fun you have. Neither Marks & Spencer nor its supplier could have achieved this technological development alone. On another occasion, the same retailer was concerned with the colour-matching of different pieces of cloth used in men's overcoats. It developed equipment for use by its cloth suppliers that enabled them to ensure consistently perfect matching. That same technology is now used by other companies producing and using textiles in a wide range of different areas, from producers of high-fashion clothing to the fabrics used to cover airline seats.

Marks & Spencer also sells food as well as clothes. It faces the problem of competition from supermarkets that stock a wider range of groceries and so it has tried to compete by offering high-specification and innovative prepared foods. It was keen to improve the taste, nutrition and appearance of its prepared foods and wanted to offer dishes that would be fresh and not frozen. This is relatively easy to do if the dishes are produced in delicatessen departments in each store. But Marks & Spencer wanted to achieve the lower costs and consistency that could only come with centralized production. To develop and implement the concept of sophisticated chilled food dishes produced on an industrial scale, it had to work with food producers on meal design and food safety. It had to cooperate with packaging companies to produce innovative packs that ensured freshness over a reasonable shelf-life. It had to work with refrigeration companies to be assured of precise temperature control in its stores and with a logistics company to develop reliable, chilled distribution over the whole of the country. Each of these companies and Marks & Spencer contributed their individual technologies to the development with the effect that chilled food has largely displaced frozen prepared food in its stores and more widely in other UK retailers.

There are no rules about who does what, who knows what or who has which technologies between customers and suppliers or indeed anywhere in a network. Some of the variations in approaches to technology taken by different companies are illustrated in Box 4.2.

Box 4.2   Technology Choices[2]

Alfa and the electronic lock

"Alfa" (name disguised) is a small company in Trondheim, Norway. It is in the business of "making" ASICs (Application Specific Integrated Circuits). But actually, it doesn't make them. It developed an ASIC to meet the requirements of a company that makes the locks for hotel room doors. This company understands the technology of locks, but not of microelectronics. It wanted to be able to offer locks operated by memory cards, containing an ASIC, to its customers in the hotel business. These could be programmed in hotel receptions and, compared to the company's mechanical door locks, offered additional functionality for guests and the hotels. The ASICs are actually made by Alcatel, a large French electronics company, which has a "foundry" for making silicon devices.

Even in this simple network situation, who the customer is, who the supplier is, who has which technologies is not fixed.

Alfa could choose to buy the chips from Alcatel that were produced to its design. It could then sell the chips to the lock maker. Alternatively, Alfa could sell the design to the lock maker who would then buy the chips from Alcatel. In fact in this case, Alfa retained the design and bought the chips from Alcatel and sold them to the lock company. By developing the ASICs for the lock company Alfa had developed its own technological ability in ASIC design. It then faced the task of effectively exploiting this technology. The lock project was delayed, which reduced Alfa's sales income. But Alfa was subsequently able to exploit this technology by producing ASICs for another company that wanted sophisticated controls for its range of electric room heaters. In this way Alfa made profits through the wider exploitation of its technology in different applications.

Clarks, Ecco and Keen: DIFFERENT TECHNOLOGICAL APPROACHES TO SHOES

Three successful companies supplying shoes have very different approaches to the activities that they carry on inside their companies.

Ecco was founded in the small Danish town of Bedebro in 1963. In 1980 it introduced the first high-tech production equipment as the first move in a strategy of developing the most advanced production methods in the world shoe industry. Following further developments, companies in Japan, Cyprus, Argentina and the Czech Republic were licensed to produce Ecco shoes, using Ecco's process and product technologies.

Ecco buys animal hides and produces its own leather from them in a joint venture company in Indonesia and in tanneries in Holland and Thailand. It has a large research facility in Holland and is responsible for the development of all its own product and process technologies for the design and manufacture of shoes. Ecco has its own production unit in China. It sells its shoes through over 3,000 of its own retail outlets. It employs 9,000 outside of these stores and sells 12 million pairs of shoes each year.

[2] These cases were developed from the work of Espen Grossetvold and Mike Redwood.

The British shoe company Clarks was established in 1825. Until fifteen years ago, it manufactured all its own shoes, most of them produced close to its original location in southwest England. The company had a strong reputation for design, material innovation and process sophistication. Clarks is a much bigger company than Ecco and it sells over 41 million pairs of shoes each year. It still has its design function in the UK, but it now owns no production. All its shoes are bought from suppliers in China, Brazil and Eastern Europe. Global turnover in 2005 was £955 million.

Keen Footwear follows a very different strategy for its technologies. It only employs 40 people, but it is the fastest-growing footwear company ever. It owns and fully controls almost nothing. Keen was founded in 2003, based on one concept; a sandal with an ugly rubber protection on the toe. This made it safe to use on the deck of a racing yacht, and also struck a cord with walkers in the US. The company had $30m of sales in 2004, was quoted as trading at the rate of $100m by mid- 2005 and if press reports are to be believed will pass $300m in 2006.

Keen has combined the modern possibilities of communications, globalization and new business formats to create such a large business so quickly. Heavy marketing has been avoided and the brand has been promoted by word-of-mouth or "buzz" marketing. It does not look as though this was all perfectly planned, and certainly some of it was fortuitous, such as Steve Jobs launching the Apple iPod wearing a pair of Keen sandals. Yet Keen exploited this ruthlessly and had the shoes given to trekking guides and other influential users as far away as New Zealand. They also got mentions in highly influential websites such as Metacool.

Added to buzz marketing in its first year the company instructed its then only salesperson to tell three out of four callers that they were "sold out", yet making sure the shoes stayed in influential stores. This created more talk in the industry and at the trade shows in 2004 it was impossible to get on their stand for the crowds. In January 2005 $1m budgeted for advertising was given to charity.

The company wanted to jump from being just a sandal company without being burdened with costly infrastructures and this required it to expand its product range very quickly. To do this they exploited their industry knowledge by using freelance designers to develop a wide range of shoes to a precise look and technology consistent with the look and feel of Keen and utilizing the distinctive toe-covering technology. They also made arrangements with their suppliers from China to book production capacity rather than wait to accept orders for specific designs.

Keen has limited investment in product or design technology. It has no investment in process technologies. This approach gives it flexibility. It means that even a few days before a major trade show Keen can continue to complete and finalize the range and still meet the shipping deadlines needed in an overcrowded market where inventory must be in place at the right time.

Decisions on which technologies to hold "in-house" and for which to rely on others are among the most important and longest-term that businesses ever have to take. Unfortunately, many companies don't even recognize that strategic decisions about technology have to be taken, or they stumble into those decisions or take them without a clear idea of their importance or based on narrow short-term cost considerations. A particular technology or set of technologies, such as those that enable a company to design or make a particular part of its offering is rather like a train. In order to stay on the train and keep up-to-date with the technology, the company will have to commit itself to continued long-term development. If it goes for the wrong technology or too many technologies it may jeopardize its whole business. But if the company gets off a particular technology "train" by stopping a development that will be important in the future, it will soon be left behind as others develop the technology further. This may damage the value of its offerings or simply make them obsolete. If it wants to get back on the train in the future, it is likely to be a difficult, time consuming and very expensive investment.

Technology decisions affect a company's ability to solve the problems of others and they provide the structure to its interdependence with its suppliers and its customers. Business marketers don't need to be technologists. But they must understand the nature and value of the technologies of their own company and of those around them. These technologies are the basis of their activities. Indeed, one interpretation of business marketing is that it is concerned with effectively exploiting the marketer's company's own technologies and linking those technologies with the technologies of their customers and others. Business marketers also have an important role in setting the direction for the development of their company's technologies. In Chapter 1 we saw the problems that may arise for the business marketer if he takes a *sales approach* and sees his job as selling his current products to his customers, or if he takes a *market approach* and sees his customers as a homogeneous market, or if he takes a *single purchase approach* and sees his job as trying to win a series of single sales. Instead, we suggested that the business marketer should take a *network approach*. This network approach will be vital to us if we are to understand how technologies form the basis of business marketing and purchasing.

Technology and the Company

All companies face similar problems to do with technology, whether they are those companies we used to call "manufacturers" or "retailers", or whether they are so-called "product" or "service" companies, or consumer or business companies or "high" or "low" technology companies. These problems can be outlined as follows.

The rate of technological change outside the company is likely to be accelerating and competitors are often engaged in a desperate race to introduce new technologies into their operations and offerings. For example, aluminium is starting to replace steel in the construction of car bodies. This poses major design and production challenges for those car companies who have no experience of using this material in large volumes.[3]

New competitors often arrive in established industries using innovative technologies that have been developed in quite different applications. For example, traditional banks face severe competition from grocery retailers, insurance companies and entirely new entrants, all of which have the technologies to operate telephone call-centres and web-based sales. Many banks have responded to this by using the services of specialist customer-service companies. In other words, technological innovation has led them to contract a central area of their business to an outside supplier.

---

[3] We will consider exceptions to this situation of rapid change later in this chapter and suggest how sometimes technology may be a force for stability.

The cost to the company of developing the technologies on which its offerings are based is likely to increase with each new generation of offerings. For example, financial service companies face higher costs in developing each new investment or insurance offering because of the greater costs of compliance with tougher government regulation.

More and different technologies are needed to offer and implement each subsequent generation of a company's offering. For example, grocery retailers now operate websites and home-delivery services and offer financial and mobile, land-line and web-based telephone services as well as sourcing and managing an ever-wider range of nonfood lines in order to maximize the return on their assets. Thus, if we think of each company having a box of technologies, then that box will get wider with each new technology that is necessary for its operations and the increasing cost of each generation of technologies means that the box will get deeper.

Technology Decisions for the Company

We will use the diagram in Figure 4.1 as a first step towards understanding the decisions that business companies must take about their technology. These decisions all relate to three major tasks that are faced by companies concerning technology, as follows:

- The first task is to *acquire* the technologies that the company needs for its operations and its offerings.
- The second task is to fully *exploit* these expensively acquired technologies in the company's own offerings or by other means.
- The third task is to *manage* these two processes effectively in a complex organization.

We can examine these three tasks in more detail as follows:

THE TASKS INVOLVED IN A STRATEGIC APPROACH TO TECHNOLOGY

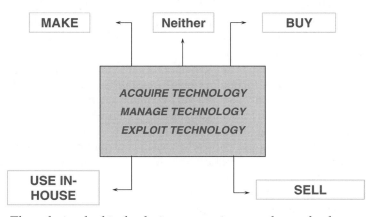

Figure 4.1   The tasks involved in developing a strategic approach to technology.

Acquiring technology

Companies need constantly to review and update their technologies and acquire new ones that they need for their operations. For example, cathode-ray tubes have been used almost universally for televisions for 75 years. They are now being displaced by liquid crystal display (LCD) and plasma screens. At the moment it isn't clear which of these will become the dominant technology. But it is clear that any electronics company that is unable to offer equipment based on the winning new technology will be out of business.

Companies can acquire technology in two ways, as follows

- **Make:** A company can "make" its own technology by developing it in its own research and development facilities. This method may be slow, risky and expensive, but it is an important way of maintaining the company's research capability, its "stock" of technologies and its competitive position.

- **Buy:** A company can also buy technologies in a number of ways.

  Firstly, it can take a licence on the technology of another company. This is what happens when a company buys the right to manufacture gas-turbines to the designs of General Electric or when someone buys a licence, or "franchise" to open a fast-food outlet using the skills or technologies of the McDonald's corporation, or to operate a Holiday Inn using the skills or technologies of the Holiday Inn Corporation. Licensing is often a much quicker way to acquire a technology than by developing it internally. However, licensing may mean that the company can only acquire obsolete technologies or technologies that are also available to its competitors.

  Another way to buy technology is simply to buy a company that already has it. This method has been used by many large pharmaceutical companies in recent years to acquire the technologies of small biotech companies. Buying a company is likely to be expensive and it may not be possible to successfully transfer the technology from the acquired company. These problems are often expressed in the saying, "Don't buy the dairy, just because you want a glass of milk". On the other hand, buying a company may also provide access to its relationships and to a new part of the network.

  A company can also buy technology by commissioning a contract-research company to develop a technology for it. This is happening at the moment as European car producers use independent research companies such as Ricardo in the UK in their struggle to catch up with Japanese developments in "hybrid" petrol/electric cars. Contract research is likely to be relatively quick, but expensive, and the acquiring company does not gain the ability to develop future generations of technology for itself.

  A company can also buy technology by hiring staff from a company that has skills and technology that it wants. This is a very common method; but to be successful, it is essential that the company has or can develop a culture in which the new staff feel comfortable and can develop further. Another alternative is for a company to enter into a joint venture with another company, where each contributes part of the funds and/or part of the expertise needed to develop a technology. Joint ventures are useful where the company has some, but not all of the skills or finance available for a development. But by entering into a joint venture the company will have to give up some control over the direction of that technological development.

The final method is to not buy the technology! A company can try to copy or "reverse-engineer" the technology from another company. Copying may be low-cost, but it can cause problems if the company falls foul of patent laws. It also means that the company becomes a technological "follower" and may also lose some of its abilities to solve customers' problems.

- **Neither make nor buy:** A third alternative for a company is simply to *not* acquire the technology. Instead, the company can buy an offering from a supplier, *based on the supplier's technology*. In this way it gains the benefits of the supplier's technologies, but it does not acquire the technologies themselves, nor does it incur the costs of developing them. We refer to these technologies on which a company depends, but does not own as its "external technologies".[4] The approach of not acquiring technology has obvious advantage for a company: it can save it the time and costs of its own development and its R&D budget can be used for other and perhaps more important technologies. Also, the supplier of the offering will be able to spread its costs of developing the technologies on which the offering is based over a number of customers. Thus, the supplier may be able to charge a low price for those offerings. But buying an offering, rather than developing a technology, has the disadvantage that the customer will become dependent on a particular supplier and its technology. The company is also likely to receive an offering which is technologically indistinguishable from those of other customers, who may be its competitors. This is unless it develops a very special relationship with the supplier.

Companies are increasingly not acquiring many of the technologies that they need for their business. They tend to have fewer internal technologies and rely more on complex relationships with their suppliers. This situation, where suppliers effectively manage technologies on behalf of their customers is the one in which business marketers increasingly operate.

The decisions that a company takes on which technologies to acquire and which not to acquire are critical for that company's survival. Its ability to develop and fulfil its future offerings will depend on having the right technologies available at the right time, whether from inside or outside of the company. Decisions on how to acquire them will affect the time when they are available, their costs and their suitability. It is important that a company chooses the appropriate method of acquisition, depending on the future requirements of its customers, the urgency of the situation, the availability of alternatives and the age of the technology.

But technology decisions are often taken by companies without clear strategic analysis and earlier studies indicate that few companies take a coherent approach to technology acquisition decisions.[5] A number of functions need to be involved in these important decisions, in addition to the company's most senior management, as follows:

---

[4]A useful example of this process is the watch on your wrist. By buying it you acquired the benefits of the technologies of the producer. You have a beautiful and reliable timepiece but you did not acquire the technologies themselves. You cannot reproduce the watch for yourself. The technologies remain with the supplier. As far as you are concerned, they are external technologies.

[5]Earlier studies in both the USA and the UK indicate a sharp difference between a small number of companies that use a variety of technology acquisition and exploitation methods and the larger majority that use licensing as an ad hoc way to cope with a technological inadequacy, see D Ford and M Saren (2001) *Managing and Marketing Technology*, London, International Thomson, p 29.

- R&D staff are obviously the most qualified people to assess their own competence in a particular technology and those of potential external suppliers. Unfortunately, R&D people also invented the not-invented-here syndrome! They are often keen to convince management that they should develop their own version of a particular technology in-house. A wrong decision to develop in-house can lead to delays, high costs or failure.
- A company's purchasing staff should have an important role in decisions on whether to acquire technology. They are responsible for the company's actual or potential relationships with suppliers. They should be able to advise on whether suitable technologies exist in suppliers and whether these could be translated into valuable offerings as a substitute for in-house development or external acquisition.
- Business marketers should also be involved in technology acquisition decisions. Their input should be based on their knowledge of what customers are likely to require in future offerings, what technologies they currently use and plan to acquire and how these relate to the technologies of the company and its suppliers.

Exploiting technology

Companies face similar choices in exploiting their technologies, as follows:

- **Internal exploitation:** This is the most obvious way for a company to exploit its technologies, by using them in its own processes and offerings. Internal use of technologies is likely to lead to lower costs and improved offerings. But it is only a limited way of recovering the company's investments in its technologies.
- **External exploitation:** This is where a company exploits its technologies by selling them to others, most commonly by licence, but also by offering a "turnkey" package where it provides the production equipment and product design and the customer simply has to "turn-the-key" to start operations. External exploitation has the advantage of generating additional revenue for the company. The disadvantage is that it may involve selling to competitors those technologies that are critical to the company's future. This is often referred to as "selling the seed-corn". A different sort of external exploitation is a joint venture with another company where both companies contribute their own technologies and gain the benefit of those of each other. A joint venture can develop new technologies through the efforts of both companies, as well as solving customer problems that would be beyond the resources of one company acting alone.

The wider, external exploitation of their technologies is often disregarded by companies and by business marketers and many opportunities for revenue and profit are missed. Also, companies often take individual exploitation decisions without sound strategic analysis. It is relatively easy for a company to spot an inadequacy in its own technologies when its sales start to slump. It may then look around for a company from which to license an up-to-date technology. In contrast, few companies actually analyse their inventory of technologies and develop ways to exploit them fully. Few companies actually have a clear idea of what skills and technologies their company has and what value they might have to other companies. This is illustrated by studies in the USA and the UK that show that in the majority of licence deals, the initiative was taken by the buyer, rather than the seller.[6] An attempt to solve this problem at Siemens is illustrated in Box 4.3.

Box 4.3   The Problem of Managing Technology Effectively

This problem has been highlighted by many managers in the saying, "if we knew what we know, we would be unbeatable". However, Siemens is attempting to deal with the problem among its 470,000 employees in 190 countries by setting up "Sharenet", an internal system on which knowledge is posted for use throughout the company. For example, Siemens Malaysia used this system when it wanted to bid to supply a high-speed data link between Kuala Lumpur and its new airport, but lacked the necessary know-how. Through the Sharenet it found that Siemens was already working on a similar project in Denmark. The Malaysian company was able to adapt what had been done there and won an order for a pilot project. The chairman of Siemens hopes that the system will enable him to say in future, "Siemens knows what Siemens knows" (*Economist*, June 2nd 2001, p. 103).

Full exploitation of technology is likely to be achieved only by using it in-house and externally at different stages in the life-cycle of the technology (see later), with different counterparts and in different applications. Business marketers need to be involved in planning for this phased exploitation. For example, a company may use a new type of design in its own offerings for a period of time and then license it to others in different countries or for different applications. The car industry has many examples of this. For example, General Motors licensed the designs of earlier models of its cars to Daewoo, and Mitsubishi licensed designs to Proton that it was no longer using.

Unfortunately, business marketers are often too preoccupied with generating sales from the company's offerings, rather than being concerned with maximizing the return on its technological assets. Also, the potential customers for a technology licence are very often the company's competitors and marketers are often unwilling to take any risk of helping a competitor even if the revenue prospects are attractive or the technology is old.

Managing technology

This third task includes the important issue of how the company can speedily and economically commercialize new technologies and bring them to its customers. It also includes how the company can transfer knowledge around the company so that each operating unit can gain from developments elsewhere in the company so that the same problems are not solved several times. Finally, it also includes the critical task of developing and implementing policies for technology exploitation.

[6]D Ford and M Saren (2001) *Managing and Marketing Technology*, London, International Thomson, p 37.

In many companies, these activities are fragmented and this causes considerable problems for the business marketer. Often, a marketer who is responsible for solving the problems of a customer in a particular relationship will have difficulty in finding out whether similar problems have been solved elsewhere and how it was done. Also, the business marketer will have to take an active part in the commercialization of technology both across different relationships and in specific offerings.

We will revisit these problems in Chapters 7 and 8 when we look at the development and implementation of offerings.

Examining the Technologies of a Company

Any offering that will solve a customer's problem will be based on a number of different technologies, from a large number of different companies. The business marketer will therefore be dealing with an offering that includes the output from his company's many suppliers. This offering will also be based on his company's own technologies as well as those of other companies with which it cooperates.

It is important for the business marketer to be able to understand the role of these different technologies in his company's efforts to solve customer problems. A way for the business marketer to examine his own company's technologies and those of others is to use the following categories for analysis:

- Firstly, it is useful to examine the different *types of technology* that are within a company.
- Secondly, we can separate each of these technologies according to their importance for customers, depending on whether they are *distinctive or basic*.
- We can also examine whether these technologies are actually possessed by the company concerned or whether they are the technologies of suppliers to that company, so-called *external technologies*.
- Finally, we can examine where the company's technologies and the offerings based on them are on their respective *life-cycles*.

We will now deal with each of these categorizations in turn:

Types of technology

A company's technologies can be separated into two broad types for the purposes of analysis and marketing development:

- **Product technologies:** These technologies provide the ability to design a particular type of offering. Product technologies are the basis of the company's problem-solving abilities. For example, McDonald's have product technologies that they apply to the design of offerings that solve the customer problem of needing to eat quickly and to be served speedily. A "Big Mac" is one of the many current outputs from these technologies. McDonald's could apply the same technology to the design of a pizza. Similarly, Bic have the product technologies to design small, disposable, plastic products. They have applied these technologies to a range of products such as pens, razors, lighters, etc. Axa, the international insurance company has the product technologies to enable it to design complex investment and insurance offerings. It uses these technologies to develop offerings that comply with the diverse regularization regimes in different countries.

- **Process technologies:** These technologies provide the ability to produce or implement an offering, on time, in the right place, to the right specification, at the right price and to do all these things consistently. Process technologies are the basis of the company's transfer ability. Black & Decker claim to have strong process technologies used in the production of small electric motors. These process technologies have had a strong effect on their marketing strategy. They have exploited these technologies by finding many different things to "wrap round" these electric motors and so have introduced innovative, affordable and reliable electric drills, lawnmowers, hedge cutters, paint strippers, electric saws, etc. McDonald's have process technologies that enable them to produce their fast-food fast. For example, they designed a scoop that allows their operators to stack French fries neatly in a carton with only two hand movements. The scoop is not the technology, but it is an output from it. McDonald's have recently started to exploit their product and process technologies more widely in two areas. Firstly, and close to their original business, they have opened a number of coffee shops. Further away from their main operations, McDonald's have opened the first "Golden Arches" hotels. The technologies to operate a budget hotel are similar to those required to run a fast-food outlet. They involve skills in providing consistent, speedy service to deliver a carefully designed, standardized and restricted packaged offering, just like a burger. Similarly, Axa have the process technologies that enable them to operate systems that receive and invest huge premium income in multiple currencies and process claims from business and consumer customers efficiently and accurately.

A combination of product and process technologies is always needed to satisfy the requirements of a customer. Even innovative technologies must be combined with already existing technologies in order to be usable. A very clear example of the importance of technological combination is provided by digital computing. It was necessary to combine these new technologies with old-fashioned QWERTY keyboards to achieve widespread impact. Similarly, an innovatively designed car is of little use to a motorist unless someone has the process technologies to produce it. Both types of technologies may be located in the same company that supplies the offering. But this is not always the case. In many situations it is the customer that possesses either or both of the necessary product and process technologies. For example, we have seen in the Marks & Spencer case that many retailers specify the design (product technology) of the offerings that they wish to buy and manufacturing methods (process technologies) that will be used to produce the offerings. In this case the customer has incurred the costs of developing the offering and so will expect to pay a much lower price than for an offering that has been developed by a supplier.

In other situations a company may design an offering (product technology), but either by choice or necessity it may rely on another company with the appropriate process technology to manufacture it. For example, when Amgen developed Epoetin alfa, its first treatment for anaemia (in other words, a product technology), it did not have the ability to either manufacture or distribute it, so it launched a 50:50 joint venture with Kirin Brewery which had the manufacturing and distribution presence in major Asian markets (process technology).[7]

The use of the technologies of different companies may be coordinated by a third company that has a relationship with end-customers. This is common in the fashion industry. Here retailers liaise closely with independent designers on what garments are required and then use suppliers that "cut-make-and-trim" garments to those designs for their stores. Similar approaches are increasingly used in aerospace, as illustrated in Box 4.4.

Box 4.4   Approaches to Developing and Exploiting Technology in the Aerospace Network

Developing a new airliner carries huge technical and commercial risks. The latest Airbus 380 had cost $12 billion before its first flight and the new Boeing 787 will probably cost around $10 billion to develop. Both companies face uncertainty over whether airlines and passengers will want to fly them. The two companies have followed different technological strategies until recently. Airbus grew rapidly by taking advantage of the different technologies of its constituent companies and suppliers throughout Europe. For example wings for all Airbus aircraft have been designed and built in the UK by BAE Systems and then shipped to Toulouse for assembly. Until recently, Airbus used the Anglo-French company, Messier-Dowty to design and produce undercarriages to its requirements that it specified in terms of dimensions, weight of aircraft and landing speed.

In contrast, Boeing has traditionally designed most of the constituent parts of its aircraft, including their undercarriages. This required Boeing to hold and develop a vast range of product technologies. It then contracted with US manufacturers, who have the necessary process technologies, to produce undercarriages and other items to that design, often referred to as "make to print".

The product and process technologies of a company affect its position in a business network, its relationships with its customers and suppliers and its ability to compete. But these networks are not stable and marketers must be aware of the constantly shifting relationship and technological situation. For example, in the aerospace network:

• The US producers of undercarriages we referred to above will have had a particular relationship with Boeing, based on their own process technologies and Boeing's product technologies.
• European companies will have a different relationship with Airbus based on their own product and process technologies.
• The European suppliers may find it difficult to work with Boeing because both supplier and customer would have their own versions of similar product technologies.

---

[7] Alberto Torres (1999) Unlocking the Value of Intellectual Assets, *The McKinsey Quarterly*, no 4, 28–37.

They would also find it difficult to compete on price with US suppliers who did not have to cover the same overheads of research and development.

- The US manufacturers would find it difficult to build a relationship with Airbus, unless they invested heavily in their own product technology. But recently a US supplier, BF Goodrich, did commit itself to these investments and won a major order from Airbus for the main landing gear for the A380. However, Airbus has sought to maintain its relationship with Messier-Dowty by awarding it the contract for the nose-wheel mechanism for the aircraft.

Boeing faces many of the technology issues we have described above. It cannot continue to develop in-house many of the technologies on which it depends, so it is seeking relationships with suppliers where they are responsible for developing the necessary product and process technologies and for carrying the financial risks associated with that development. In the 1960s only 2% of its best-selling 727 was made outside the USA. But at least 70% of the new long-haul 787 will be made outside America, mostly in Japan, and the 787 will spend only three days in final assembly by Boeing in the USA. This process will turn Boeing into an integrator of many different companies' technology. At the same time Boeing's change of strategy will facilitate technological acquisition by a number of Japanese companies, such as Mitsubishi, Kawasaki and Fuji that previously had no significant position in this network, funded in part by $1.6 billion of launch aid from the Japanese government.

Basic, distinctive and external technologies

A company's technologies aren't all of equal importance to its customers. Business marketers need to know how their company's different technologies are viewed by customers and which of them are more or less important to customers' problems. It is equally vital for a business marketer to know where the technologies on which his company depends are actually located in the network: in his own company or externally. In order to make this analysis, we need to use the following threefold categorization of technologies:

- **Basic technologies:** These are the technologies on which a company depends and without which it could not operate in a particular network. For example, car companies must have the necessary process technologies to run an assembly line. They must also have the product technologies to enable them to design a safe passenger compartment. Similarly, a bank must have the process technologies to be able to clear the cheques presented in its branches. But for most companies, these are basic technologies. They are necessary for a company to operate at its position in the network, but not a sufficient condition for competitive success.
- **Distinctive technologies:** These are the technologies of a particular supplier that are seen by customers as somehow "special" and are the source of that supplier's competitive advantage. These distinctive technologies are likely to be different for different competing suppliers. So, for example, when other companies had similar, basic process technologies, Toyota developed distinctive technologies in vehicle assembly. Not only did

these reduce its inventories, but they also improved the "build-quality" of its cars. For many years customers saw these distinctive technologies as the basis of the reliability of Toyota cars. In contrast, Volvo has a distinctive product technology in safety engineering. In both cases, customers do not necessarily have to understand the technologies, as long as they can recognize their effects. Also, it does not matter whether or not the company's technology in these areas is actually better than that of other companies, at least in the short term. If customers believe it to be better, then it is distinctive!

The separation between basic and distinctive technologies has important implications for business marketers. A company's offerings will depend on all its own technologies as well as those of its suppliers. Nevertheless, its distinctive technologies are likely to be the basis of its ability to solve customer problems. It is important for marketers to have a realistic view of which of their company's technologies are seen by its customers as basic or distinctive – and how they relate to customers' problems. For example, a company may produce electronic components whose performance is identical to those of its competitors (based on basic product technologies), but it may have distinctive process technologies that enable it to supply components with very low failure rates. The company may be able to build productive relationships with those customers for which absence of failure is far more important than absolute level of performance.

- **External technologies:** Very often a customer will establish a relationship with a supplier rather than develop the technologies necessary to produce a similar offering for itself. In this way the technologies used by the supplier are "external" for that customer.[8] It is important for marketers to understand that the choice of establishing these relationships with a supplier is not just made by customers on the basis of the supplier's price, "quality" or features, but on the basis of the customer's assessment of its current technologies and its willingness to continue developing each of them. This practice of "externalizing" technologies is increasing as companies try to limit the costs of technological development and managerial activity. In some cases customers are happy to receive similar offerings from their supplier to those received by their competitors. But in other cases, the customer may seek to build a relationship with its supplier that is based on a distinctive technology developed by that supplier solely for one customer. For example, the lubrication company, Castrol, has close relationships with a number of developers and producers of additives for its oils. These suppliers use their distinctive technologies to produce dedicated offerings just for Castrol.

A marketer needs to be involved in these decisions on which technologies his own company should "externalize", based on his understanding of customer requirements and how these relate to the company's technologies. For example, one large European bank has outsourced its customer call-centre operations to suppliers in India. However, it has found that its retail customers don't like speaking to operators on international phone lines or they feel that those operators are not in touch with their problems. The bank is not able to easily reverse this move. It has disposed of its own call-centre facilities and the staff with the expertise to set up and operate these. A major marketing opportunity often exists for

[8] For a discussion of the concept of External Technologies, see D Ford and M Saren (2001) *Managing and Marketing Technology*, London, International Thomson, pp 64–66.

suppliers when companies externalize some of their technologies. An example of these opportunities can be seen in the growth of "contract manufacturers", such as Flextronics, Solectron, etc. Contract manufacturers undertake production for other companies and currently account for about 11% of the world production of electronic hardware. Contract manufacturing is growing at around 20% per annum. Contract manufacturers have developed relationships with component suppliers and buy their own materials. They have distinctive process technologies and they are able to advise their customers on product design to ease manufacturing. The largest companies have factories in several countries. This enables them to increase production quickly to get new products to market for their customers. Also, if demand in one country increases rapidly, they can literally fly in an entire production line from somewhere else.

An example of the use of technology analysis is provided in Box 4.5.

Box 4.5   An Analysis of Basic and Distinctive Technologies in a Food Ingredients Company[9]

The matrix in Figure 4.2 was produced for a supplier of food flavourings, seasonings and ingredients. It shows the percentage of the company's total gross-profit contribution generated by offerings that were based on distinctive or basic product and process technologies. The majority of its contribution came from offerings based on basic product and process technologies (Cell 1, 66%). An example of this is the seasoning for sausages, for which the technologies of formulation (product) and production are well known. In contrast, the design of flavourings for snack foods is an area where customers recognized that the company had some distinctiveness, although there was nothing special about its production skills. These offerings accounted for 19% of total contribution. Emulsifiers are used to bind water and fat together in food. The technology for designing these is widely known, but the company was seen to have distinctiveness in their production (Cell 3). But these offerings only represented 1% of gross contribution. Finally, only 13% of the company's gross contribution came from offerings based on technologies where it had both distinctive product and process technologies. This was in the area of textured gluten for the relatively new area of prepared vegetable meals.

Despite being heavily dependent on low-margin offerings, based on basic technologies, the company was financially successful. Further analysis indicated that this success was based on the speed with which it was able to spot emerging trends amongst ultimate consumers and on its good relationships with food producers. These enabled it to develop new flavour offerings to meet these requirements, often within 48 hours. However, the company was concerned that too much of its effort was devoted to short-term customer response and it was locked into the low-margin Cell 1. It addressed this by putting more effort into longer-term relationship building and particularly technology acquisition programmes enabling it to offer more innovative products.

---

[9]Developed from the work of Richard Brewer, research student, University of Bath.

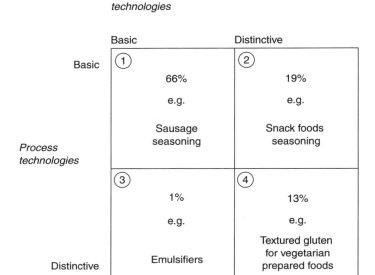

Figure 4.2 The contribution of different product and process technologies.

Source: D Ford and M Saren (2001) *Managing and Marketing Technology*, London, Thomson Learning.

Technology, offerings and life-cycles

The life-cycle positions of its technologies and offerings are the final method of categoriz-ing a company's technologies. Most business marketers are familiar with the idea that a company's offering is likely to move through some sort of "life-cycle", during which sales in-crease, reach some sort of stable level and then decline as the offering has been adopted by most potential customers or is replaced by better offerings from competing suppliers. These simple life-cycles are not predictive devices and the pattern of a company's sales can depart from an expected pattern for many reasons, such as changes in customers' problems, com-petitive innovation or wider macro-economic factors. But product life-cycles do explain important elements of the business marketer's task and this is illustrated in Figure 4.3.

Suppose that a company develops an offering (1), either alone or in cooperation with a customer. The company will then seek to introduce the offering to a number of customers, perhaps in a different form to each one. In this way it will try to achieve a return on its development expenditure. The costs of this development are likely to be considerable. For example, one major electronics company estimated that on average it needed to achieve 15% of the world market for an offering just to recover its development costs, before taking into account production or marketing expenses. The offering will progress through a life-cycle of sales. At some point, the company will withdraw or radically change the offering. It is important that the business marketer is able to do this before the offering is outdated by the competition, to the detriment of his relationships with his customers. But the marketer faces two problems:

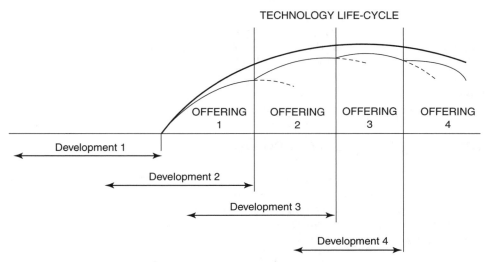

Figure 4.3   Technology and offering life-cycles.

- The time that the offering is likely to provide the best solution to customer problems is likely to be short, either because the problems themselves change or because competitors develop better offerings. Another major electronics producer refers to "six-month markets". Clearly, if the company in this situation is two months late with its offering, then it has missed a third of the available market.
- The length of time that a new offering takes to develop means that the development of offering 2 must often start before the first offering has been launched.

Figure 4.3 also shows the sales curve for offering 2. If the company has managed the development and transition process well and the new offering relates well to customer problems, then this curve will show an upward trend. Similarly, the marketer will need to develop and time the transition to offering 3. Each succeeding offering will largely be based on modifications to earlier offerings and thus is likely to require less development expenditure than its predecessors. This may lead to higher profits, even though sales growth may be lower. However, each of the offerings will be based on one or more technologies. Each of these technologies will have a life-cycle and these technologies will become increasingly outdated. This is illustrated in Figure 4.3 by the Technology Life-Cycle that lies above the offering curves.[10]

A business marketer must face the decision of whether to develop a further generation of offering based on existing technology or whether to switch to new or different technologies. Obviously, the time taken to make a major change in technology is likely to be longer and more costly than that required simply to introduce a new version of an offering based on "old" technology.

[10]David Ford and Chris Ryan (1981) Taking Technology to Market, *Harvard Business Review*, March–April, 117–126.

This means that business marketers must not just be involved in the development and introduction of successive generations of offerings. They must also be involved in much more critical decisions about the development, timing and full exploitation of the technologies on which their offerings depend. They need to coordinate both internal and external means of achieving a return on the company's technological assets. For example, it is often possible to exploit technologies that are no longer usable internally by licensing them to other companies, in other countries, or for different applications.

Technology in Supplier and Customer

Business marketing takes place at the interface between the technologies of supplier and customer. This interface raises at least two important issues for the marketer. The first concerns the interaction between supplier and customer in the technological development process and the second concerns the gap between the respective levels of technological understanding of the two companies.

Involving customers in technological development

The active involvement of customers has frequently been shown to be one of the key factors in successful new product development and launch. Indeed, Håkansson[11] has shown that the majority of technological development in business networks does not take place in either supplier or customer, but interactively between them. Often the potential users of an offering initiate its development by searching out and working with potential suppliers. At other times suppliers seek a "lead-user" to be closely involved in the development of a product or process technology or an offering based on them.[12] Customers are important to suppliers in technological development for several reasons:

- Customers have to face the problems of using current offerings and have the greatest knowledge of how a new offering can provide an improved solution.
- Customers know how a single offering can be used in combination with others from different suppliers.
- Customers know about alternative and substitute offerings and how a new offering compares to alternatives.
- Customers know how the offering will be used by their customers and at other points in the network.
- Perhaps most importantly, customers are likely to be committed to the development process because they will benefit from improved performance.

It is the business marketer's task to locate potential development partners among customers, to establish a relationship with them and to manage interactions with them during the development process. In doing this, it is important that the marketer understands and is able to communicate the benefits to the customer of a developmental relationship with a supplier. Some of these customer benefits are as follows:

[11]Håkan Håkansson (1987) *Industrial Technological Development: A Network Approach*, London, Croom Helm.
[12]EA von Hippel (1988) *The Sources of Innovation*, New York, Oxford University Press.

- Suppliers have a range of different technologies that the customer can never match.
- By using the efforts of several suppliers, the customer can gain the benefits of their combined technologies.
- A company can increase its total development capacity substantially by mobilizing its suppliers, without having to make all the required investments itself.

A customer's suppliers may in turn be able to mobilize their suppliers to create a large development network to support the customer's own development activities. In this way, suppliers can relate the developments in their fields to the evolving requirements of a customer. However, for this to be successful, both companies must effectively manage the relationship between them.[13] An example of successful technological development between Cummins and Toshiba is illustrated in Box 4.6.

Box 4.6   Effective Development between Customer and Supplier[14]

Ceramics have excellent insulating and high-temperature strength properties. Cummins is a producer of diesel engines and it started to develop ceramics with the idea of using them to make a diesel engine that didn't need a cooling system. It then became clear to Cummins that fine ceramics were very resistant to wear and could be used in applications other than insulation. Cummins made a thorough survey of all the potential materials and suppliers. The result of these efforts was that silicon nitride was selected as the most promising material and a patent search showed that Toshiba had by far the best patent position in regard to this material. The studies also indicated a good fit between Cummins and Toshiba. Both companies seemed to have staff with similar personalities, similar ways of working and common business objectives. After a number of meetings Cummins decided to choose Toshiba as partner for its development programme.

The core group involved in the development consisted of three to four full-time people from Cummins and eight to nine part-time people from Toshiba. This group had already started to work together before the formal agreement was signed. Cummins concentrated on design (product) technology and Toshiba on manufacturing (process) technology. The group jointly decided which components to develop and test and the joint project team evaluated the results.

Despite a number of problems, the joint development effort was considered a success and a joint company was established, Engineering Ceramic Technologies Inc. (Enceratec). The main task of this company is to market ceramic components in the US market.

This case study shows how productive cooperation between supplier and customer can advance technology and can also develop new businesses to exploit that technology more widely. However, it also shows that these benefits are not achieved easily or without a great deal of effort.

---

[13] Lars Erik Gadde and Håkan Håkansson (1994) The Changing Role of Purchasing: Reconsidering Three Strategic Issues, *European Journal of Purchasing and Supply*, vol 1, no 1, 27–36. A Lundgren (1995) *Technological Innovation and Network Evolution*, London, Routledge.

[14] J Laage-Hellman (1997) *Business Networks in Japan: Supplier–Customer Interaction in Product Development*, London, Routledge.

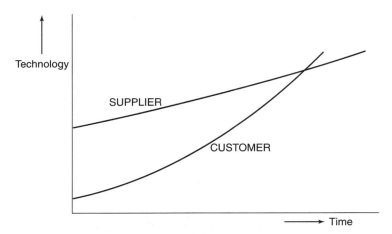

Figure 4.4   Technology in supplier and customer.

Differences in understanding of technology between customer and supplier

In the previous chapter we saw that customers often face uncertainties about what is the right solution for their problem. These uncertainties relate to their level of understanding of the technologies that are involved in different approaches. The "gap" between the level of understanding of customer and supplier will have a profound effect on the relationship between the two companies. This "gap" is illustrated in Figure 4.4.

The supplier in a relationship is likely to have greater knowledge than the customer of the technologies on which its offering is based at the start of that relationship. The customer's limited understanding is likely to be an important factor in its need uncertainty. Over time, the supplier's knowledge will increase, *but so too will that of the customer*. The gap between the two curves is likely to narrow and they may eventually cross. In this case, the customer knows more about the technologies on which the supplier's offering is based than does the supplier itself. This situation is common in business networks. For example, many retailers in textiles and other areas know more about the product and even the process technologies involved in what they sell than do their suppliers. They specify to these suppliers the design, materials and how the products are to be made. Hence they operate to the right of the diagram in Figure 4.4 where their suppliers have little to offer their customer other than low costs of production. Generally, the width of the gap between the two lines is a good indication of the profit margin of the supplier. Hence, for example the margins of textile suppliers to retailers are likely to be very low.[15]

---

[15]For example, one European retailer of household textiles and ornaments with a strong design function receives a profit-margin of around 64% of the final retail price, which is much greater than that of their suppliers.

It is important for business marketers to continuously monitor their position on these curves. Suppliers who move close to or past the intersection of the lines are unlikely to earn high margins and will need to invest in their technological contribution to the relationship to do so – effectively moving their position to the left of the diagram.

Technology in the Network

A network consists of companies, each having different product and process technologies. A company in the network is dependent on the technologies of its suppliers that are incorporated in their offerings and which it transforms using its own technologies to provide offerings for its customers, and so on. A combination of the technologies from many companies is needed to provide an offering that will meet the requirements of an end-consumer. The relationships between the companies in a network enable this process to take place. Companies operating in complex business networks can only make sense of their marketing by understanding how different skills and technologies are distributed throughout the network and the impact of this on the priorities of customers and suppliers and on the company itself.

Stability and change in technology

The impact of the network on a company and its technologies is neither simple nor predictable. At least two dimensions can be identified:

- Firstly, technology may tend to stabilize the networks in which business marketers operate and restrict their freedom to innovate. This can be explained as follows. The technologies that a company develops will lead it to invest in operational facilities and a range of offerings to exploit those technologies. Its customers and suppliers will make similar investments using their technologies. There is an incentive to use these investments, once they have been made and paid for. Each of these investments will be influenced by investments in surrounding companies. This leads to pressure on marketers from their own companies to produce offerings that use existing process facilities or product designs, so as to maximize the company's return on its technological investments. It also leads to pressure from customers and suppliers for the company to work within their technological boundaries. This pressure for continuity may also affect the direction of the company's future development.
- In contrast, successive refinements of existing technologies and the birth of new ones are probably the most important factors for change affecting companies. Developments can occur at any point in a network and affect even distant companies through the interconnections of relationships. This makes it important for the business marketer to scan the wider network for technological developments that may be significant for his company and also to look for opportunities to exploit the company's technologies in new applications. Developments in technologies change the internal operations of a company but they also affect the relationship between the company and its counterparts. For example, a supplier may be able to reduce a customer's costs of inspection of

delivered items by developing its own process technology to produce more consistently to specification. Similarly, by introducing new process technology, a supplier may be able to undertake activities previously carried out by the customer.

Adapting to the network

Companies operating in business networks develop technology themselves, but they must also adapt to the technological development of other companies around them. Indeed, they rely on this technological development by others to complement their own. Consequently, business marketers need to be concerned with the technological developments that their company can and should be doing and what surrounding companies are also doing. In other words, they must know how their company can influence what is happening in the network and how it should take part in what others are initiating. A company's developments must take place in interaction with important counterparts: customers and suppliers and others. Each company is involved in a sequence of actions, reactions, counteractions, cooperation through which different companies' technologies and offerings are developed in relation to each other. We referred to this process as "co-evolution".

- **The company's own developments:** In order for a company to take advantage of technological opportunities, it is important for it to have a number of development projects of its own as well as an intensive internal debate about suitable directions for development. Both these projects and the debate must systematically include external parties such as customers and suppliers. Marketers have a primary role in discussions about these developments with both customers and suppliers, who often need to be involved in major developments.
- **Relating to developments elsewhere in the network:** Business marketers also have an important role alongside that of purchasing and development staff in monitoring current and potential developments in existing and potential customers, in competing or complementary suppliers as well as in research institutions. These developments elsewhere in the network can be of vital importance for the company.
- **Managing technology in relationships:** Business marketers are involved in technological issues across a range of different relationships within a complex network. Relationships act as pipelines bringing the technologies of the two companies together. They create the framework within which technological development takes place and they influence the direction of technological development in and between both companies. Hence a relationship becomes a technological resource for the two companies.

However, to be successful, the process of technological development within each relationship needs to be carefully managed. Business marketers have an important role in this management. In some cases a customer will accept the offering from a seller and adapt itself to it. In this case the customer accepts the product and process technologies on which the offering is based as a given. In other situations the supplier will provide an offering that is completely designed by the customer, including the way it is delivered. Most situations are somewhere between these extremes, with both parties involved in development and in making adaptations.

Business marketers face important questions about the developments and adaptations that they and their customers should make and about how to manage the process of adaptation. If the technological strand of a relationship does not work, then the whole relationship will be in trouble. We can identify some of these questions for each relationship as follows:

- Who should be responsible for adaptations and changes? Adaptations are not the responsibility of marketing or technical staff alone. Instead there must be continuous discussion between marketing and technical departments about the costs and benefits of specific adaptations for different customers.
- When and how can the technical resources of a customer be activated? A common problem for business marketers is to find ways to get more people from the customer's company involved in a relationship. Greater involvement can lead to wider opportunities to develop the relationship and to gain from the technological strengths of the customer. But at the same time, greater involvement will mean increased investments by the supplier and customer. It is important that this investment is worthwhile or the relationship will be damaged.
- When and how should the technological issues and investments made in a relationship be evaluated? In order to increase objectivity, this analysis should be carried out by someone who is not closely involved in the relationship.
- How should the company organize itself to cope with the technological issues in a relationship? Marketing companies often organize themselves using key-account managers or key-account departments. This approach assigns responsibility for coordinating all the interactions with a customer to a single individual or group. However, it does not automatically solve the problem of the interface between marketing and R&D. Innovations in offerings and in processes will always affect customer relationships and vice versa and there is a need for a close link between the two. It is also vital to realize that a company's relationships and its technologies are equally important and neither should be de-emphasized. Key issues in both must be addressed together. Similarly, there is an important interface between marketing and operations. Most obviously this concerns questions of implementation, such as the daily problems of delivering the offering minor customer complaints. But the longer-term issues of the link between developments in relationships and the company's process technologies also demand close liaison between marketing and operations staff.

There are also a number of issues that concern adaptation and development across several relationships:

- How can the company handle relationships that are very different from each other? This is a key issue in the interface between the internal organization of a marketing company and its portfolio of relationships. On the one hand it is important to maximize the technological similarities between relationships, so as to reduce development costs and take advantage of previous investments in the design of offerings or in production processes. Yet on the other hand, standardization reduces the opportunities to gain knowledge from the unique features of a customer or a relationship. This means that business marketers need to think carefully about the potential and costs of a relationship and liaise with technical staff to assess the technological benefits of adaptation.

- How should the technological content of different relationships be related to each other? Each relationship will be based on one or more offerings from the supplier that will in turn be based on some of the supplier's technologies, development efforts and physical resources. Business marketers need to be involved in continuous discussion with technical staff about the best use of scarce resources in different relationships and the possibilities of starting new relationships to make better use of spare resources or of investments that have already been made.

- How can developments in different relationships be related to each other? Each of a company's relationships is a potential source of technological development. A major challenge for business marketing is to capitalize on this potential, so that developments in one relationship can be applied elsewhere. All too frequently, problems solved in one relationship have to be solved again in others because the company has not transferred the learning across its operations. This problem is particularly acute in companies that operate internationally. It can only be reduced by good flows of information between those responsible for different relationships and for technical issues in each operating area.

Conclusions

Most business marketers are not technologists and there is no necessary reason why they should be. Nevertheless, they do need to have an appreciation of the issues that their companies face in technology. This chapter has emphasized that a company's technologies and its relationships are its prime assets. Neither is a free resource. Each has to be expensively acquired and neither has any value without the other. Relationships are essential to exploit and develop technology. Technology is essential if a relationship is to have any value to customer or supplier. A relationship can add to the technologies of the customer and the supplier as well as solving immediate problems for them and generating short-term revenue. It is true to say that much of the technology of business companies actually exists in their relationships.

One view of a company's technology is that it is the sum total of all that exists "between the ears" of its staff. Technology includes patented designs of physical products and services and complex operating processes. But technology also includes the company's experience of how to put offerings together that will solve customers' problems, how to make things work and how to consistently and accurately fulfil the promise of an offering. Business marketing has the responsibility, with others, of maximizing the rate of return on these technological assets.

Technology is a widely but loosely used term. All too frequently managers talk of "high-tech", "core technologies" or "distinctive competences" without thinking what they really mean. Business marketers need to be proactive in making sure that their companies have a clear idea of the technologies they really have, both product and process. They must realistically assess which are truly distinctive and which are basic and common across all their competitors. This understanding is essential as a basis for exploiting technologies in a portfolio of relationships, whether for the sale of an offering or for external exploitation via licence or joint venture.

Finally, when a customer takes a decision to buy an offering from a supplier it is doing so because it believes that the supplier has the ability to design, develop and implement an offering that will solve a particular problem for it. This ability is based on the problem-solving and transfer abilities of the supplier. These abilities in turn depend on the supplier's product and process technologies, when combined with those of the customer. All of a supplier's technologies must be related to the problems, operations, buying processes and organization of its customers. It is to these issues that we turn in Chapter 5.

Further Reading

David Ford and Mike Saren (2001) *Managing and Marketing Technology*, London, International Thomson.

Håkan Håkansson (1987) *Industrial Technological Development: A Network Approach*, London, Croom Helm.

Håkan Håkansson (1989) *Corporate Technological Behaviour: Cooperation and Networks*, London, Routledge.

Håkan Håkansson and Alexandra Warluszewski (2002) *Managing Technological Developments: IKEA, the Environment and Technology*, London, Routledge.

Eric von Hippel (1988) *The Sources of Innovation*, New York, Oxford University Press.

I Nonaka (1990) Redundant, Overlapping Organisation: a Japanese Approach to Managing the Innovation Process, *California Management Review*, Spring, 27–38.

CK Prahalad (1993) The Role of Core Competences in the Corporation, *Research Technology Management*, November–December, 40–47.

P Smith-Ring and A van de Ven (1999) Development Processes of Cooperative Interorganisational Relationships, *Academy of Management Review*, vol 19, no 1, 90–118.

Assignment for Chapter 4

New technology at Wallace

The Wallace Company's business consists almost entirely of the design, manufacture and sale of specialized equipment for the plastics industry.

The Wallace Company now has approximately 100 customers. No single customer accounts for more than 15 % of sales, but the ten largest customers account for about 50 % of total sales volume. Direct export business amounts to about 5 % of total sales.

The company maintains a research and development department designed to meet the specialized and peculiar needs of the plastics industry in the development and improvement of production machinery and equipment. Because of the close integration of Wallace's products and customers, the Sales Manager and one Salesman handle all sales through personal contact.

Wallace has been concerned for several years that it has not been able to secure higher profits from its equipment. It has been working on a development in the area of production automation that it believes would provide considerable value to its customers. Customers currently buy complete moulds from specialized suppliers that are used to produce each of their plastic products. These moulds are hand-made by the suppliers. They are expensive and late delivery and teething troubles often lead to major delays for the plastics producers.

The new idea would be for Wallace to provide the moulds for use on its machines. Its customers would be provided with software that would enable them to specify the moulds and transmit the specification to Wallace. Wallace would then produce the mould to the customer's design and deliver it by courier. Not only would this innovation reduce the costs for the plastics companies, but it would also increase the speed with which they could respond to orders from their customers and enable them to increase the variety and sophistication of product shapes that they could produce.

However, the technology is still in the development stage and is likely to be expensive to bring to the market. It also involves Wallace moving from simply supplying equipment to also selling moulds on a continuing basis. The chairman is concerned that although the idea is to make things simpler for the plastics producers, it would involve Wallace in providing continuing advice and it would have to produce moulds on a continuous basis. The new moulds would probably involve modifications to the chemicals that the plastics producers use as their raw materials. Wallace has not previously been involved in the design of moulds.

Questions

Advise the chairman on the issues he should address before making a decision on the new innovation?

Do you think that Wallace should embark on the new innovation?

What are the risks involved?

What are the possible reactions of other companies in the network to the new innovation?

Are there any other approaches that Wallace could consider for this innovation?

What alternative technology strategies are open to Wallace?

UNDERSTANDING CUSTOMERS 5

Aims of this Chapter

- To examine the activities and importance of business purchasing and the purchasing function in a customer company and how this affects suppliers and business marketers.
- To analyse the nature of customers' problems and the role of purchasing and suppliers in solving these.
- To highlight the actual behaviour of customers in solving their problems.
- To examine the important dimensions of purchasing strategy of a customer and their implications for suppliers.

Introduction: The Importance of Purchasing and Suppliers

We emphasize throughout this book that the starting point for business marketing is the problems of their customers. Business marketers must understand where they fit within the operations of their customers and the problems that these customers face. In other words, it is important that business marketers are able to see themselves and their companies through the eyes of their customers. In this chapter we will examine the problems of business customers from the perspective of the customers themselves and look at how those customers try to use suppliers to address those problems.

Effectively using the skills, resources and the offerings of their suppliers is of major strategic importance for most companies. For example, Ford and General Motors spent $76 billion and $62 billion respectively, on purchases from suppliers, while Hewlett Packard's procurement costs for production materials amounted to $43 billion in 2004.[1] Purchases from suppliers account for more than half of the total costs of most companies and in

[1] *Purchasing Magazine*, June 17 2004.

some industries, such as electronics, telecommunications, construction and automotive, this portion can be considerably higher.

The importance of suppliers has grown as companies have concentrated more of their efforts on a limited part of the total activity structure of the business network in which they are involved. Specialization reduces a company's costs of technological development and leads to economies of scale in operations. But it means that a company becomes more reliant on inputs from suppliers and so effective purchasing is vital to reduce a company's costs. It is also important as a way of ensuring that a supplier's offerings are effective from its customer's point of view, by making the best use of the skills or technologies of suppliers. The purchasing function has a central role in this process and hence a substantial proportion of the resources available to a company are handled by the purchasing function. The significant contribution of individual suppliers to the operations and the offerings of their customers is illustrated in Box 5.1.

Box 5.1   The Importance of Individual Suppliers

A survey of 123 Swedish companies representing various sizes and industries showed that on average ten suppliers accounted for more than two-thirds of the total purchasing spending.[2]

Motorola's top 25 suppliers account for about 50% of its spending, an increase in two years from about one-third.[3]

Its reliance on its suppliers for technology development is one reason why Hewlett Packard have centralized their purchasing on a small group of suppliers: 80–85% of HP's production spend is with just 35 suppliers.[4]

Sun Microsystems say that they have gone from building 100% of their systems internally to building about 10% of their systems internally in a span of three years.[5]

The supply side of companies has also come more into focus because what happens at the interface between a supplier and customer has increased in importance. Ideas such as "just-in-time deliveries" (JIT), total quality management (TQM) and the zero-defect principle increase the importance of the relationships between a company and its suppliers. Applying these techniques makes the boundaries between suppliers and customers unclear. It means that a customer's internal costs are greatly affected by what goes on at the interface with its suppliers. Efficiency improvements in logistics related to JIT and TQM require the active involvement of both customer and supplier and affect benefits and costs

---

[2] H. Håkansson (1989) *Corporate Technological Behaviour*, London, Routledge.

[3] *Purchasing Magazine*, September 16 2004.

[4] *Purchasing Magazine*, June 17 2004.

[5] *Purchasing Magazine*, June 5 2004.

for both parties. In addition, the ambitions of suppliers to develop customized offerings have put build-to-order production at the top of the management agenda. This has further accentuated the importance of the interfaces between companies.[6]

The Dimensions of Supply

A customer's set of supplier relationships reflects the scale and complexity of its operations and there are no "normal" or "typical" supplier relationships. Some suppliers may be important to a customer because of the volume of purchases that it makes from them and the immediate financial effects of this. Other suppliers may be involved in long-term development of new offerings or ways of working and the contributions from these may only become apparent over time. The impact of each individual supplier relationship depends on how it fits into the problems and the operations of the customer and the way it affects the customer's other supplier and customer relationships. There are large variations in supply relationships across types of business and companies, but also for an individual customer over time. The variety of customers' approaches to their suppliers can be described in three dimensions:

- **The scope of its supply:** This describes the extent to which a company uses external suppliers as a complement to its own operations. Purchasing accounts for the dominant portion of total costs for many firms but other companies have a higher internal value-added and purchases have much less impact on their total costs. For example, some traditional airlines carry out most of the activities of booking, check-in, food service, pilot training and aircraft maintenance for themselves. Other more recent airlines contract out all of these activities to others, perhaps including to some of their competitors.
- **The configuration of its supplier base:** This refers to the make-up of a customer's supplier portfolio. Many companies require a large number of different offerings provided by many specialized vendors. But even if a company uses hundreds or even thousands of suppliers, the offerings of only a few of them may account for the major portion of purchasing costs as illustrated by Box 5.1. Some suppliers may be important for other reasons, for example by being responsible for offerings such as components, raw materials or services that are critical to the operations of the customer from a technical point of view.
- **The nature of its relationships with suppliers:** A customer's supplier relationships will vary substantially in the level of activity links, resource ties and interaction between the individuals. Some relationships are characterized by extensive interpersonal contacts, some by joint development of offerings. Some suppliers are kept at arm's length with minimal interaction. Some work solely to the customer's specification. Some suppliers deliver products "just-in-time", while others deliver to the customer's inventories. This variety can be illustrated by three examples:
  —Firstly, high-volume purchases of a commodity-based offering such as cement or cash transfer services will involve interaction between many individuals at different

---

[6] The problems and opportunities related to build-to-order production are illustrated in a case study of Volvo Cars presented in Chapter 8.

operating locations, such as construction sites or retail banks, particularly regarding deliveries. The operations scheduling of supplier and customer will have to be coordinated, but there will be few, if any, adaptations of the technical features of the offering.

—Secondly, a relationship involving a specialized offering, such as that for components and systems or operating software may have extensive mutual adaptations of the offering and facilities, but only moderate levels of activity coordination.

—Thirdly, a relationship that involves extensive service provision, such as food service or JIT deliveries will entail very tight coordination of the activities of the two companies, but the offerings may be standardized and there may be only limited interaction with other functional areas in the companies.

These variations in relationships lead to a distinction that we will use throughout this chapter between *high-* and *low-involvement* relationships. High-involvement relationships are those either with extensive activity links, resource ties or actor bonds, while low-involvement relationships score low on all of these.

The Customer's Problems

Business customers are interested in solving or coping with their problems. They are not particularly interested in suppliers' products and services per se. This is nicely illustrated by the purchasing director of the US company Pilgrim:

> In selecting a supplier for MRO (maintenance, repair and operating) goods and services we are not searching for a company to sell its widgets. We need suppliers that will come into this facility and help us identify opportunities and share them with us across the company.[7]

In the same spirit the CEO of a US distributor argues that "it is more about providing solutions than just selling parts". He continues by saying that customers come and ask "what can you do to help me design the products and get to market faster and what can you do to help me reduce costs?".[8]

The problems of customers can arise for many reasons, but they all relate to two basic activities of customers, which they will look to their suppliers for support in achieving. The two activities are rationalization and development.

Rationalization

Rationalization concerns the customer's need to carry out its day-to-day operations as efficiently and economically as possible. Faced with a particular operating problem, a customer may consider changing the specification of the offering it buys from a supplier or the way that it is produced or delivered. It may change suppliers, or it may choose between

[7] *Purchasing Magazine*, March 3 2005.
[8] *Purchasing Magazine*, April 21 2005.

making or doing what it needs itself or buying an offering from a supplier. The purchasing function contributes to these decisions through its knowledge of the capabilities of different suppliers and by relating these to the internal needs of the company's development, design and operations.

Rationalization requires customers to be concerned with both the direct and indirect costs of what they buy. Direct costs comprise the amount of the invoice from a supplier and the other costs that can be directly traced to the specific transaction, such as transportation costs. Concern with direct costs is likely to be greatest when the customer's need and transaction uncertainty are low and the specific problem is not closely related to other problems. When faced with this situation, it would be important for a supplier to benefit from economies of scale and offer a low purchase price by adopting a standardized offering.

Indirect costs are all the other costs of purchasing. They include the costs of running the specific relationship in which the purchase is made and the more general costs of its purchasing operations. Indirect costs are more difficult to trace than direct costs because they do not normally show up in company records, but they are often substantial, for example, Kodak estimates that these "hidden costs" are 250% of its direct costs of purchased items. Hence, in many cases a customer is likely to gain more by trying to reduce its indirect costs than by chasing for lowest price. We will examine the supplier's costs in detail in Chapter 9 when we consider pricing in business markets.

The administration of purchases, from enquiry to order to payment, provides huge opportunities for reducing indirect costs (see Box 5.2 for an illustration). These indirect costs may be greater than the total value of the purchase, especially for frequent purchases of low-valued items. One US study estimated the costs for handling a single purchase order for uncomplicated items such as for maintenance, repair or operations (MRO supplies) to be at least $20. For more complex purchases the costs ranged from $75 to $150. These figures emphasize the importance for companies to develop effective routines to deal with a huge number of transactions rather than to concentrate on optimizing each one. However, because each purchase is relatively unimportant, many companies have neglected to undertake these rationalization efforts. Hence they struggle with a huge number of fragmented purchases from a large supply base and an unnecessary administrative burden. Other companies have analysed and reduced their supply base, and concentrated their small purchases with a single supplier that then delivers offerings from other suppliers on their behalf.

Development

The second source of a company's problems is its need to develop its operations and its offerings. Purchasing has become more important in development as companies have concentrated their own operations and relied more on suppliers as an important resource. This means that the internal development activities of a customer need to be coordinated with those of its suppliers and so purchasing must be involved in developments at an early stage and then bring the right suppliers into the process. Early supplier involvement means that the vendor's product and process technologies can be fully exploited to enhance design

Box 5.2   Rationalization and Development of Customer Operations

Joint development between Bang & Olufsen and suppliers

System suppliers or strategic suppliers are the suppliers with whom B&O has a very close collaboration and in which co-development of unique components takes place. The system suppliers are involved both in the design and development stages. They have on-line access to sales forecasts, production plans, and materials requirements. They are often part of a Vendor Management Inventory (VMI) agreement. Open-book calculations are used and yearly productivity improvements are agreed upon. The investments in specific assets are high and in several cases, B&O develops unique technology in collaboration with the system supplier.[9]

Rationalization at BMW by "Automating" administrative processes

In this system a buyer at BMW generates an Excel spreadsheet of spare parts from the company's ERP (Enterprise Resource Planning) system and emails it to the appropriate supplier. The supplier enters details of pricing and lead-time and emails it back to the buyer. After analysis and negotiations the buyer uploads the spreadsheet into the ERP system which updates the scheduling agreement. The system then emails a purchase order in PDF format via EDI (Electronic Data Interchange) to the supplier who confirms receipt via the BMW supplier website.[10]

and to reduce later costs. The importance of this is emphasized by studies that show that up to 80% of the total costs of a new offering are determined in the design phase. Early supplier involvement can also reduce development lead times. This thinking has led companies such as Ingersoll-Rand to involve its important suppliers when new projects are "only a gleam in the eye of the marketing manager"! Box 5.2 exemplifies the role of suppliers in rationalization and development.

Who is Involved in Purchasing?

Purchasing is complex; it is not a simple process of search, evaluation and ordering. It often does not have a clear beginning and end. It is not just concerned with a set of discrete and separate transactions. Each purchase is affected by those that have been made before and ones that are planned for the future. Purchasing is not something that is only done by those with the job title of "buyer". Instead, the importance of purchasing to the

---

[9] J Mikkola and T Skjoett-Larsen (2003) Early Supplier Involvement: Implications for New Product Development Outsourcing and Supplier–Buyer Interdependence, *Global Journal of Flexible Systems Management*, October–December.
[10] *Purchasing Magazine*, August 11 2005.

rationalization and development of a company's operations means that many of the company's staff and functions are involved in it. The idea of the "buying centre" provides a way to make sense of this complexity.[11] A buying centre is not a formal group that exists in the company, but a way for us to classify different roles that individuals can perform in purchasing, as follows:

- **Buyers:** People with this job-title are likely to have a major role in managing an existing supplier relationship and dealing with the contractual arrangements in most purchases. They are also likely to have a role with others in selecting and establishing relationships, but they rarely act alone when important problems arise in either case. Sometimes a customer will have relationships with a group of suppliers that have been approved by other functions in the firm. Then the buyer will often be responsible for negotiation about the offering and fulfilment for a particular episode. In other cases a supplier may be chosen from within a portfolio of suppliers that have been decided on by someone else in the company and the buyer's task is then to administer the order.
- **Influencers:** These are able to affect the choice between existing suppliers in a portfolio. They can also introduce new suppliers into consideration or question the presence of existing suppliers. Influencers can be found in almost any part of a customer firm. For example, the marketing department may have preferences for a certain supplier, because its offering can improve the buying firm's offerings for its own customers. Development staff can be important influencers based on their evaluation of the technical content of different offerings and the technical capabilities of various vendors. Buyers can also influence supplier choice because of their experience of the reliability of suppliers, so too can accounting staff who know about the financial position of suppliers. Individuals who are potential *users* of suppliers' offerings can also be important influencers. The importance of users has increased as companies have appreciated that listening to them is a good way to enhance future productivity.
- **Gatekeepers:** These control the flow of information into the customer. Buyers often act as gatekeepers because they are the customer's primary interface with existing suppliers and they are likely to receive sales efforts from new ones. Gatekeepers can often prevent a potential new supplier getting access to important influencers in a company and hence may be a source of problems for a potential supplier's sales and marketing staff.
- **Deciders:** Finally, in some cases it is possible to identify one or more deciders. These may be individuals who specify a supplier, or an offering, in such a way that choice is limited to only one company. Sometimes development staff or senior managers take on this role and there is no "choice" for the buyer. In other cases it may be difficult to identify either a single decider or the point at which a decision is taken. Alternatively, a particular purchase may be made within an existing relationship without additional evaluation.

It is important for business marketers to be aware of the roles of different functions and individuals in a customer company and who is carrying them out. The more difficult or

[11] FE Webster and Y Wind (1972) A General Model of Organisational Buying Behaviour, *Journal of Marketing*, vol 36, no 2, 12–19.

Box 5.3   Two Examples of Multifunctional teams

General Motors has 150 "Creativity Teams" that form part of its globalization efforts. They combine people from purchasing, engineering, design, quality, marketing and finance. Their main task is to coordinate sourcing decisions for everything from door handles to anti-lock braking systems on a global basis. The members of the teams live in different countries and have telephone meetings twice a week. According to the purchasing director, these people together, "bring the skill levels up for our buyers" and often uncover new strategies and sourcing opportunities. When developing parts and systems for future models GM relies on "advanced purchasing teams" of buyers and engineers during the design stage for a new vehicle. Together they decide on the functional requirements and ask suppliers for proposals. Based on these proposals, the advanced purchasing team makes a final recommendation to the sourcing committee.[12]

Purchasing teams at Genentech are usually led by purchasing and are made up of members from quality assurance, quality control, manufacturing, process development, process sciences, inventory, materials planning, production planning and top management. Formal teams are in place to discuss performance of existing suppliers and to work toward continuous process involvement. These teams meet weekly to review the performance of suppliers with whom high-volume or single-source agreements have been made and discuss specific incidents of nonconformance of raw materials and delivery. Less formal teams are often formed to handle new projects or sourcing of a new raw material.[13]

important the problem is, the larger the portfolio of potential suppliers, the more complex the process and the more people who are likely to be involved, especially as influencers. Any one individual may occupy several roles, especially in small companies. Sometimes more formal multifunctional groupings exist in companies, as illustrated by Box 5.3.

The people in the buying centre will have different information needs because of their different responsibilities, so a buyer is likely to be more interested in price and contractual details than is a user. Yet behind these roles there are individuals who will have their own perceptions, expectations and objectives based on their personalities and backgrounds. Thus an analysis of the different roles in a buying centre needs to take personal as well as functional characteristics into account.

How Companies Buy

When academics try to explain how companies buy, they usually describe a number of stages in a supposedly "rational" decision-making process for a single purchase. This process

[12] *Purchasing Magazine*, August 15 1996.
[13] *Purchasing Magazine*, February 8 2001.

moves from need-recognition to the selection of a supplier and subsequent delivery of an offering. However, customers do not treat each purchase as an isolated event. Instead, they will relate the purchase to a number of factors particular to themselves, as follows:

- The particular problems they are addressing and the uncertainties they face.
- Their experience of dealing with this problem or similar problems in the past, within each of their relationships.
- Their expectations of the future of those relationships.
- Their own organization and resources.
- Their view of the wider network and of the other relationships in which they are enmeshed.

These factors help to explain why business customers most commonly start by looking for solutions to their problems in their *existing* supplier relationships. We refer to this process as Buy-cycle 1: "business as usual".

Solutions from existing relationships – Buy-cycle 1

A customer will have a supply base made up of a variety of existing relationships and it will vary widely in its involvement in them. Both high- and low-involvement relationships provide different opportunities for customers to solve their problems and this variety of relationships also reinforces continuity in the supply base.

The customer (and the supplier) in a high-involvement relationship use some of their limited resources to adapt their offerings and operations to suit each other's requirements. Because of this, the customer will have an incentive to stick with its current supplier to gain the benefits of these investments.

A low-involvement relationship requires only limited coordination of activities between the companies, few adaptations and little interaction. However, a customer will still be inclined to continue with it for routine problems, provided that it is effective and requires little attention. In this way, the customer avoids the costs of searching for and evaluating potential new suppliers. For example, it has been shown that "durable arm's-length relationships" in some situations represent the most appropriate type of involvement with suppliers.[14]

The importance of long-term supplier relationships is illustrated by Table 5.1 showing the age distribution of the relationships in the supplier portfolio of a vehicle manufacturing company. The data covers the period 1964–2003 and describes the total number of suppliers used for procurement of ten different components.[15] These components account for about one-third of the buyer's total purchasing costs and represent components and materials of varying complexity.

[14] J Dyer, D Cho and W Chu (1998) Strategic Supplier Segmentation: The Next "Best Practice" in Supply Chain Management, *California Management Review*, vol 40, no 2, 57–76.
[15] A Dubois, L-E Gadde and L-G Mattsson (2003) Change and Continuity in the Supplier Base. *Journal of Customer Behavior*, vol 2, no 3, 409–432.

Table 5.1   The duration of supplier relationships.

Relationship duration	Number of suppliers
1–4 years	18
5–9	11
10–19	11
20–29	6
30–39	5
Total number of suppliers	51
Average length	11.4 years

There is a strong continuity in many of the relationships. This is illustrated by the fact that eleven suppliers have been used for more than 20 years. Five vendors have delivered for over 30 years and four of them were still being used at the time of the study. Another indication of long-lasting conditions is that the lengths of the relationships in most cases represent consecutive periods of delivery. This means that once a supplier is used it stays until it is definitely removed. Some of the long-term relationships involve extensive adaptations. However, in some of the relationships the supplier has delivered standardized offerings with no specific adaptations, every year for more than 25 years. In another case, two competing suppliers have been used for the same component and both of them have delivered each year.

An existing relationship may be important because it involves large payments or contributes to technical development or is valuable to another company in the customer's network. Both high and low involvement can be important and all important relationships tend to be long-term. This is the case even when there are no apparent barriers to the entry of other suppliers, but it does not mean that a customer will continue with its less important relationships just for convenience. Often a customer will have two or more relationships simultaneously and alternate purchases between them. A customer is likely to consider the value of its existing relationships, its previous efforts to develop them, its evolving problems and the costs of searching for, evaluating and developing new ones, before it makes a change to a different supplier. These conditions imply that a company sometimes continues relationships with counterparts they don't like. For example, a German study identified "the paradox of unsatisfying but stable relationships" between car manufacturers and their suppliers.[16] In this case a group of suppliers were "notoriously unhappy" with the relationships to the car makers. In spite of this the relationships continued because of site-specific investments and adaptations of various kinds. Similar situations are not unusual on the buying side of companies.

Business-as-usual is a rational approach in most cases. A customer will often have made major efforts to find the best solution to its problems and find a suitable supplier. Often this will involve adaptations towards specific suppliers and so it would be rather surprising if a customer turned readily to a new solution and new supplier.

[16] K Backhaus and J Buschken (1999) The Paradox of Unsatisfying but Stable Relationships – a look at German car suppliers, *Journal of Business Research*, vol 46, 245–257.

However, business-as-usual does not mean a lack of change. Customers' problems constantly evolve in even the most "stable" of relationships. Suppliers' offerings also shift as both companies look for opportunities to improve the fit between them. The amount of change in a relationship is affected by how important both of them think that the relationship is. Sometimes the revisions are initiated by the customer as new problems emerge. But often it is the supplier that proposes a change, perhaps based on its experience in other relationships, or its problems in this one. Often it is difficult to trace a clear origin to these changes and they simply arise from the continuous interaction between the firms. Altogether this means that the process of seeking solutions from existing relationships in Buy-cycle 1 is highly dynamic.

Searching outside existing relationships – Buy-cycle 2

Sometimes a customer may look for solutions outside its existing supply base, even though this may require investments of time and money. We refer to this as Buy-cycle 2 and the cycle can start for a number of reasons, as follows:

- The customer may face new problems, or it may find it necessary to change its requirements for internal reasons. For example, it may decide to change the organization of its operations and search for a supplier of a new business system.
- On other occasions problems and solutions are redefined because of changes outside the customer. For example, it may be presented with offerings from new suppliers. These may provide new types of solutions or lead the customer to see some of its problems in a new light. Sometimes the customer's own customers may change their requirements or its competitors may introduce new offerings. Hence the customer will have to change its offering and thus seek new suppliers. Sometimes a customer may use an innovative offering from one supplier to solve a particular problem and then other problems may arise and solutions may need to be redefined.
- The customer may simply not be satisfied with the way that established suppliers are implementing their offerings. Perhaps deliveries or service provision has declined or prices have become uncompetitive.
- The existing supplier itself may cause a relationship to end. This could be because the supplier considers that the required investment in the relationship outweighs the potential benefits, or because it wishes to devote more resources to other customers. Suppliers have a portfolio of customer relationships and they have to evaluate how individual relationships contribute to the portfolio as a whole. Suppliers must choose the customers with which to be highly involved and investments in one relationship may hinder investments in others. Once a supplier has made its evaluation, it may not stop supplying the customer, but simply stop investing in the relationship until the customer itself chooses to switch.

Buy-cycle 2 involves a customer in searching outside its existing supplier-base. Depending on the reason for this, the customer may start with any one of these activities:

- Re-evaluating potential solutions.
- Redefining the problem.
- Seeking an alternative supplier.

Business marketers must be prepared to be involved in any of these activities if they wish to develop a new relationship or break into an existing one. The marketer will have to compare the solution that her offering provides to a range of other potential solutions, some of which may be unfamiliar to her. She must also be prepared to help the customer to define its problem, especially if this has changed. She must relate her offering to this problem, rather than simply describe its features.

Finally, she must be able to compare her offering with those of alternative suppliers *as a potential solution* to the customer's specific problem, rather than simply contrast the specifications of the alternative offerings.

No relationship will exist between the customer and the potential supplier when Buy-cycle 2 commences and both companies are likely to have considerable uncertainties. Both will need to invest time and possibly make adaptations to suit each other's offerings and operations.

Information Exchange in Business Transactions

The relationship between a customer and a supplier may encompass only one transaction, such as when a utility company buys a new generating station from a particular supplier or an insurance company employs a consulting firm for a major culture-change project. More commonly each relationship involves a number of transactions or episodes, such as the regular delivery of batches of components or monthly payment for a public-relations contract. Each of these episodes can only be understood in the context of the relationship of which it is part and each relationship can only be understood in the context of the network in which it is enmeshed. Despite this, business marketers must remain closely involved in their relationships and need to be aware of what happens in each of many episodes. This task of monitoring and controlling the interactions in a relationship will involve marketing in liaisons with many different functional areas in the company. Often this will involve the marketer in attempts to influence managers in these functional areas, who may be much more powerful than they are. This coordination is a major source of problems for both marketers and their customers. A single episode can vary in the time that it takes and in the number of functions and individuals from the customer and supplier who are involved. It can also vary in the type and amount of information that the customer and its supplier need. Business marketers have a prime role in managing information in a relationship. This is to provide information for the customer and for the marketer in order to monitor the relationship and to develop, communicate and implement its offering. It is useful to distinguish between three different types of information: administrative, commercial and technical.[17]

Administrative information is needed for a transaction to be fulfilled. It covers a chain of activities from inquiries, offers and orders, to delivery notifications and invoices. This is the major portion of the information that is exchanged between supplier and customer in simple episodes in Buy-cycle 1. When transactions between companies are frequent and the offerings are low-value, then the costs of handling the flow of information will be a large

---

[17] L-E Gadde and H Håkansson (1993) *Professional Purchasing*, London, Routledge.

proportion of the customer's total costs. In these cases, customers will be interested in suppliers that can help to reduce these costs. For example, many customers now make many of their small purchases from a single web-based intermediary. This reduces the number of suppliers with which the company has to deal and consequently reduces its administrative costs.

Commercial information is necessary to identify existing and potential suppliers and to continuously evaluate their offerings and their ability to implement them. A substantial amount of information will be needed to evaluate new, potential suppliers in Buy-cycle 2. Customers often use comprehensive rating schemes for new suppliers, but they may still find that they can only assess how well they implement their offerings after they have been used for some time. Convincing new customers of their implementation abilities is often a major challenge for marketers. In contrast, many customers omit to continuously evaluate their existing relationships. This omission can mean that an existing supplier can "get away" with things. This is particularly the case if the customer does not check on how up-to-date is the supplier's offering, or how well it is being implemented. It can also mean that supplier's best efforts are "taken for granted" by its existing customers. Both cases can mean problems for the marketer.

Technical information is often critical for a customer when making an initial evaluation of both offering and implementation. However, once a relationship is established, it can be stable for a long time. This means that the need for technical information is not necessarily determined by the complexity of an offering. For instance, technical exchanges between a car manufacturer and its component suppliers are much less complicated once a model of car is in serial production. Administrative information then becomes more crucial for a time. But an intense exchange of technical information may follow when the customer seeks a new solution or the supplier plans to modify its offering and each tries to take advantage of the technologies of the other.

Using systems for efficient exchange of information in buyer–supplier relations is thus a crucial issue. Various types of information technology portals have been developed recently and Box 5.4 describes some of the features of the portal used by Rockwell Collins and their suppliers.

Resources for Purchasing

The importance and complexity of business purchases mean that customer companies have to face the difficult issue of how they should allocate resources of people, time and money to particular episodes in each relationship. Figure 5.1 illustrates some of the factors in this resource allocation.

Uncertainties

A customer is likely to devote more resources to a purchase episode when it faces greater uncertainties:

- Need uncertainty is likely to lead a customer to involve more staff to try to establish its requirements and relate these to available offerings and to liaise with potential suppliers. A useful strategy in these situations is to stay with known suppliers.

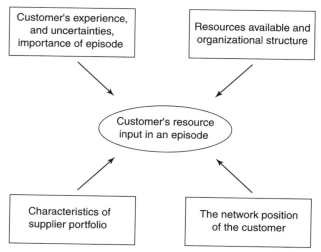

Figure 5.1   Purchasing organisation and resources.

- Market uncertainty means that a customer will need to gather commercial information about technological changes in the network and about a number of potential suppliers, unless it already has relationships with those suppliers.
- Transaction uncertainty may lead the customer to either devote resources to improving the fulfilment performance of its current supplier or to use a number of suppliers.

The importance of an episode will also affect the resources that a customer puts into it. For example, a purchase may involve little risk, such as when it is just one of many similar purchases, or it may be of low monetary value. In this case it is likely to involve few resources within an existing relationship, following Buy-cycle 1. In contrast, a purchase may be risky because the problem involved is difficult to solve or is critical to the company's operations, or it may be of high value. In this case the company is likely to devote considerable resources to it by involving many company functions. It may even use consultants or it may restrict its detailed discussions to only a few trusted suppliers to try to reduce its need uncertainty.

Organizational structure

A company can organize its purchasing activities in two different ways: either centralized or decentralized. By bringing all its purchasing activities into one centralized function, a company will hope to coordinate all its contacts with each supplier and achieve cost savings through large order quantities. Centralized purchasing also improves resource allocation and professionalism because purchasing staff can specialize in buying particular items, such as professional services or components.

Box 5.4   Information Exchange Through Rockwell's Portal

The first functionality targeted for Rockwell's portal was the efficient exchange of technical documents and information between suppliers and buyers. An E-drawings tool allows suppliers to log on to the portal and access large technical drawings online instead of via email or CD.

To further streamline functionality an e-RFQ (request for quotations) application was developed that searches the ERP-system for contracts that are coming up for bidding six weeks out and sends alerts to suppliers to bid on them through the portal. The system evaluates the bids and can automatically send a purchase order to the winning bidder or let a buyer evaluate the bids.

The Supplier Scorecard module on the portal provides data on each supplier's quality and delivery performance. Suppliers are sent an email every month with the data including current scores as well as six-month averages to help identify longer-term trends.

The Order Status application lets the highest-volume suppliers see all their open orders and confirm delivery dates, push-out dates, split orders and change quantities.

A forecast tool lets suppliers see Rockwell's future demand expectations for the items they supply and plan appropriately based on the forecast.[18]

In decentralized purchasing the various business units within a company can make the supplier choices they prefer. This has the advantage that buyers can relate more closely to the particular requirements of the users of their purchases but it does mean that they have to work across a broader range of offerings.

The choice between centralization and decentralization will always be a compromise and companies try to combine the advantages of both approaches. For example, a decentralized purchasing organization may be supplemented by a central unit that is responsible for group agreements so as to benefit from economies of scale. Similarly, centralized purchasing can be supported by local buyers who are in close contact with the company's operations. An example of this approach is illustrated in Box 5.5.

One organizational issue at the top of today's purchasing management agenda is "global purchasing", ie firms' efforts to economize on total purchases over the world. By leveraging common commodities across the company's operations a firm may save huge amounts of money. For example, Motorola used to have 65 different agreements globally with one supplier for the same software licence. Motorola's software team, in cooperation with the supplier, negotiated a global agreement which reduced costs by 50% of what they had been paying for the 65 different agreements. Similarly, Motorola was able to reduce the 27 buying centres located in Asia to only one.[19]

---

[18] *Purchasing Magazine*, January 9 2005.
[19] *Purchasing Magazine*, September 16 2004.

> ### Box 5.5 Purchasing Organization at Dupont[20]
>
> To overcome the many challenges of purchasing in the specialty and fine chemical areas, Dupont has combined the specific market knowledge of buyers in each of its separate business units with the leverage and perspective possible only with a centralized sourcing structure.
>
> Dupont's purchasing structure has buyers and contract administrators at each of its locations and within each of its 18 strategic business units. These buyers handle the purchasing task of the business on a day-to-day basis.
>
> Sourcing personnel focus on the more strategic procurement task and are grouped in the company's global services business unit. Headed by the chief procurement officer and three directors (two for sourcing and one for logistics), the global services business unit includes many purchasing professionals. These specialize in various areas of strategic sourcing, including energy and raw materials, specialty chemicals, contract manufacturing, equipment, transportation and logistics.
>
> In addition to the sourcing and purchasing divisions within Dupont's central and localized purchasing models, sourcing personnel are also stationed within the business units, having dual responsibility – to the business units and to the company's central sourcing structure.

Supplier portfolio

We have emphasized that a customer's existing supplier relationships affect the evolution of its problems and the solutions it seeks. The characteristics of these relationships also have a major impact on the resources that a customer puts into its buying operations. Most of these resources will not be devoted to single episodes, but are used to maintain the relationships and also to develop long-term exchanges with suppliers. High-involvement relationships are resource demanding, both at the beginning and in their continuous maintenance. It is important for a customer to manage its portfolio so that it has a range of suppliers that relate closely to its existing and emerging problems. At the same time it is important that the customer does not incur the costs of maintaining a wider portfolio of supplier relationships than is needed to meet its requirements.

Therefore companies strive to reduce the sizes of their supplier portfolios. Some of the companies discussed previously in this chapter are good examples of this trend. For example Bang & Olufsen reduced suppliers from 1000 to 300, and Hewlett Packard reduced its suppliers of production materials by 53% and its logistics suppliers by 68%. Factors contributing to this reduction include efforts to consolidate the purchasing volume with fewer suppliers, increasing reliance on systems sourcing, and enhanced attention to single sourcing.[21]

---

[20] *Purchasing Magazine*, May 6 2001.

[21] L-E Gadde and H Håkansson (2001) *Supply Network Strategies*, Chichester, John Wiley & Sons, Ltd.

Network position

We have previously defined network position as a company's portfolio of relationships and the rights and obligations that come with these. The network position of a customer company may have important effects on its purchasing.[22] For example, other companies in the surrounding network may affect the way that a customer allocates its resources to its supplier relationships. These other companies may include the customer's own customers or its other suppliers, or companies operating elsewhere in the network that have similar problems. For example, an important customer may pressurize a supplier to invest more heavily in its relationship with a particular component supplier. On the other hand, the network position of some major companies, such as Microsoft or Intel can more or less dictate many aspects of the way that surrounding companies do business.

A company's network position may also restrict its ability to change suppliers. For example, a company may have previously bought all its requirements from a wholesaler. It may now wish to buy some of these directly from a manufacturer. The manufacturer may refuse to supply it directly for fear of harming its relationship with the wholesaler. Some companies, such as those in the fashion or household products business have a network position that involves them in relationships with numerous actual or potential suppliers, each able to offer different combinations of price, product sophistication and delivery. They are also likely to have relationships with independent product designers and media companies that fuel rapidly changing fashion and customer demands that affect the whole network. Box 5.6 illustrates how one company tries to reduce the problem of dealing with multiple relationships in a complex network.

Box 5.6   Reducing the Problems of Network Complexity

The British fashion and house-wares retailer, Next, sources supplies from a wide range of suppliers around the world. It would be difficult for Next to manage each of these supplier relationships effectively in a rapidly changing and fashion-driven network. One way that it avoids this problem is to use the services of Li and Fung. Li and Fung were originally established in Hong Kong to help companies from the west to buy from China without having to locate, establish and manage relationships with suppliers from there. It now has offices and provides similar services in many countries. For the purchase of ceramic house-ware from Portugal, Next outlines its requirements to the Portuguese office of Li and Fung, based on the work of its internal designers and its interpretation of fashion trends. Li and Fung then approach around twenty ceramics producers in Portugal and assemble a display of their products aimed at Next's requirements. Next makes its choice and the purchase, quality assurance and delivery is handled by Li and Fung. Li and Fung charge Next a small percentage on their total purchase amount for their services. In this way, Next substitutes one "supplier" relationship for twenty.[23]

---

[22] For an extensive discussion on managing in networks see D Ford et al (2003) *Managing Business Relationships*, Chichester, John Wiley & Sons, Ltd.

[23] Postgraduate student Helena da Silva provided the information for this illustration.

Strategic Choices in Purchasing

We saw in earlier chapters that the choices facing a single company are strongly affected by the surrounding network. This means that the ability of a company to develop an independent purchasing strategy is severely limited by its existing relationships and the wider network that impacts on these.[24] Despite these limitations, companies do face clear choices in their purchasing strategy and these have important implications for business marketers. We can examine these issues by using some of the terms we have developed in this chapter.

Determining the level of involvement with suppliers

As we have suggested previously, it is possible to see two simultaneous but contrasting approaches to a customer's involvement with its suppliers: low-involvement relationships and high-involvement relationships.

Low-involvement relationships

When a customer and supplier establish close activity links, resource ties, or actor bonds, then both will become dependent on each other. Sometimes customers strive to avoid this dependence on individual suppliers to give themselves freedom to change. So-called "arm's-length relationships" have four major advantages:

• They are cheap to operate.
• A number of suppliers can help overcome short-term problems related to implementation, such as delivery failures, problems with product or service "quality" or fluctuations in demand.
• Limiting investment in a particular relationship means that the customer may avoid being "locked in" to that supplier in the long term.
• Limiting involvement with any single supplier may encourage different suppliers to compete by improving their offerings or reducing their prices.

The low-involvement approach to supply relationships considers suppliers as more or less efficient producers of *identical* inputs. This view is implicit in purchases by competitive tender, which is common in government buying and in the construction industry. Each project tends to be evaluated in isolation and on the basis of each supplier's price for a *defined* offering. This price orientation ignores the effects of the indirect costs of a purchase, the wider problem-solving abilities of particular suppliers and the additional benefits to a customer that may come within a developed relationship. It is also rather adversarial, so that a price reduction is perceived as a gain for the customer and a loss for the supplier and vice versa. In practice, a low-involvement approach can work when the customer's problem and the required solution are clear and need not be questioned and there are a number of suitable suppliers available. Examples include contracts for waste removal or

---

[24] We deal fully with overall issues of strategic choice and limits to independence in Chapter 10.

office cleaning. Although, even in these cases, differences between the way that each company implements its offering can cause problems and cost increases for the customer.

High-involvement relationships

High-involvement relationships are based on another idea of purchasing efficiency and a different view of the role of suppliers and the nature of relationships. Companies increasingly have to rely on the resources of outside suppliers and this means that many of the customer's activities must be coordinated with those of its suppliers. This need for coordination means that the two companies will have to adapt some of their activities and invest dedicated resources in the relationship. These adaptations create interdependencies and these restrict a customer's ability to switch suppliers frequently. An illustration of this is provided in Box 5.7.

A customer taking a high-involvement approach will not try to optimize the price it achieves in each single transaction. Instead, it will aim to improve its operations in the long term by using the resources of its suppliers more effectively. This involves attempts to reduce the total direct and indirect costs of the relationship by effective adaptations by both companies. Examples of this include building activity links to enable a data company to process a customer's data overnight in a low-cost location such as India, or linking the manufacturing operations of a component supplier to those of a car assembler, or introducing Electronic Data Interchange (EDI) to enable a textile supplier to reduce the in-store inventories of a fashion retailer.

A high-involvement approach also involves a customer in using suppliers in the development role of purchasing, to enhance its offerings for its own customers. Examples of this would include: a supplier and a customer working together on joint developments to improve the service level in the customer's call-centre; or joint development of the product

---

Box 5.7   High-involvement Relationships at Sun Corporation

John Shoemaker, Vice-President for Purchasing, has witnessed how supply management at Sun has evolved: "When I first got here, Sun had a highly tactical strategy with suppliers. We did not work with them. We had adversarial relationships with them." However, Sun began forging long-term relationships with suppliers and took a more strategic approach to supply management. It signed long-term agreements with suppliers who were travelling down the same technology path as Sun. It developed an "open kimono" approach to suppliers who became involved earlier in Sun's new product developments. "It's totally changed from the old days when you didn't want suppliers to know too much. Now it's the opposite. They know as much of our business as we do. That's how you maximize their value-added."[25]

---

[25] *Purchasing Magazine*, September 19 1996.

element in a supplier's offering to enable the customer to change its own offering to provide a higher performance offering to its customers.

Joint development with suppliers has become increasingly common over time. Integrating resources with suppliers can reduce the lead-time in developing new offerings and decrease total development spending. It can also increase the profits of both companies by contributing to more effective relationships between the buyer and its own customers. However, a high-involvement approach is always costly. Achieving the benefits of integration requires adaptations to offerings and resources, coordination of activities and intense personal contact between individuals.

A marketer must find out the approach that a customer is likely to take to involvement in their relationship and adjust her own approach accordingly. But her task is also to develop and manage a portfolio of customer relationships and she faces a limit to the resources she has available. She must determine the opportunities and problems of each relationship, based on the customer's approach to it, the approach she would prefer, the resources the relationship will require and its contribution to the portfolio as a whole.

Configuration of the supply base

Low-involvement relationships often lead to a large supplier base as customers use multiple competing suppliers to try to drive down prices. However, customers have become increasingly aware of the indirect costs of handling suppliers and this has made them eager to reduce the number that they use. One way that they have done this is to encourage some suppliers to become systems-suppliers and take responsibility for bringing together the activities of a number of sub-suppliers, as we saw in Chapter 2 in the case of Toyota.

The trend to high-involvement relationships has also affected suppliers' portfolios. This is because customers often have to use a single source for each problem or offering in order to achieve the benefits of integration. Business marketers will often only consider investing heavily in a relationship in return for exclusivity. High-involvement relationships are resource-demanding for customers and, as previously argued, suppliers and customers cannot handle too many of them. This was very clear when Sun entered high-involvement relationships with suppliers. Five years before the strategic change, Sun spent 80% of its purchasing budget with about 100 suppliers. After the change, 89% went on 20 suppliers and the top five accounted for 65% of its total spending.[26]

Even greater benefits of high involvement can be achieved if it can be extended to cover the supplier's suppliers and the customer's customers. This can promote activity coordination and resource combinations throughout what is often referred to as the customer's "supply-chain". However, the major benefits for customers are likely to be attained if a wider "supply-network" perspective is used. Customers need variety in the level of their involvement in their supplier relationships and it is the combined efforts of all suppliers that comprise the external contribution to them. Box 5.8 illustrates the variety in the supplier relationships of two companies.

[26] *Purchasing Magazine*, September 18 1996.

Box 5.8 Two Examples of Variety in the Supply Base

Bang & Olufsen[27]

"Standard suppliers" supply B&O with commodity components. Price, specification, consistency and delivery are important criteria for the choice of these suppliers and typically the relationships are of arm's-length type. Electronic market places are used to compare and select the suppliers.

"Capacity suppliers" perform simple production and assembly processes according to specifications set by B&O. These suppliers are mainly used in periods of peak loads on B&O's own production capacity. B&O regularly searches for new potential vendors, and current suppliers have to demonstrate productivity improvements.

"Key suppliers" provide proprietary key technologies important for B&O's final products. These relationships involve specific investments imposing interdependences. There is also a collaboration agreement between the parties and B&O has access to the supplier's roadmap for technological development. A committee of top managers from both parties meets at least once per year.

"System suppliers": Crucial features of the development aspects of these relationships were described in Box 5.2. Because of their high asset specificity and technological complexity, these relationships are usually based on single sourcing. This type of supplier—buyer relationship is very resource-demanding and so currently B&O has only about twelve system suppliers.

Kodak[28]

Level One: "World-source suppliers" have global capabilities, are a designated standard source for specific products, and have established global pricing/discount contracts in place; a formal variance process is applied to any request to purchase these specific products from other sources.

Level Two: "Preferred suppliers" comprise a few specific, selected suppliers per product who may have either global or regional pricing or discount agreements. Although their use is encouraged, it is not mandatory as it is for world-source suppliers. The opportunity exists for these suppliers to eventually become a world-source supplier.

Level Three: "Niche suppliers" are for specific applications in a specific manufacturing segment where it does not make good business sense to change the installed base. They may not be retained in the long term.

---

[27] J Mikkola and T Skjoett-Larsen (2003) Early Supplier Involvement: Implications for New Product Development Outsourcing and Supplier–Buyer Interdependence, *Global Journal of Flexible Systems Management*, October–December.

[28] *Purchasing Magazine*, March 7 1996.

These characteristics imply that it is vital for suppliers to understand their position in the total network that surrounds a customer and how that customer sees the relationship between that supplier and the rest. Encouraging cooperation within the total network of complementary suppliers can produce major benefits and a number of major companies are following this route. In order to improve the performance of the supplier-network a customer may share its knowledge and resources with suppliers and actively intervene in their operations. One way of doing this is through so called "expatriate programmes" whereby technicians from the buying company may become more or less permanent staff in supplier factories. A further source of technical progress is transfer of technology, both from the customer and between the various suppliers.

The scope of supply

The final set of strategic choices in purchasing concerns the extent to which the customer should make-or-buy the inputs to its operations. This has been an issue in companies for a long time, but was traditionally handled at a relatively low level in purchasing organizations. Decisions were mainly based on the expected level of capacity utilization and historical cost data. Depending on conditions, the make-or-buy decision could be changed from year to year. Such changes caused no major problems because the subcontracted items were either highly standardized or designed by the customer.

Only recently has make-or-buy been regarded as a strategic issue, based on the sort of technology analysis we described in Chapter 4. This has led companies to rely more and more on "buy" rather than "make". Outsourcing has extended far from the subcontracting of manufacturing operations to other activities such as administration, logistics, market intelligence, process design and product development. In the previous chapter we explained how the reasons for this centred on companies' need to concentrate on a small number of distinctive technologies, rather than attempt to maintain a presence in all of the technologies needed to produce their offerings. Specialization means that a customer can use suppliers that can achieve economies of scale in their operations, so that focused suppliers can contribute to the rationalization role of purchasing. A supplier working with several customers is also likely to be better at choosing and following the "right" direction for technical development, when compared to a customer with its narrower experience and focus on its own operations.

Corporate attitudes towards resource control have also been modified. Owning resources provides a high level of autonomy in their utilization and companies have traditionally shown preference for ownership control, but investments in highly specialized resources can lock a firm into a structure which might become obsolete as technologies develop. On the other hand, outsourcing can provide flexibility. Companies increasingly realize that they can still achieve some control over the direction of development and the operations of their supplier's resources within high-involvement relationships.

The increased level of outsourcing places greater emphasis on the relationship management skills of both buyers and business marketers. It provides opportunities for suppliers as their customers ask them to take on more responsibilities. Changes in attitudes to resource control have also fostered new ways for suppliers to connect with customers through links, ties and bonds. A supplier can actively promote customers' outsourcing activities by making its wider capabilities available. But this requires marketers to move away from a narrow orientation towards their offering and take a greater interest in their company's operations, their resources and their technology. All of these are increasingly brought into play in their relationships with customers.

However, suppliers should also be aware that the current increase of outsourcing will not necessarily continue. We believe that today's one-sided prescriptions for outsourcing need to be supplemented with an argument for in-sourcing. For various reasons a customer may benefit from taking back activities in-house. Such decisions can result from changes in cost–benefit considerations, strategic analysis of the technologies that are likely to be critical in the future, and/or changes in other parts of the network.

Conclusions

This chapter has examined some of the complexities of business purchasing and their implications for business marketers. Customer problems are at the core of business marketing. These problems go beyond concerns about which offering to choose for each transaction. They include the wider questions of how to carry out the development and rationalization roles of purchasing, what type of relationships to seek and how to manage them effectively. Different types of relationships provide quite different kinds of benefits to a customer. High-involvement relationships are costly, but may contribute more to rationalization and development. In other situations, a customer is likely to gain more through a low-involvement approach. Sometimes a customer might benefit from having suppliers that compete with each other to offer the lowest price for a standardized offering. In other cases a customer might gain from staying with one supplier for a long time and perhaps developing a dedicated offering for its requirements. Every customer needs a mix of supplier relationships characterized by variety in the level of involvement. The main issue in supply strategy is how to handle this mix and to modify it as conditions change.

The ways in which customers handle strategic issues in purchasing have profound implications for business marketers. Customers are not interested in the specification of a supplier's product, but only what that supplier's offering can do to address their problems. Marketers must be closely in touch with these customer problems and also make choices about how to handle customers, based on their own resources and aspirations in the light of customers' evolving purchasing strategy. For some customers a standardized offering will be appropriate because any adaptations would involve it in more costs than benefits, or it may simply not be possible to convince the customer of the benefits of adaptations, or it may negatively affect the supplier's relationship with another customer. In some cases a customer may be interested in developing a high-involvement relationship. In this case the marketer must evaluate the potential long-term costs and benefits of such an arrangement and, if it goes ahead, must continue to monitor the relationship throughout its life.

Further Reading

R Axelrod (1997) *The Complexity of Cooperation*, Princeton University Press.

B Axelsson and F Wynstra (2002) *Buying Business Services*, Chichester, John Wiley & Sons, Ltd.

T Davis (1993) Effective Supply Management, *Sloan Management Review*, Summer, 35–46.

D W Dobler and D Burt (1996) *Purchasing and Supply Management*, 6th edition, New York, McGraw-Hill.

D Ford (ed) (2001) *Understanding Business Marketing and Purchasing*, London, International Thomson, especially readings 5.1–5.6.

L-E Gadde and G Persson (2004) Developments on the Supply Side of Companies, in *Rethinking Marketing*, H Håkansson, D Harrison and A Waluszewski (eds), Chichester, John Wiley & Sons, Ltd, pp 161–186.

R Lamming (1993) *Beyond Partnership: Strategies for Innovation and Lean Supply*, London, Prentice-Hall.

M Mol (2003) Purchasing's Strategic Relevance, *Journal of Purchasing and Supply Management*, vol 9, no 1, 43–50

J Morgan (1999) Purchasing at 100. Where it's Been, Where it's Headed, *Purchasing*, November 18, 72–94.

T Nishiguchi (1994) *Strategic Industrial Sourcing: The Japanese Advantage*, Oxford, Oxford University Press.

M Sako (1992) *Prices, Quality and Trust: Buyer–Supplier Relationships in Britain and Japan*, Cambridge, Cambridge University Press.

A van Weele (2005) *Purchasing and Supply Chain Management*, London, Thomson.

J Womack and D Jones (1994) From Lean Production to the Lean Enterprise, *Harvard Business Review*, March–April, 93–104.

Case for Discussion

United Steel's new offering

United Steel Ltd has developed a new offering – sheet steel based on cold-rolled steel coated with a thin layer of a zinc-aluminium alloy. This coating improves the corrosion resistance of the sheet, which is a crucial feature in some user applications. United Steel and many other companies are currently supplying galvanized steel – a standardized sheet coated with a layer of zinc only. The new coating enhances the corrosion resistance of the steel considerably. In comparison with galvanized steel, laboratory tests indicate an extension of life by three to four times. Current users of galvanized steel therefore represent a prime target for the new product. In addition, the features of the product might make it competitive in other applications too. Some users of sheet materials currently buy stainless sheets or aluminium sheets because galvanized steels do not provide the corrosion-resistance required in their applications. These other materials are much more expensive than United Steel's new product and in particular applications its features might be good enough.

A few potential customers have been involved in the development of the new sheet and the features of the coating have to some extent been determined by their specific applications. The serial production of the new coating is planned to start within eight months and company representatives of United Steel are currently working hard to convince potential buyers to change to this new material. The typical customer uses the sheet as an input material for what they offer their customers, for example ventilation ducts, automotive components, garage doors etc. The new sheet should also be interesting to current users of aluminium and galvanized steel because its technical features make it possible for buyers to use thinner sheet than at present. This provides benefits from a cost perspective and opportunities for alternative designs of their own products. United Steel assumes buyers working with products aimed for "corrosive environments" to be those most interested in the offering, for example manufacturers of car mufflers and equipment for sewage systems and drains.

Questions for discussion

It is important for United Steel to consider the situation from the buying firm's point of view when attempting to get potential customers to change to the new offering. These firms are not particularly interested in the product and its characteristics per se. From a potential customer's perspective the main concern is in what way a change would make its situation better, for example in terms of increased revenues, lower costs or other types of benefits.

Question 1: In what respects would a customer be better off by changing to this new material?

Question 2: What inconveniences might be associated with change?

Question 3: What differences concerning Questions 1 and 2 can be expected with regard to three types of potential buyers:

- those currently buying galvanized sheets from United Steel;
- those buying galvanized sheets from another supplier;
- those buying stainless or aluminium sheets

Changing to a new material is an important strategic issue for any customer which leads to the following questions:

Question 4: What types of uncertainties can be expected to arise in the customer?

Question 5: What actions can be undertaken by the customer to reduce these uncertainties?

Question 6: What can United Steel do to affect these uncertainties?

Again it might be relevant to make a distinction between the three types of potential customers.
    At a typical meeting with a potential customer:

Question 7: What functions of the customer would you expect to be present?

Question 8: Discuss what you think will be the main concerns of the various functions and also what information they might require from United Steel.

MANAGING RELATIONSHIPS WITH CUSTOMERS

6

Aims of this Chapter

- To examine the tasks facing business marketers in managing their relationships with individual customers.
- To explain a process for auditing these relationships.
- To examine the management of an overall portfolio of customer relationships.
- To highlight the importance for the business marketer of understanding company relationships in the wider business network.

Introduction

It is not a matter of choice for a supplier whether or not it should have relationships with its customers. All companies have relationships now and all companies have always had them. In fact it is difficult to see how a company could operate or buy or sell without relationships. But as we have discussed in Chapter 5, business relationships vary in content, strength and duration: not all relationships are close, complex or individually important to the supplier and/or to the customer. Many companies also have hundreds or thousands of relationships that are individually less important, but which collectively are vital to it. All of these have to be managed if the companies involved in them are to be successful.

A company's relationships are actually a mixed blessing for it. On the one hand, relationships are an asset. They are the source of problem solutions, sales, purchases, profits and often technology and new ideas. But relationships are also a costly burden for a company to carry. They require investments of time and money and they involve risk, uncertainty and dependence on others.

Hopefully, the earlier chapters of this book have equipped us with some concepts that will help us to understand what happens in relationships with customers. We have learned that:

- Each relationship is founded on the individual problems and uncertainties of both customer and supplier.
- Business marketers and their customers are likely to be involved in adaptations to their offerings and operations to cope with this individuality. This must happen within the difficult constraints of their own costs and profit responsibilities.
- Time is a defining feature of a relationship. Both the past and the future affect current behaviour in a relationship and experiences, expectations and promises underlie the interaction within it. Managing a business relationship is likely to be a long-term activity.
- Each of a company's relationships is part of a wider portfolio of relationships. Together, these relationships define the company's position in the network. The network provides a structure for each relationship and the technologically based interdependencies within it.

The importance of time, uncertainties and problems as well as the individuality of each relationship, its financial significance, and the technological interdependencies within it, all mean that business marketers must shift away from conventional approaches. Specifically, they must *not*:

- Try to sell the offerings they have to whoever might buy them – *the sales approach*.
- Try to approach all companies in the same way – *the market approach*.
- Concentrate on winning each order, project or deal that comes along – *the single purchase approach*.

Instead, business marketers need to work with two interconnected units of analysis: firstly, their current and potential customer relationships and, secondly, the technological resources of their company and of the customer. Their aim is to maximize the return to their company of its investments in each of its relationships and technologies.

Analysing Customers

Understanding customers and their problems is at the core of business marketing. Acquiring this understanding is the most important task for the business, or indeed for any marketer. It provides our starting point for the management of customer relationships.

A customer will use its existing relationships or seek new ones in order to solve one, or a combination, of its own problems, such as the need to improve a production process, or to develop a new customer offering, or to increase the reliability of a key service. Each individual and sub-group in the customer will have their own problems and these will all affect the way that the company interacts within its relationships. For example, the operations department of a customer may feel overloaded by frequent changes in the company's offering. It may be keen to develop a relationship with a supplier of flexible services or equipment. The development department may have difficulty in attracting technologists because the range of its work is too restricted to provide them with interest or career development. It may try to build relationships with new suppliers so that it can use their development skills. The company's Head of Finance may be under pressure to contract-out much of the company's accounting function to an outside supplier and thus may fear that he will lose status or salary. He may try to get the company to invest in new operating software that will "lock" it into doing its own accounting, or even try to damage the company's relationships with potential suppliers of accounting services.

We have also seen in Chapter 3 that irrespective of its problems, a customer is likely to approach its relationships with uncertainties. A customer will also bring its demand and transfer abilities to a relationship. These uncertainties and abilities will all affect a customer's approach to each of its relationships.

Researching customers

Researching customers for the business marketer is complicated because of the variations that are likely across the marketer's portfolio of customers. Many suppliers have a small number of important actual or potential customers that will justify investment in individual research, extensive development and significant adaptation in offerings. A supplier may only have a limited number of important customers for many reasons: there may only be a few potential customers that have the particular problems in which a supplier specializes; or only a few customers may have requirements that call for extensive supplier investment; or the supplier's technical, financial, human or physical resources can sustain complex relationships with only a few customers.

These few, important potential customers will justify individual research by the marketer before a relationship is established and on a continuing basis thereafter. This research is often carried out by the marketer's sales force, when visiting prospective customers. To be effective, this research will have to be systematic and be supported by analysis of the customer's public statements and financial reporting, as well as by information provided by trade journals, exhibitions and industry experts. This research should produce a detailed profile of each customer and its actual or potential problems. It should also produce information on what the customer could contribute towards the problems of the marketing company. The outcome of this analysis should lead to a detailed plan of how the customer should be approached, who should be seen and in what order and who in the company has what problems and requirements. An illustration of some of the issues in researching a customer and building a relationship based on particular problems is illustrated in Box 6.1.

Those companies with a large number of customers that are individually less important face a somewhat different research task. Here, it will not be possible to examine each new

Box 6.1   Building a Relationship for a Big Sale: the Case of Service Providers and Software Suppliers[1]

Service is becoming an ever more important element in the offerings of companies. For example, companies like Cisco supply their customers with equipment for their communications. If these fail, the whole of the customer's network stops. To deal with this customer problem, suppliers have to guarantee a maximum down-time in their equipment. This means that in turn, these equipment suppliers face a number of difficult problems in living up to this guarantee: How can we manage our service personnel? How many expensive replacement parts should we keep and where should we keep them? The problem of replacement parts is made worse because many of these have only a three months life before technology change makes them obsolete.

Equipment suppliers are likely to look towards suppliers of innovative software to help them solve the twin problems of achieving high levels of service to their customers and minimizing their inventories of replacement parts. This software is expensive: it involves an initial licence fee of up to £2 million, with recurring maintenance fees of around 15% of this each year and further continuing charges for professional services. This means that a well-managed relationship between a software supplier and an equipment company can last many years. However, the process of developing those relationships and making an initial sale is complex and difficult. It is likely to involve a number of different individuals in supplier and customer, each with their own agenda.

Because the business problem for the equipment suppliers is relatively new and because the software is innovative, customers are unlikely to already have relationships with potential suppliers. But, whether the customer approaches the software supplier or vice versa, it is likely that the requirement to exercise "due diligence" will mean that the customer will quickly want to talk to at least two or three potential suppliers.

A software supplier will have to manage the sales process over six to nine months and a Sales Account Manager will probably only be able to manage two or three sales at one time. Thus, building these relationships requires nerve on the part of the Sales Account Manager as he may have to wait a year or more before making his first sale! During this time the software supplier will have to commit more and more resources as the process proceeds, so it simply cannot afford the time or resources to waste on the wrong prospects. This means that the sales account manager must constantly evaluate the developing relationship as follows:

- **Customer's business plan:** What is the precise problem that is driving the decision to buy software and is there a real sense of urgency? Does this problem fall within the supplier's area of expertise?
- **Initial prospect assessment:** Is there a clearly defined project in the customer to address this problem? Has a budget been allocated? What is the competitive activity?

[1] This box was produced following interviews with Leighton Morgans, industry expert and super-salesman!

- **Schedule of key activities:** Is there a clear timeline at the customer for key project activities such as proposal development, access to the project team, access to decision makers?
- **Individual relationships:** What are the roles being played by each of the prospect's team? What will we have to do to deliver "wins" or specific benefits for each of them?

This evaluation needs to be aligned against a well-defined sales process by the Sales Account Manager, as follows:

- **Interest:** This is the time of first contact between customer and supplier.
- **Building credibility:** This occurs when the supplier finds out about the specific nature of the problem that is being addressed by the customer. If qualification has been properly carried out, he will be able to say, "We solve those problems" and "This is what we have done and this is who we have done it for".
- **Proof:** This is when the customer prepares a "Request for Proposals" or an "Invitation to Tender". The different suppliers will make a formal response to the tender document, usually followed by an extended presentation. If the supplier is successful to this point then it and perhaps one other supplier may be asked to deliver a "Proof of Concept": the customer will supply data from its business and the supplier will run it on its software. Several hundred person-days of supplier time will have been invested in the relationship by the proof stage.
- **Negotiation:** During the sales process different elements will increase in their importance and it is crucial for the supplier to be aware and react to these changes. For example, price will initially rule suppliers in or out, depending on how close to the customer's budget they are. Later, technical issues become paramount and price is de-emphasized. Finally, pricing becomes vital during the negotiation stage.
- **Close the sale:** You hope!

potential customer relationship in detail.[2] However, irrespective of the size or importance of a relationship to either the customer or supplier, that relationship will still be based on the problems and uncertainties of both of the companies involved. When dealing with many small customers, it is common for business marketers to rely on market research, often carried out by a separate agency, as a way of finding out about and tracking customer perceptions. Unfortunately, this market research is often designed to ask respondents what they think of the supplier that is commissioning the study, when compared to others that the supplier thinks are its competitors and on dimensions that the supplier thinks are important. An illustration of this approach is provided in the questions in Figure 6.1. This type of research is likely to fail to identify customer problems, or indeed why customers are "small". For example, it may well be that these "small" customers have important and/or large-scale problems that are currently unsolved or are solved by others. Research into a large number of small relationships is better if it is based on focus group discussions to

---

[2] For simplicity, in this and other chapters, we refer to an *individual* customer, rather than to a group of customers.

Market Research Study for Frigidaire Refrigerators

Q1: We are interested in your overall opinion of five companies that manufacture refrigerators.

Please rank them from 1 to 5 with 1 being the best and 5 the worst.

Company	Rank
General Electric	____
Westinghouse	____
Frigidaire	____
Sears	____
Whirlpool	____

Q2: We would like to have your opinion on a few statements that could be used to describe

Frigidaire and the refrigerators they make.

For each statement: How much do you agree or disagree?

If you *agree completely* you should give it a *10* rating.

If you disagree completely you should give it a *0* rating.

Or you can use any number in between which best expresses your opinion.

They are a modern up-to-date company   ____

Their refrigerators offer better value than those made by other companies   ____

Their refrigerators last longer than those made by other companies   ____

They are a company that stands behind their products   ____

Their refrigerators have more special features than others   ____

They are a well-established, reliable company   ____

Their refrigerators are more dependable than others   ____

Their refrigerators offer higher-quality construction than others   ____

Their refrigerators have a better guarantee of warranty than others   ____

Q3: If you were buying a refrigerator today, what make would be your first choice?

Your second choice?   Your third choice?

Brand	First choice	Second choice	Third choice
General Electric	_____	_____	_____
Westinghouse	_____	_____	_____
Frigidaire	_____	_____	_____
Sears	_____	_____	_____
Whirlpool	_____	_____	_____
Other (specify)	_____	_____	_____

Figure 6.1   A "typical" market research study.

Adapted from C McDaniel and R Gates (1995) *Contemporary Marketing Research*, St Paul, MN, West Publishing Company.

identify customer problems and creative segmentation of customer groups based on their problems and uncertainties.[3]

Understanding Yourself

It is important for a business marketer to examine his own company's situation as well as that of actual or potential customers. A supplier will seek a relationship with a particular customer as a way of solving some of its own problems, such as the need to generate cash, or to earn profit, or to develop new skills that may then be applied elsewhere, or to cope with a loss of business from other customers. Individuals and sub-groups in the supplier will also have their own problems that can affect the interaction. Examples may include: a salesperson down on his targets and desperate to make a sale at almost any price; an operations department anxious about the reliability of its production and eager to learn from the skills of a customer; a finance department keen to achieve quick sales to count in this year's financial results; senior managers wishing to make a strategic change in their company's network position by selling to entirely different types of customers; development staff wishing to move towards a new generation of technology to be developed in cooperation with a customer.

A supplier will approach all its relationships with uncertainties. These may be about the amount of its offering that it is likely to sell (its *capacity uncertainty*), about how customers might want to use the offering (its *application uncertainty*), and about whether a particular customer will actually do what it has said it will do in the relationship (its *transaction uncertainty*).

The supplier will bring to the relationship its problem-solving and its transfer abilities. Problem-solving ability will enable it to develop an offering with the customer consisting of a combination of product, service, delivery, advice and price and cost. Transfer ability will enable it to actually provide that offering and implement it. These abilities are not just based on the supplier's own physical and financial resources, but also on those of other companies in the network, with which it has relationships, such as component suppliers, finance houses, trucking companies or distributors. The supplier's relationships may be of great value to the customer.

Managing a Single Relationship

Well developed customer relationships provide important benefits for both customer and supplier:

- They reduce or eliminate the costs of searching for new customers or suppliers.
- They enable the marketer to learn about customers' problems and uncertainties, as well as their abilities, and to develop its offerings accordingly.

---

[3] For a thorough discussion of segmentation of business customers see, TV Bonoma and BP Shapiro (1983) *Segmenting the Industrial Market*, Lexington, MA, Lexington Books, and A Clarke and P Freytag (2001) Business-to-Business Market Segmentation, *Industrial Marketing Management*, vol 30, 473–480. For a useful discussion of business marketing research see N Malhotra and D Birks (2005) *Marketing Research - an Applied Approach*, London, Pearson Education.

- They reduce the costs of adaptations, once the initial investments have been made in the relationships.
- They reduce many of the costs of interaction, such as time spent in selling and buying and in checking deliveries, etc.
- They enable the business marketer to concentrate resources on its important customers.

The management of each single customer relationship is at the heart of business marketing. But business marketers cannot manage a customer relationship on their own. They will need to liaise closely with other functional areas, such as operations, finance, purchasing and corporate strategy. Each of these is involved in a business relationship and many will interact directly with customers. Business marketers must also accept that they cannot completely manage or control a relationship. How a relationship develops will depend on the resources and actions of both customer and supplier and the *interaction* between them. Each will have its own idea of what they want to get out of the relationship and what they are prepared to give to it. Both will have their own idea of its importance and both will look at the relationship in the context of all their other relationships. We use the term relationship *management* to describe this interactive activity rather than the term relationship *marketing* which indicates a supposedly one-sided activity. In relationship management both customer and supplier are involved in influencing each other (see Box 6.2).

Box 6.2 Relationship Marketing and Relationship Management

Many consumer marketing companies have adopted the idea of "relationship marketing". Relationship marketing is based on the idea that the selling and promotional costs of attracting one new customer (establishing a relationship) are likely to be much greater than the costs of retaining an existing customer. Relationship marketing is made possible by the availability of proprietary databases on customer life-styles and purchase behaviour and on analysis of the company's own customer purchase data.

Some business marketers have also embraced the idea of relationship marketing, particularly those with a large number of small customers, such as those providing delivery services or office products. Figure 6.2 shows some of the differences between relationship marketing and relationship management. A relationship, by definition is two-sided. But much of what is called relationship marketing has not really got much to do with relationships at all. It is based on a series of individual one-way communications with customers and an analysis of how effective each communication is in generating purchases. Both customer and supplier are involved in interaction and in managing their relationship. Relationship marketing implies that it is only the supplier that is involved in the process. Any conversation with a business buyer will show how unrealistic this idea is!

We now turn to the tasks facing the business marketer in managing within each single customer relationship. We will use the listing of these tasks provided in Figure 6.3.

RELATIONSHIP MARKETING	RELATIONSHIP MANAGEMENT
DISTANT	CLOSE
DISCRETE/ONE-OFF ACTIONS	EACH ACTION IS AN EPISODE THAT IS PART OF OVERALL RELATIONSHIP MANAGEMENT
AIMS TO INFLUENCE INDIVIDUALS IN COMPANY	SEES EACH INDIVIDUAL AS ONE ELEMENT IN RELATIONSHIP WITH THE COMPANY AS A WHOLE
CONCERNED WITH SINGLE TRANSACTIONS	CONCERNED WITH EPISODES IN A RELATIONSHIP
DOES THINGS *TO* PEOPLE	DOES THINGS *WITH* AND *FOR* PEOPLE
CONCERNED WITH ACHIEVING RESPONSE TO STIMULUS	CONCERNED WITH THE WHY AND HOW OF INTERACTION
BASED ON SUPPLIER'S VIEW OF RELATIONSHIP	BASED ON BOTH COMPANIES' VIEW OF THE RELATIONSHIP
MEASURES EFFECTS (DO YOU LIKE WHAT WE'RE SENDING?)	MEASURES REASONS (TELL ME WHY IT WAS USEFUL?)
DEALS WITH A REDUCING SET OF ADDRESSES (RESPONDERS ONLY)	MAINTAINS AND BUILDS RELATIONSHIPS

Figure 6.2   A comparison of relationship marketing and relationship management.

Figure 6.3 The tasks of managing an individual customer relationship.

Task 1: Managing learning and teaching with the customer

The business marketer must constantly learn about the customer and its operations, resources and technologies (including those things that she can use in her other relationships). She must learn what the customer needs from the relationship and what she can offer to it. The marketer will also have to learn about more subtle and complex issues, such as what a counterpart means by the things they say and the attitudes they show. She must learn how predictable the customer is and how much it can be trusted. The marketer must also try to *teach* the customer. This includes providing information and advice to the customer about the marketer's own company.[4]

The way that a relationship develops and the interaction between the individuals involved in it will depend on what the two companies feel that they need to learn about each other's uncertainties and abilities, on their willingness to learn and on their ability to learn. Learning helps the companies to reduce (but never eliminate) their uncertainties. Marketers must also learn how to live with some uncertainties that cannot be reduced.

A supplier needs to support the customer's learning through being actively involved in teaching. Developing the capabilities of other companies is a prerequisite for developing the performance of the company itself. Teaching by the supplier will have its point of departure in formal assessments or audits of the customer relationship. Where the performance level of the relationship does not meet the supplier's expectations and standards, measures will have to be taken to improve conditions. Joint training and development programs have been shown to be an important way to achieve these improvements. There are three significant issues to handle in teaching a counterpart company. The first is to identify what knowledge areas are crucial. The second is to determine what role the customer can play within these areas. The third is to define what development activities are required.

[4] The role of teaching is more thoroughly discussed in L-E Gadde and H Håkansson (2006) Teaching in Supply Networks, in M Gibbert (ed), *Learning in Networks*, Strategic Management Society Book Series, Oxford, Blackwell.

To get the most out of these efforts "the teacher" must analyse how much the counterpart company needs to be familiar with its own internal characteristics and the wider business context. The other development projects of the two companies also need to be taken into consideration in the design and implementation of teaching programs. These network conditions make teaching (and learning) complicated. A number of actors simultaneously are involved in teaching programs in order to affect a particular business counterpart. All of these have different views of the current and potential capability of this company. Therefore their objectives and means of teaching will differ as will their aspirations for relationship development in relation to this particular counterpart.

Task 2: Managing distance between the companies

The business marketer's ability and willingness to learn about the customer will have an important affect on the "*distance*" between the companies. This distance has a number of aspects of which the marketer must be aware and which it must seek to monitor and control:[5]

- Social distance is a measure of the extent to which individuals in the two organizations are familiar with each other's ways of thinking and working and are at ease with them.
- Cultural distance is the degree to which the norms and values of the two companies differ because of their place of origin, or because of their corporate cultures.
- Technological distance refers to differences between the levels of understanding between the customer and supplier of the technologies involved in the relationship. For example, the interaction between a retailer that is seeking to buy products to its own specification from an inexperienced, low labour-cost supplier is likely to be very different from that between a manufacturer of industrial robotics and an experienced buyer from the automotive industry.[6]
- Time distance is usually at its greatest in the early stages of a relationship, when there is a considerable time before either supplier or customer is likely to have to deliver on its promises, or to receive benefits from the relationship. Hence, their interactions are likely to appear rather unreal and little trust will have developed between them.

Social, cultural and technological distance can only be reduced by social interaction between individuals and the development of actor bonds. Time distance can be reduced by arranging for the customer to receive some benefit from a relationship at an early stage.

It may not always be sensible for the marketer to try to reduce distance. The less distance between them, the more knowledge the customer has of her and hence the more predictable she may be. This may encourage a customer to take advantage of the supplier, based on knowing what it can get away with.[7]

---

[5] Jan Johanson and Finn Wiedersheim-Paul (1975) The Internationalisation of the Firm, Four Swedish Case Studies, *Journal of Management Studies*, vol 2, no 3, 305–322.

[6] The implications of differences in technological understanding between the companies in a relationship were discussed in Chapter 4.

[7] D Ford, H Håkansson and J Johanson (1986) How do Companies Interact?, *Industrial Marketing and Purchasing*, vol 1, no 1, 26–41.

Task 3: Investing in the relationship between the companies

Investments build relationship assets. Marketers must constantly assess current and planned relationship investments against the benefits they can realistically expect to receive from them, both immediately and in the future. They also need to consider whether the investment planned for any one relationship would be more productive if applied in others. Relationship investments are likely to include the time of staff that is used to develop contacts between the companies and to give and receive information and advice. There may also be investments in product and process technologies to develop different elements of either company's offerings, or to improve or change the companies' procedures to make interaction more effective and efficient.

Making the most of a supplier's high-involvement relationships also requires investments by the customer. Since these relationships are accompanied by high costs, in terms both of investments and maintenance, the prospective customer will have to be motivated and mobilized to make them. A supplier with the ambition to develop a relationship with a customer must convince the customer that the benefits of increased investments outweigh the costs. Because a customer's resources are limited, its investments in a particular relationship will require it to redirect some of its investments from other current suppliers. It is not only the attractiveness of the new supplier that will affect a customer's investment decision. Sometimes, it is the state of the customer's connections to other suppliers that may be a more decisive influence on further investments in a particular supplier-relationship. The outcome of a supplier's efforts to mobilize a customer will not just be determined by the customer's view of the current or previous performance of the relationship. Instead, it is the customer's view of the future prospects of the supplier, of their relationship and of the wider network that are likely to be critical.

Task 4: Making and controlling adaptations in the relationship

Most suppliers (and customers) will invest in each of their relationships to at least some extent. At one extreme, this investment may simply be the normal time spent by the supplier's sales force in advising each customer. At the other extreme, it could mean that the supplier always changes or develops a new offering for each customer. In contrast to these "normal" investments, adaptations are when a particular customer is treated in a unique way. Any formal adaptations are likely to be laid out in the contract between the customer and supplier. *Informal adaptations* are those that are agreed to cope with a problem that arises or at the request of the customer. For example, the supplier may agree to reduce deliveries from the contractually agreed level for a short time to cope with a sales downturn at the customer, or the customer could change the design of its own product to cope with a production difficulty at its supplier.

Informal adaptations to suit a customer are often critical to the development of a relationship. But a supplier's adaptation of its offering or operations may adversely affect its efficiency and its costs. Also, a supplier's adaptations are often made without a proper assessment of their costs or effects and this can cause difficulties for the supplier. Examples of these difficulties could be when a salesperson agrees to a price reduction for a single customer, without thinking through the effects on profits, or on other customers if they should find out; or when informal adaptations for different customers lead to uncontrolled proliferation of types of offering. Unfortunately, many companies do not have the appropriate costing information to accurately assess the real costs of informal adaptations, or the benefits that they achieve.

The business marketer must fully assess the costs and effects of each adaptation against their benefits and the potential of the relationship. She must seek to monitor and control informal adaptations made by individuals. Where possible, the marketer should try to reduce the costs of adaptations for each relationship by making a single investment that can benefit a number of relationships.

The investments and adaptations of supplier and customer companies build actor bonds, activity links and resource ties between them. They are also part of the process by which they come to rely on each other and to co-evolve (see Box 6.3). In other words, the companies actually change their characteristics and ways of working because they have a relationship with a particular customer or supplier.

Box 6.3   Co-evolution between a Customer and Supplier in a Relationship

Cargo is an industrial wholesaler that has 30,000 customer relationships. Many of these are with small electronics companies involved in designing, developing or maintaining equipment. Many of the relationships are very long established. The company issues a rolling electronic catalogue containing 200,000 items of maintenance, repair, development and operating items. Customers order on-line or by telephone for next-day delivery, almost anywhere in the world. The average size of each order is low. Cargo's high prices mean that it is not a competitive supplier to customers that require high volumes of material for use in production.

Cargo and its customers have co-evolved, but in different ways from each other:

- Cargo's operations and indeed its whole culture have been dictated by its large number of distant, impersonal relationships. Its operations are dominated by the need to constantly refine the efficiency of its interactions, each of which involves virtually no differentiation between individual customers.
- The evolving efficiency of Cargo has meant that its customers do not have to maintain stocks of the ever-widening range of products on which they depend. Many customers have great faith in the supplier's ability to "speak their language" and to select products for their catalogue that are "right" for them. Their relationships with this supplier mean that they do not have to think ahead about their requirements. Unlike the supplier, their evolving culture does not emphasize planning, order and efficiency. Instead, the relationship means that they can react quickly to the random nature of their research, development or maintenance requirements.

This co-evolution has also affected Cargo's other relationships with its few large customers. These customers each place many low-value orders and each requires the supplier to adapt some aspects of its operations to suit their requirements. Cargo has found it difficult to develop a way to deal with these large customers. Its management and staff are unused to the idea of dealing with separate customers in a differentiated way and its internal systems and procedures do not cope well with it.

Task 5: Developing and demonstrating commitment and trust between customer and supplier

Many relationships fail to develop after an initial contact. This may be because the problems of the customer or supplier disappear or can be solved more effectively in other relationships. Some relationships are long-lasting and may broaden in scope to solve a wide range of customer and supplier problems. Some potentially valuable relationships fail because either of the companies lacks the skills or resources to develop them, or because the companies do not understand their true value. A relationship can also fail because the companies do not demonstrate commitment to it, or do not trust each other. An important way for a business marketer to demonstrate commitment to a relationship is by agreeing to adapt her offering or promise. Adaptations show that she is willing to incur immediate costs for the prospect of later reward.

It is easy for a marketer to demonstrate a *lack* of commitment to a relationship by declining to adapt a production schedule to suit a customer's requirements or by refusing to alter a fixed price for a volume order. Similarly, it is easy to destroy a customer's trust. For example, the marketer could reduce the calibre of staff assigned to a customer, or it could increase the price of an offering at a time of shortage. But relationships are two-sided and a supplier's commitment may not be shared by the customer. For example, a customer may encourage the supplier to invest in their relationship, even though it plans to change to a new supplier in the near future.

Relationships vary widely: sometimes each company will willingly incur considerable costs so that both gain in the longer term. Sometimes the parties will be entirely trustworthy in their dealings, other times they will behave with guile. On some occasions they will show genuine altruism, but other times they will simply cheat.

The behaviour of the two companies will not always be predictable, or indeed make any sense when set against their stated individual aims or even their best interests. Every single relationship will have a history of how the parties have treated each other and the degree of trust and commitment that has been built up.

It is important for the business marketer to understand that commitment and trust in a relationship cannot be built by making promises, but only by fulfilling them by implementing her offering. A customer with high need-uncertainty about what is the right offering to buy may initially rely on its trust in a particular supplier's brand, or reputation. But if the reputation of the supplier is not fulfilled then the customer's trust will soon evaporate. Customers also have long memories of previous promises made by suppliers and whether or not they were fulfilled.

The business marketer must make a clear decision about whether she wishes to develop a particular relationship. If she does, then she must demonstrate commitment to it by a controlled process of formal and informal adaptations. She must also monitor how much the customer trusts the supplier and check the fulfilment of her offering to build that trust. The marketer must also closely monitor the commitment of the customer and its investment in the relationship, as well as the customer's trustworthiness in carrying out that commitment.

Task 6: Managing interdependence and power in a relationship

Sometimes the dependence of one company on another in a business relationship may be immediately apparent. For example:

- In one case, a supplier may be very dependent on a particular customer for a large proportion of its sales or profits.
- In another case, a customer may be very dependent on a particular supplier because it is the only available source of a particular type of offering, or because the supplier is the only company that has the resources to supply all its requirements.

Both of these two cases could exist *simultaneously* in the same relationship. This is because the relationship between a customer and supplier is based on their dependence *on each other* to solve particular problems. Interdependence may be based on the difficulty of their problems, their respective resources, the technological distance between the companies or the investment that either or both of the companies have made to build the actor bonds, activity links and resource ties between them. Thus for example, it is very common for a supplier to be dependent on a customer because of the volume or financial value of their relationship. *At the same time*, the customer may be dependent on the supplier for a particular technological solution or more simply because of its knowledge of the customer and its ability to diagnose emerging problems.

The interdependence between companies is likely to increase as that relationship develops and as the companies invest in the relationship. This increase in interdependence has advantages and disadvantages for both of the companies. For example, if a customer becomes dependent on the technology of a supplier, then it may not retain the ability to do some things for itself (as we discussed in Chapter 4). However, dependence on the supplier's technology may free up resources for the customer to invest elsewhere. Similarly, if a supplier becomes more dependent on the business from a customer, then its thinking and its resources may become more oriented towards that customer and it will be less able to develop other relationships. However, dependence on the customer may enable the supplier to benefit from the customer's investments in that relationship and to learn from the technologies and skills of that customer.

Of course the extent of the dependence of the two companies on each other may not be the same. For example, many small suppliers of textiles and food items are much more dependent on their large retail customers than the customers are on them. This imbalance in dependence allows the retailers to exercise considerable *power* over what the suppliers should produce and what prices they should charge. Similarly, many customers in the automotive or aerospace industries have power over their subcontractors that manufacture to the customers' design and do not have their own design capability. Suppliers often have power over their customers when they have a strong technological position in an area that is important to a customer that has no similar ability itself.[8] Suppliers are also powerful when a customer needs an adapted offering from a supplier, but is unable to order in large volumes.

---

[8] In other words, the technology is *external* for the customer. See Chapter 4.

A marketer may choose to exercise power in a relationship by taking advantage of a customer's dependence for short-term gain, for example, by increasing price or requiring the customer to make adaptations in order to use the supplier's offering. Alternatively, the marketer may choose not to use her power in the short term, but to incur short-term costs as a way of increasing the customer's dependence on her and her long-term power. Before exercising power in a relationship the marketer must consider the extent of her own dependence on the customer, the purpose of the relationship and the long-term effects of any action.

Task 7: Managing conflict in a relationship

Conflict in business relationships can take many forms. At the most obvious level, for example, companies must have a minimum level of agreement with each other in order for business to take place. But they can then argue about everything to do with that business! Richard Gettell once referred to this phenomenon as "pluralistic competition".[9] There may be conflict between customer and supplier about the overall direction of their relationship. For example, the supplier may wish both parties to invest for the long-term development of a relationship to solve a number of problems for both of them, but the customer may see this supplier only as a short-term stop-gap for an immediate problem. There can also be conflict over the division of activities between the two companies, such as when a department store wants a supplier of designer clothes to pay the salaries of sales staff in an area dedicated to that supplier's garments. Conflict can also occur because of the past or the future actions of either of the parties. An example would be because a problem with previous service delivery meant that a customer had lost one of its own valued clients, or because a customer insists on a guarantee of future compliance with specification.

When a business marketer is faced with disagreement or conflict in a relationship, she must balance the exercise of her power to achieve her immediate aims against the chance that this will reduce the customer's trust and generate further future conflict. Any decision must be based on an assessment of the long-term value of the relationship to his company.

Even in cases where customer and supplier fully agree on common objectives for their relationship, they are likely to have different opinions about the most appropriate action to take within it. Therefore, it should come as no surprise that conflicts arise even in what seem to be "well-functioning" relationships. Conflict may actually increase with increasing collaboration because of the need to coordinate more activities and actions. In fact, the absence of conflict in these relationships is likely to reflect that the two companies have not really "clinched" with each other, and have made insufficient efforts to exploit the full potential for collaborative action. Close relationships tend to be larger reservoirs of conflicting behaviour than arm's-length relationships.

The obvious conclusion is that collaborating companies cannot escape conflict. Close relationships are full of conflicting interests, which are important for their long-term

[9] RG Gettell (1950) Pluralistic Competition, in *Theory in Marketing*, Reavis Cox and Wroe Alderson (eds), Homewood, IL, Richard D Irwin, pp 89–99.

development. However, in the short run conflict tends to cause problems because it may hamper day-to-day operations. Therefore, conflict must be managed properly so that it can be a breeding ground for creativity. It is important that neither party in a relationship sacrifices its own aims and interests. The only way for the parties involved to establish long-term well-functioning relationships is to have the courage to work on the basis of their own ambitions, and at the same time to accept that the counterpart may have different motives, which must also be taken into account.

Task 8: Managing interaction and communication

Communicating with customers is frequently associated with the sales force. But for the business marketer, communication is not just to persuade a customer to give the first or subsequent orders, to sell the supplier's "product". Instead, communication is part of the broader theme of "interaction", which is also about influencing others. Communication is important for all of the relationship management tasks we have been examining.

The sales force is likely to be part of the important "actor bonds" between the supplier and individuals in the customer company. This means that it is important for the business marketer to ensure that the sales force is "on message", or working within the company's aims for that relationship. One common example of lack of sales force control is when a salesperson agrees to reduce price to achieve a sale, without realising the full impact that this would have on profitability. We will return to this issue in Chapter 9. The marketer may also face problems if she allows a business relationship to become dependent on the actor bond involving a single salesperson or an individual in the customer company.

But in many relationships there are likely to be numerous contacts between individuals from different functional areas in both companies and within each customer about a single relationship. Figure 6.4 illustrates the scale of inter-company communication for a company supplying an international customer in the computer industry. Figure 6.5 shows the associated communication patterns within the supplier.[10] Each of these contacts involves communication and influence. Coordination of these is important to ensure that each interaction fits into an overall approach to the relationship. It is the responsibility of the business marketer to determine what this overall approach should be, what resources should be invested and how the relationship should fit into the wider portfolio. Traditionally, the sales force had the job of coordinating the interactions with customers. But nowadays, companies face a number of problems in coordinating their customer communications, as follows:

- The role of coordinating interaction has become more difficult as more communications media are used such as call-centres, sales and service depots, websites and portals, etc.
- The problems of customers have become more complex and their reliance on suppliers has become greater. Customers now require more complex offerings involving many functions within the supplier. Customers often require several of their different suppliers to cooperate with each other and have complex relationships between different

[10] Figures 6.4 and 6.5 are from the work of Sally Hughes, postgraduate student, University of Bath.

SUPPLIER		Customer Corporate			Customer-Europe				Customer-USA			
		Commodity management team	Process project managers	Process development engineers	Fab general management	Site purchasing	Engineering project managers	Process engineers	Fab general management	Site purchasing	Engineering project managers	Process engineers
Corporate	General management	✓			✓				✓			
Marketing	Marketing Director	✓			✓							
	Key account managers					✓	✓		✓	✓		
	Customer care account handlers (UK)					✓						
	National sales centre (USA)	✓								✓		
	Onsite Managers at Customer	✓			✓	✓	✓	✓				
	Site service team						✓	✓				
	Customer care account handlers (UK)	✓				✓			✓	✓	✓	✓
	Site service team (USA)									✓	✓	✓
	Business development (Europe)	✓			✓				✓			
	Product management (USA)	✓								✓	✓	
Product Management	UK operations management team	✓	✓			✓	✓					
	US operations management team	✓	✓	✓								

Figure 6.4 Customer–supplier communication matrix.

		Product Division, UK Operations Management Team				
		Operations director	Operations manager	Assembly cell leader	Project engineers	Manufacturing support engineers
Corporate	General management	✓	✓	✓		
Customer Facing Division	Marketing director	✓	✓			
	Key account managers		✓	✓	✓	
	Customer care account handlers (UK)			✓	✓	
	National sales centre (USA)			✓	✓	
	Customer site team manager (Europe)		✓	✓	✓	
	Site service team (Europe)			✓	✓	✓
	Customer site team manager (USA)			✓	✓	
	Site service team (Europe)					
	Business development (Europe)	✓		✓		
	Product management (USA)	✓		✓		

Figure 6.5   Internal communications matrix.

customer divisions and headquarters in different countries. Many salespeople lack either the technological competence or standing within their companies to effectively coordinate this evolving interaction.

- Some companies have tried to overcome this coordination problem by appointing technically qualified, senior relationship managers to handle important relationships. Others have introduced project managers in the case of those relationships centring on a single major project (see Box 6.1). In this situation, the sales force becomes more of a service function working within the overall control of the relationship or project manager. This can lead to problems of low sales force morale and to poor communications between project managers and marketers.

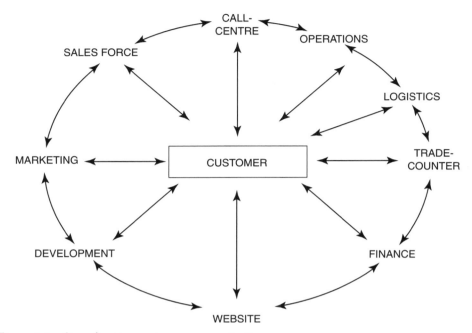

Figure 6.6 Co-ordinating customer communication.

- In many companies, marketing is only responsible for a limited number of support activities such as direct mailing and publicity and has no responsibility for the sales force. In this case, marketing will lack the stature in the organization to enable it to influence other functions, such as development, finance or operations. This problem is likely to be particularly acute when the company has a strong, experienced or senior sales manager or director.

Figure 6.6 illustrates the need to coordinate all of the interactions with a customer that involve different functional areas, each of which may have their own relationships with individuals and their own agenda to pursue. A common problem is that each function may interact with a customer, indicated by the radial lines. However, the links and coordination between these functions, particularly those involving marketing may not be well developed.

Task 9: Auditing a business relationship

This final task of managing a single customer relationship integrates all of the others. Because a marketing company's relationships are its primary assets, without which neither its skills nor its physical resources can be exploited, the marketer needs to maximize the rate of return on these assets. A regular audit of each important relationship is a useful starting point for relationship management. Less significant relationships can be audited as a group. An outline of the questions that may form such an audit is provided in Figure 6.7.

1 HISTORY AND CURRENT STATUS

- WHAT IS THE HISTORY OF THE RELATIONSHIP?
- WHAT IS THE CURRENT PURPOSE OF THE RELATIONSHIP FOR BOTH PARTIES?
- WHAT IS THE SUBSTANCE OF THE RELATIONSHIP: ACTOR BONDS, ACTIVITY LINKS AND RESOURCE TIES?
- WHAT IS ITS FINANCIAL PERFORMANCE?

2 ATMOSPHERE OF THE RELATIONSHIP

- HOW COMMITTED ARE BOTH COMPANIES TO THE RELATIONSHIP AND TO THAT INVESTMENT?
- WHAT IS THE DISTANCE BETWEEN THE TWO COMPANIES?
- WHAT IS THE POWER AND CONFLICT POSITION IN THE RELATIONSHIP?

3 POTENTIAL AND INVESTMENT

- WHAT IS THE POTENTIAL OF THE RELATIONSHIP FOR BOTH PARTIES?
- WHAT INVESTMENT IS REQUIRED FROM BOTH PARTIES TO FULFIL THAT POTENTIAL?
- WHAT ARE THE THREATS TO THE RELATIONSHIP?

4 NETWORK

- WHAT IS THE NETWORK POSITION OF THE RELATIONSHIP?
- WHAT IS ITS ROLE IN THE COMPANY'S PORTFOLIO?

5 CURRENT OPERATIONS

- IS CURRENT MANAGEMENT OF THE RELATIONSHIP IN LINE WITH OVERALL STRATEGY?
- IS THE CURRENT PATTERN OF INTERACTION APPROPRIATE?

Figure 6.7   The relationship audit.

1: History and current status

Questions in this section may include:

- Which company started the relationship and why?
- What has happened in the relationship?
- What has gone right and wrong and why may crises have occurred?

Customers have long memories of a supplier's good and bad performances and these may strongly affect current and future business. An analysis of relationship history will explain much about current resource ties, activity links and actor bonds and contribute to a sound description of the current state of the relationship.

A customer and supplier are unlikely to have the same view of the purpose of a relationship or of what has happened in it. For example, the customer may see the relationship only as a source of basic items with a restricted potential, while the supplier considers it to be a potential source of technological learning. These differences in views will affect the marketer's assessment of the potential of the relationship and the tasks necessary to achieve his aims for it.

The financial performance of a relationship is an important indicator of the value of the relationship to the marketer. It is important that financial analysis for a relationship audit should extend beyond recording sales volume or superficial "profit" achieved from each customer. The analysis should show the return achieved in the relationship by relating sales volume to the direct costs of purchased items, production, service, advice and delivery. Indirect costs, or those which are incurred irrespective of sales volume, should also be assigned to particular relationships. This would include the costs of developing or adapting an offering or investing in production facilities or providing dedicated deliveries. Less significant relationships will have to be financially analysed as a group (see Chapter 9).

2: Relationship atmosphere

The questions in this section deal with the level of commitment of both companies to the relationship, which will be strongly affected by their previous experience and their assessment of the potential of the relationship (see below). An assessment of the distance between the companies and the extent of their interdependence are important indicators of whether the supplier will be able to change the current state of the relationship. These factors may indicate that changes will be needed in the way that the supplier communicates with the customer or that it should seek to reduce its dependence on it.

3: Potential and investment

Questions in this section must examine the relationship from the perspective of both customer and supplier, as there are likely to be differences between their views. The potential of a relationship may include the generation of cash, or "profit" at various levels of cost allocation, or the acquisition of new technology or access to other relationships. It is common for a marketing company to fail to fulfil the potential of its relationships, either because it is unable to convince the customer of that potential, or because the marketer is unable to secure the necessary investment from the customer or from his own company. This emphasizes that skills of communication and influence are needed both inside the marketer's own company and with the customer.

4: Network position

The potential of a relationship can never be assessed in isolation from the marketer's other relationships and the wider network position of both companies. By analysing the connected relationships of the customer the marketer can find out where her relationship fits in with those of the customer's other suppliers and its customers as part of the process of providing an offering for a final user. The problems, potential and investment prospects of any one relationship must be compared with the prospects of the other relationships in its portfolio. Also, each relationship within a portfolio must complement the others.

5: Current operations

It is important for marketers to check that their current way of working in a relationship is related to their overall strategy for that relationship. All too often the actions of individual marketers, or of other staff in the company, are out of line with that strategy or with each other. For example, a development department may fail to respond to a modification request from a customer because it is concerned about the costs involved. This may jeopardize the future of a high-potential relationship. The pattern of interaction with a customer refers to such issues as the frequency of sales calls on the customer and the seniority of those making the calls. Paradoxically, this is a relatively unimportant aspect of the overall management of a relationship, but in many companies it receives a disproportionate amount of attention. This is because these companies have failed to take a strategic approach to their relationships and instead are more concerned with short-term cost and revenue issues.

Managing a Portfolio of Customer Relationships

Each of a supplier's customer relationships forms part of its portfolio and the business marketer must manage that portfolio as a totality. Each relationship in the portfolio will differ in the problems it solves and the contribution it makes to the portfolio. For example:

- Some relationships might be useful to both companies for the regular sale and purchase of standard offerings. They will contribute to the supplier's cash flow and to the basic operations of the customer. They may account for a major portion of each company's activities. These relationships may be safe and reassuring, rather like a marriage.
- Other relationships may solve some particular technological or operational problems for one or both of the companies and lead to different ways of working or interacting. They may be exciting, but perhaps unstable and could damage both companies if things go wrong, just like an ill-considered affair.
- Some relationships may be unimportant themselves, but together with other similar ones may constitute a vital part of the supplier's portfolio.

- The position of a particular relationship within the portfolio of a customer or supplier is also likely to change over time. For example, the supplier or customer may divert their resources into other relationships, in order to gain greater benefits when they consider that the first one is well established, or is losing its importance. Both might simply become bored with each other if their relationship is no longer progressing.

Managing a relationship portfolio has some similarities to managing a portfolio of investments in different shares, fixed-interest accounts or government bonds. Each financial investment will have a different combination of risk and return that the investor tries to balance to achieve his financial goals and in line with his personal attitude to risk. Business portfolio management also involves resource investment for both supplier and customer with the aim of maximizing the return on relationship investments, within a particular attitude to risk. But business portfolio management involves a number of complexities when compared with managing a financial portfolio, for example:

- Relationship portfolio management requires companies to choose between relationships in their portfolio, in terms of their respective contribution of revenue or "profit". The revenue from a relationship may be relatively easy to determine, but it is often difficult to find out about relationship costs and profit. Many so-called "Customer Relationship Management" (CRM) software packages will provide a company with information on a customer's order size and cumulative sales. Also, they will assign *standard* or *allocated* costs to provide a profit figure. However, they are unlikely to take into account the up-front investments and the real costs of adapting offerings, operations, delivery or advice. Most company accounting systems are based on individual products and operating units and they report accordingly. We have seen that customer service is likely to be a key aspect of most offerings. But many accounting systems treat service as a general cost and allocate it to all products. This cost-based approach is one reason why inadequate service provision is often a reason for the failure of a supplier's offering to solve a customer's problems. Company accounts are rarely set up to produce figures for relationship profit after all the relevant costs are taken into account. Nor are they able to calculate the return to the company from its investment in a particular relationship. These accounting problems make it much more difficult for business marketers to manage either a portfolio of relationships or individual customers within it.
- Relationship portfolio management also involves investing resources in a number of relationships that make a *different* contribution to the company. For example, some relationships may be important sources of new technology. Others may provide access to other relationships or experience in meeting harsh commercial criteria etc. This means that a narrow financial assessment of a relationship portfolio is unlikely to be realistic for the business marketer.

Categorizing the companies in a customer portfolio

Figure 6.8 outlines a simple categorization of relationship types that has proved useful for purposes of customer portfolio analysis. The terms used are merely illustrative and modified categories may be required in analysis for particular companies.

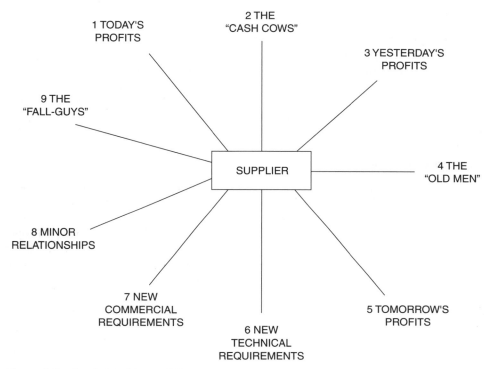

Figure 6.8   A relationship portfolio.

Category 1: Today's profits

These relationships generate current profits for the supplier. A full analysis of the costs of managing the company's relationships may show that only a minority of the company's re-lationships make a profit. These profits will be based on previous investments made in the relationships, probably by both supplier and customer. If the customer's requirements change, then these investments may no longer be appropriate. In this case further investment may be required or the relationship will move into one of the other categories listed below.

Category 2: The "cash cows"

These relationships contribute the highest current sales volume for the company, but not necessarily the highest profit. This can be because these high-volume customers are likely to expect significant adaptations by the supplier. These adaptations may result in very high relationship management costs. Also, because the supplier is likely to feel highly dependent on these relationships, the customer might be able to force it to lower its prices. Because of the costs and problems of this type of relationship, they were also referred to by one manager as "bottomless pits"! A well-carried out relationship audit of these relation-ships will provide insight into their true characteristics.

Category 3: Yesterday's profits

Relationships in this category no longer contribute the same level of profits as previously. This can be because of changed customer requirements, or the efforts of competing suppliers, or the failure of the supplier (or the customer) to make the necessary adaptations. The sales volume may still be high and unless the marketer has good cost information she may not be aware of the reduced profits. This category emphasizes how important it is to constantly manage relationships throughout their life. It also emphasizes how important it is for marketers to know the real "cost-to-serve" of a relationship.

Category 4: The "old men"

This category is a more extreme form of the previous one and includes many long-established relationships that have become "inert".[11] These relationships may be based on an offering and a way of interacting that suited the problems and conditions of long ago. These "old men" relationships are likely to be popular with long-serving salespeople who may value the personal interaction with old friends. But a full relationship audit (see above) could show that they tie up expensive resources that could more profitably be invested in other relationships.

Category 5: Tomorrow's profits

These relationships have the potential for future growth. However, they are unlikely to be profitable at the moment because of the costs of investing in the relationship and developing the offering. This time-before-profit can be considerable and so it is important that the marketer makes a clear assessment of the development funds required, the potential of the relationship, the likely pay-back period and the risks involved. This category emphasizes how important it is for a marketer to choose which relationships to develop and which to discontinue, as opposed to simply taking whatever business is on offer.

Categories 6 and 7: New technical or commercial requirements

Customers in these relationships have demanding technical or commercial requirements. Satisfying them requires the supplier to invest in its product or process technologies, in its order processing, or in its skills in managing relationships. Some of these types of relationships may be currently or even always unprofitable and no supplier could afford a large number of them. However, these types of relationships are important because what is learned in these relationships may subsequently be valuable in others. Hence, a supplier may be prepared to offset the losses in these relationships against the profits to be earned in others.

---

[11] Studies have shown that relationships can become inert after only a short time, if they are not properly managed, eg D Ford and P Rosson (1982) The Relationships between Export Managers and their Overseas Distributors, in *Export Management*, M Czinkota (ed), New York, Praeger, pp 257–275.

Category 8: Minor relationships

This is likely to be the largest category in many portfolios. The relationships in this category may be with small customers or those that are new to the supplier. The customers may have limited requirements or neither customer nor supplier may see the other as an important part of their portfolio. It is often easier for a supplier to manage a single important relationship than many small, but potentially valuable ones. However, developments in operations and in electronic media have made it easier to develop and fulfil tailored offerings even to small users. Relationships should not be judged solely on the volume of business that they represent. This category of relationships will need to be separated into sub-groups according to the different problems of the customers, their requirements from the supplier and their respective potential contributions. Business marketing segmentation will require at least the same creativity and continuous attention as that in consumer marketing.

A customer is likely to have a different relationship with minor and major suppliers, even for what is apparently the same type of offering. For example, the customer may use the major supplier for its large-volume, day-to-day requirements. It may use minor suppliers for more flexible, more unusual, or more technically demanding problems, or simply to keep its main supplier "on its toes". There is an obvious analogy in this between the major supplier as husband or wife with the minor supplier providing excitement as a lover or mistress! More seriously, these differences mean that a company that is used to being a major supplier may not be able to cope with being a minor supplier. Conversely, a company that is used to being a minor supplier should perhaps choose to avoid major supply situations that may not match its skills or profit expectations.

Category 9: The "fall-guys"

This final category emphasizes that managing business relationships is not solely based on mutual trust or "niceness". The category includes customers from which the supplier expects valuable volume, profit or knowledge acquisition in the short term. But in the longer term the supplier may plan to either drop the customer or at least to disinvest in the relationship, after it has learned as much as it can, or after alternative relationships have grown. However, when taking this approach, the marketer should be aware that other customers in her portfolio are likely to hear about her actions and draw the appropriate conclusions!

Managing relationship is a multidimensional and complex task. Besides the challenges associated with single relationships (see Box 6.4) we have illustrated above that each customer relationship needs to be considered as a contributor to the supplier's portfolio of customers and as part of the wider network context.

Relationships in the Network

Each company is enmeshed in a network of customer, supplier and other relationships. These relationships are the means by which it can benefit from the resources of its suppliers,

> **Box 6.4   Five Things to Remember about Relationships**
>
> 1 The customer will always have a different view from you about what the relation-
>   ship is for, what they should contribute, what you should contribute, what you
>   should receive, what they should receive, what you are doing and have done and
>   what they are doing and have done.
> 2 If you think that the relationship is important, the other party may think it less im-
>   portant. If you think it unimportant, they may think it important.
> 3 The customer always has other relationships and will assess their relationship with
>   you on the basis of their experience in those relationships.
> 4 Relationships are about time. In order to receive value from the relationship in the
>   future, you must make investments today. The return on those investments is likely
>   to take longer than you thought. The value that you may receive today is likely to
>   be at the expense of the value that you could receive in the future.
> 5 Companies in relationships have long memories — particularly when they feel
>   treated badly. If you take advantage of a customer today, they will remember the
>   episode for a long time.

customers and others and through which it gains access to the resources of the wider network. The idea of a network means that companies are not linked in a neat straight line,
comprising the "supply chain" or "distribution channel" of a single company. Managers
making simplifying assumptions of this type run the risk of misreading the dynamics of
the wider business network.

The multiple links of all companies in a network also emphasize that a network does not
just exist for the benefit of a single company. Although its relationship with a particular
customer may be important to a supplier, that relationship may be quite unimportant to
the customer because it has other far more important relationships. An understanding of
the wider network in which its customer relationships exist is vital for the business marketer and for her management of her customer relationships. This network understanding
will also have to extend to an appreciation of the dynamics of the network and how it is
likely to change over time. Networks are in continuous flux as the following examples
illustrate:

- Some of the marketer's own suppliers may seek direct relationships with our customers
  or vice versa.
- New companies may emerge and provide the marketer with useful intermediaries between her own company and her customers. This may enable the marketer to improve
  her offering to her customers with the aid of those intermediaries.
- Alternatively, a marketer's customers may insist on using new intermediaries for a range
  of its suppliers. This may dramatically alter the supplier's relationship with those customers, reducing their direct contact and scope for productive interaction.
- In other situations the marketer may choose to establish relationships with some of its
  customer's customers or even to supply them directly. These supplier relationships give it

access to their skills and these complement its own skills enabling it to have productive relationships with its customers.

- A marketer may build a relationship with one or more of her own suppliers or other previously unrelated companies to enable her to develop an innovative offering for some customers. This may involve the marketer in interacting with those customers together with these other companies.

Business marketers spend much of their time working within and trying to manage their relationships with their existing customers. Through a constant process of interaction, orders will be won or lost, offerings will be implemented, payments made, developments discussed and the relationship will develop. These developments may be within or against the direction that either of the companies might wish. This will depend on the problems, uncertainties, skills in relationship management of the two companies and developments in the surrounding network.

But current customers comprise only part of the task of relationship management for the business marketer. The importance of the surrounding network determines that business marketers must be able to develop strategy for changing their company's position in that network by seeking to develop new and different types of relationship and to abandon others. Changing a company's network position is likely to be slow and complex.[12] We will return to this issue in Chapter 10.

Conclusions

This chapter has built on the ideas presented in earlier chapters about the nature of business marketing and the context in which it takes place. At the heart of business marketing is the management of each single relationship with a customer. Some of a company's customer relationships will be individually significant in terms of their current contribution of revenue, profit and learning, as well as the access they provide to other companies in the network or their potential for the future. Each of these significant relationships will justify the effort of managing them *individually*. Other relationships may have been significant in the past, but no longer justify the costs and efforts that are involved. The marketer may have to disinvest in those relationships to lower their operating costs or to use whatever power he has to increase the contribution to them by the customer in terms of effort, resources or finance. The marketer may also have to deal with many other relationships which are not individually significant, but collectively may be of great importance. Each of these alone is unlikely to justify dedicated investment, adaptation or management time. Instead the marketer will need to seek ways to categorize these relationships according to their common characteristics and manage groups of relationships in a similar way.

This chapter has outlined a process for assessing or auditing each individual or group of the customer relationships of a company. This is not a one-off process, but one that will

---

[12] For a full discussion of the issues involved in changing network position see D Ford et al (2003) *Managing Business Relationships*, Chichester, John Wiley & Sons, Ltd, Chapter 8.

need to be repeated on a regular basis, to ensure that relationship management and operations coincide with company strategy and work towards maximizing the rate of return on the company's prime assets.

Relationship management is not a linear process leading to some ideal state or "partnership" between customer and supplier. Both companies will try to manage a relationship for their own ends. Marketers must try to build and manage a relationship over time to achieve its potential for them, within the context of the customer's problems, its aims for the relationship and its wider portfolio of relationships. Relationship management has to take a realistic view of the value of each relationship. This may lead to greater investment, more intense interaction and reduced distance between the companies but it can also lead to the marketer reducing or stopping investment and increasing the distance between the supplier and the customer.

In this chapter we have emphasized that developing an offering to solve problems for a customer is an important part of managing a relationship. In the next chapter we deal with this process in more depth. The offering is the marketer's promise to her customer. It has no value unless that promise can be fulfilled. This critical issue of implementation of offerings is then addressed in Chapter 8.

Further Reading

J Anderson and J Narus (1991) Partnering as a Focused Market Strategy, *California Management Review*, Spring, 95–113.

B Bergeron (2001) *Essentials of CRM: Customer Relationship Management for Executives*, Chichester, John Wiley & Sons, Ltd.

A Burns and R Bush (2000) *Marketing Research*, Englewood Cliffs, NJ, Prentice Hall.

B Bund-Jackson (1985) *Winning and Keeping Industrial Customers*, Lexington, MA, Lexington Books.

AJ Campbell (2003) Creating Customer Knowledge Competence: Managing Customer Relationship Management Programs Strategically, *Industrial Marketing Management*, vol 32, 375–383.

D Ford (ed) (2001) *Understanding Business Marketing and Purchasing*, London, International Thomson, especially readings 4.1–4.9.

D Ford et al (2003) *Managing Business Relationships*, 2nd edition, Chichester, John Wiley and Sons, Ltd.

N Kumar (1996) The Power of Trust in Manufacturer–Retailer Relationships, *Harvard Business Review*, November–December, 92–106.

A Lindgreen, R Palmer, J Vanhamme and J Wouters (2006) A Relationship-Management Assessment Tool: Questioning, Identifying, and Prioritizing Critical Aspects of Customer Relationships, *Industrial Marketing Management*, vol 35, 57–71.

R Palmer and P Millier (2004) Segmentation: Identification, Intuition and Implementation, *Industrial Marketing Management*, vol 33, 779–785.

J Sheth and A Parvatiyar (eds) (2000) *Handbook of Relationship Marketing*, Thousand Oaks, CA, Sage Publications.

G de Souza (1992) Designing a Customer Retention Plan, *The Journal of Business Strategy*, March–April, 24–28.

W Ulaga (2003) Capturing Value Creation in Business Relationships: A Customer Perspective, *Industrial Marketing Management*, vol 32, 677–693.

F Webster (1992) The Changing Role of Marketing in the Corporation, *Journal of Marketing*, vol 56, 1–17.

W Zikmund, R McLeod Jr and FW Gilbert (2003) *Customer Relationship Management*, New York, John Wiley and Sons, Ltd.

Assignment for Chapter 6

Customer problems and relationships at Airslash

Airslash is rather an unusual company. In 1985 two friends who loved to travel set up as an air-courier company that undertook the delivery of valuable or urgent packages anywhere in the world. The two friends then extended their business by opening a freight handling and forwarding business at Heathrow. This was also successful and quickly expanded to other European airports, such as Frankfurt, Schiphol, Charles de Gaulle etc. More recently the company acquired a number of freight transport companies operating on long-term contracts mainly for manufacturers. The company went public in 1995. Since then it has acquired and developed a parcels business. Although successful, this business is much smaller than the major competitors in the area, such as DHL, Federal Express and UPS.

You are the recently appointed Group Marketing Director of Airslash. The Chief Executive appointed you because he wanted some "real marketing – and quickly!". Fortunately you have a good assistant who has been in the company for some time. As a first step, you have asked the assistant to give you a list of some of the customers that the company currently has and of some interesting companies that they don't supply. Here is part of the list:

Electroparts

Electroparts is a medium-sized electronic parts manufacturer who supplies both manufactured and purchased parts, mainly to sophisticated electronic machinery makers (eg monitoring equipment for electricity-generating companies). Electroparts has a single plant/warehouse to supply the US market and a similar operation in France to serve the whole of Europe. Electroparts frequently have to supply parts on an emergency basis to your customers who are servicing their clients.

Airslash has provided some general parcels service to this customer.

Laura Ashley

Laura Ashley is a medium-sized English manufacturer and retailer of traditionally influenced clothing for women and soft furnishings (curtains, bedspreads/duvets, table cloths etc). Laura Ashley has shops throughout the USA, Canada and Europe. These are mostly small boutiques with limited storage space. Fashions change quickly and the company has to respond quickly.

Airslash has no significant business with Laura Ashley.

Strategov

Strategov is a state-level environmental protection agency funded by federal taxes. Strategov monitors pollution levels, pollution incidents, water and air quality and any other issues affecting the environment. It is involved in handling emergency incidents and clean-up operations and prepares the case for prosecuting offenders. It provides advice and training to companies and other organizations.

Strategov has used Airslash as a courier for the transport of urgent documents.

The Red Cross

The Red Cross is an international charity operating in disaster areas, war zones and in famine relief. It provides support services to individuals and families in distress. It provides world-wide services from bases across the globe and is funded by donations of all kinds and from private, corporate and governmental services.

The Red Cross has used Airslash for courier services, parcel deliveries and occasionally for transport.

Conway

Conway is a large building contractor based in the USA but operating throughout the Americas. It bids on between five and ten jobs per week with a success rate of 15–20%. The design and contracts department frequently work late to get bids out on time. These bids are often complex combinations of project management, direct construction work and the use of subcontractors.

Conway uses Airslash extensively for its courier services.

Mcmichael

Mcmichael is a major producer of ice-cream and frozen foods. It operates throughout Europe from several production sites and distributes products to the distribution centres of major retail chains and to its own ice-cream distribution depots.

Airslash "inherited" this customer through an acquisition and it remains its largest transport services client.

Williams, Russell and Williams

Williams Russell and Williams is a legal firm in London. It specializes in commercial legal work involving complex issues, usually of an international nature. Its clients are often, but not always, large firms who end up in dispute about a contract. It provides advice on arbitration and international settlement. It also directly represents firms in court when required to do so. However, it often has to use local legal firms in other jurisdictions and it has built up a network of reliable law firms around the world.

Williams, Russell and Williams use Airslash for courier services and sometimes for parcel deliveries.

You are keen to learn about the business of Airslash and to supply some *creative thinking* to marketing in the company. Review each of these actual or potential customers. Develop an analysis of the problems that Airslash could address for each of them. Describe the type of relationship that this would require and how you would manage it. You may use any assumptions necessary to complete your analysis, provided that you make those assumptions explicit.

Designing Offerings: Developing the Promise

7

Aims of this Chapter

- To examine the design and development of the offerings of business marketers.
- To explain how these offerings relate to the problems of customers and to the respective abilities of the supplier and customer.
- To explore the different elements from which offerings are built and to explain how these elements are related to each other.
- To examine the development processes for the individual elements of a supplier's offering.
- To consider the issues raised by the adaptation of a supplier's offering to the requirements of a single customer.
- To explore how the idea of "quality" can be applied to marketers' offerings.

Introduction: The Bases of Suppliers' Offerings

Business purchases are complex. They do not take place simply because customers "like" a product, or are impressed with its "quality". Nor is it sufficient to say that a business purchase is motivated by the customer's problems and uncertainties, although both of these are important. Whether or not a business purchase takes place will also depend on the *supplier's* problems and uncertainties, on the characteristics of the relationship between customer and supplier and on where that relationship fits within the wider portfolios of the two companies.

The problems and uncertainties of both a customer and a supplier also determine *what* is bought or sold by those companies. We refer to what is bought or sold by business companies as an *offering*. There are two crucial tasks associated with a supplier's offering, as follows:

- The first task is to design the offering. This is about developing the supplier's promise to the customer about how its problem will be solved.

- The second task is to implement the offering in the customer's operations. This is about fulfilling the supplier's promise to the customer.

We deal with the development of the offering in this chapter and with implementation in Chapter 8. We start this chapter by examining the bases of a supplier's offering.

Customers' problems and uncertainties

Customers' problems and uncertainties are the first and most obvious basis of suppliers' offerings. A particular customer's problem is often quite clear to that customer. In this case, the customer can define the problem, specify what it needs to solve it and search for a suitable supplier that will meet the customer's specification. For example, a company's office manager may receive complaints from his colleagues about the state of their offices that are cleaned by a cleaning contractor, or about the service that they receive from a hire-car company or from the hotel chain with which the company has a corporate rate. In these cases, it will be relatively easy for the office manager to determine what is required and to compare between potential suppliers and their offerings.[1] In other words, this customer is likely to have little *need or market uncertainty*, but is likely to be driven by its *transaction uncertainty* about efficiently and speedily receiving the best deal.

Other times, a customer's problem may be diffuse or the ways of solving it difficult to define. For example, an operations manager may face a corporate requirement to cut his operating costs by 12%; or a company may be concerned that its own service levels are slipping when compared to their competitors. In these cases there is likely to be a wide range of different types of offering that could provide some sort of solution to the problem. But it may be very difficult to specify which sort of solution will be best in the long or the short term, or which solution is likely to be at the lowest price or be the most cost-effective. In many other cases, the customer may not be clear exactly *what* problem they face, other than having a general concern because, for example, its sales growth is slowing. In all of these cases the customer is likely to have both need and market uncertainty.

Even in apparently simple situations, a customer's problem can rarely be solved just by purchasing a physical product or service alone. For example, the problem of a defective air-conditioning system in a heat-wave will not be solved by the rapid arrival of a service engineer. It will also need the simultaneous arrival of the single correct replacement part from among the many hundreds that constitute the system. In the case of more complex problems, such as those involving the operational control of a business, a complex software package for ERP (Enterprise Resource Planning) may be required. But this alone won't be sufficient to address the problem. A conservative estimate is that for each dollar spent on the purchase of this type

---

[1] Of course, although a customer's problem may *seem* to be clear, it is quite possible for the customer to misunderstand the real problem or to be confused about the best solution. So for example, those managers who complain to the office manager about cleaning, car hire or hotels may really be unhappy about the overall direction of the company, but have no easy way to articulate their concerns, so they are just taking it out on the poor office manager! In which case the company is unlikely to solve its real problem until it forms a relationship with a Human Resources Consultant, rather than a new office cleaner!

of software, a further five dollars will be spent on service and consulting in the choice and implementation of a system. Similarly, fashion retailers now face multiple problems of short fashion cycles, rapidly changing demand, financial pressures to reduce stock levels and price write-downs. They require that their suppliers respond to their orders for garments in days or even in hours. Not only must suppliers produce garments exactly to the customer's specification, but they must also deliver those garments in small quantities, on precise days and at precise times of day. In these cases and in order to solve their customers' problems, the ERP software supplier will need a large number of applications and implementation specialists as well as software designers. The producer of fashion garments and many other companies will find that the complexity of their customers' problems and requirements means that it will be unable to provide a suitable offering *by itself*. Important parts of the offerings that customers receive will actually be provided by other companies that produce particular subunits of the offering or act as facilitators, specialist distributors or logistics providers.

Supplier's problem-solving ability

A supplier's problem-solving ability forms the second basis of its offerings. Problem-solving ability enables a supplier to design and develop offerings that will provide a solution to a customer's problem. In turn, both of these abilities are built on the following foundations:

- The supplier's resources: physical, financial and technological (see Chapter 4).
- The supplier's network position: this position enables the supplier to use its relationships with other companies to access their resources and combine them in its own offerings and to implement those offerings.[2] The use of the resources of other companies is becoming more important as the costs and complexities of technology increase.[3]
- The supplier's ability to manage its relationships with customers: it is within these relationships that the supplier will seek to identify the customers' problems. The supplier will also take advantage of the customers' own abilities to address these customer problems (and also to address its own problems).

A customer's evaluation of a supplier will depend on much more than the characteristics of the supplier's offering. A customer is also likely to assess the supplier's organization and resources as well as its overall problem-solving and transfer abilities before it will commit itself to building a relationship with the supplier.[4] In this sense, business customers can be said to

---

[2] Transfer ability enables the supplier to actually implement its offering. We will deal with this important issue in Chapter 8.

[3] The ability to use and integrate the skills and resources of other companies is sometimes referred to as "network competence" (see T Ritter (1999) The Networking Company, *Industrial Marketing Management*, vol 28, no 5, 497–506).

[4] For discussions of supplier assessment and customer approaches to relationships see L Araujo, A Dubois and L-E Gadde (1999) Managing Interfaces with Suppliers, *Industrial Marketing Management*, vol 28, 497–506; S Talluri and J Sarkis (2002) A Model for Performance Monitoring of Suppliers, *International Journal of Production Research*, vol 40, 4257–4269; T O'Toole and B Donaldson (2002) Relationship Performance Dimensions of Buyer–Supplier Exchanges, *European Journal of Purchasing and Supply Management*, vol 8, no 4, 197–207.

"buy the supplier" rather than simply buy what it sells. The importance to the customer of this wider evaluation means that business marketers cannot just concentrate on their current offerings or on managing their relationships with their customers. Business marketers must also be concerned with the development of their company's own resources, with its relationships with its suppliers and with what those suppliers can contribute to its offerings.

Customers' demand and transfer abilities

This third basis of a supplier's offering is less obvious but equally important. A customer will be able or will choose to solve many of its problems by itself. Even when the customer decides to use a supplier for problem-solving, that supplier cannot take all the credit for the excellence of its offering or its ability to solve a customer's problem! This is because a suppliers' offering is likely to be developed, to evolve and to be implemented through interaction with customers. In this way a supplier's offering will also be based on the customer's *demand ability*. Just like a supplier's problem-solving ability, a customer's demand ability is based on its physical, technological and financial resources, on its network position and on its relationship management skills. A customer's demand ability enables it to advise the supplier of the type of offering it should produce. This is likely to be particularly important to the supplier when it is unsure of how or where the offering will be most productively used, ie when the supplier has application uncertainty; or if the supplier is unsure of the likely level of demand for that type of offering from customers, ie when the supplier has demand uncertainty. A customer's transfer ability will also be important in the development of a supplier's offering. A customer's transfer ability concerns its reliability in actually providing the promised type and volume of information and orders to a supplier. This customer ability is likely to be particularly important in those situations where the supplier is thinking of whether or not to make a major investment in order to develop a particular offering for a customer; in other words when the supplier has transaction uncertainty.

We emphasized in Chapter 6 that business marketers must *choose* the customers with which to build a relationship, rather than seek business from everywhere, or simply accept that which is offered. A supplier's customer choice must be based on the problems of both the customer *and the supplier itself*. A business marketer must assess how a customer's demand and transfer abilities will assist her in developing her offering and her relationship management skills, so that these may be profitably applied in other relationships.

A supplier with a specific problem or uncertainty may have to "buy" business from a customer in order to take advantage of that customer's abilities. *This will affect the supplier's offering for that customer and perhaps for others*. For example, a supplier may need to update its technology and so may seek a relationship with one or more technologically advanced customers. Alternatively, the supplier may already have developed a new offering and is anxious to see how it could be used by customers with particular problems. In this case, the supplier may be very keen to develop its relationship with specific customers with that type of problem. In both of these cases, the supplier may have to charge a price to these customers that does not fully reflect its costs, or spend heavily developing an offering with or for them. Similarly, a supplier may face the problem of reduced order volume. In this case, it may need to invest in developing a particular offering for customers that are able to provide the supplier with the high volume of orders that it needs.

Developing Offerings between Customer and Supplier

It is rare for offerings to be developed by a supplier alone, and it is rare for them to be launched on an unsuspecting world. For example, a producer of personal care products would be foolish to develop and launch a new hairspray without consulting with major retailers about where the new product would fit into the retailers' assortment and price range, about how the retailers and the supplier would jointly advertise it and about how it will be displayed on their shelves. In some cases, the development of consumer products is led by the retailer, such as when Marks & Spencer led the development of chilled "value-added" food products.

In the business marketing context, new offerings are mostly, but not always, developed in conjunction with one or more potential customers. In many cases development costs are shared between the customer and supplier. In others, the costs are borne by customer or by the supplier alone. Sometimes, as in the aerospace business, a supplier will only receive payment for its development efforts if and when the customer generates revenue from its subsequent sales that incorporate the supplier's offerings. The process of developing offerings is an integral part of the wider processes through which the two companies develop the technologies on which current and future offerings are based. We can use the matrix in Figure 7.1 to examine some of the development situations faced by suppliers and their

CUSTOMER / SUPPLIER	DOES NOT KNOW THE PROBLEM	DOES NOT KNOW THE SOLUTION	KNOWS BOTH
DOES NOT KNOW THE PROBLEM	Cell 1 Collaborative Investigation	Cell 2 Collaborative Investigation	Cell 3 Supply to Customer Specification
DOES NOT KNOW THE SOLUTION	Cell 4 Collaborative Investigation	Cell 5 Collaborative Development	Cell 6 Customer Specified Fulfilment
KNOWS BOTH	Cell 7 Supply to Supplier Specification	Cell 8 Supplier Specified Fulfilment	Cell 9 Collaborative Innovation

Figure 7.1   Developing offerings.

customers and see whether it is the supplier or a customer who is likely to take the lead in that development.

Cell 1 in the matrix is the case where neither supplier nor customer is able to define the nature of a customer's problem. This situation is common where a problem has its origin in the customer's customers or elsewhere in the network. For example, companies in the mobile telephone industry are currently unsure as to exactly what requirements final customers are likely to have for mobile information, data transmission, voice, pictures or music. In Cell 2, the customer can define the problem, but neither company knows what offering can provide a solution. This may mean that the customer will lead the development of an offering even though technical work will take place in the supplier. Cell 4 is the opposite of this situation, where the supplier can diagnose the customer's problem and in this case the supplier is likely to lead the development. In Cell 3, the customer understands both the problem and the required solution and the supplier understands neither. This is likely to be a low-margin case for the supplier as the customer will have little need uncertainty and the supplier is likely to be providing an offering based on the product and process technologies of the customer. In Cell 5, neither company has difficulty with problem definition, but neither knows the solution. This is when joint development is likely to take place. Cell 7 is the opposite situation. Here the customer is dependent on the supplier to both define its problem and provide a solution. This rather surprising situation is likely to occur when technologies are changing rapidly. For example, one CEO of a high-tech firm remarked: "Our customers have no idea what we can deliver next year. When we ask them what they want, they say that they want the old product". In Cell 6 the supplier understands the problem, but the solution is defined by the customer. This is a common situation where experienced producers work to the detailed design of a customer. Examples include both the fashion and automotive industries. In Cell 8, the customer understands the problem and is able to specify its requirements, but the solution will be based on the supplier's technology. Finally, Cell 9 is a situation where both companies understand both problem and current solution and so are equipped to work together on innovation.

The knowledge and ablities of both customer and supplier will impact on how an offering is developed and the form that an offering takes. Before dealing with this development process in more detail, we need to examine the constituent parts of an offering, as follows.

The Elements of a Supplier's Offerings

A supplier's offering is a promise to a customer that addresses a particular problem of that customer. Each of a supplier's offerings will consist of different combinations of the following five elements:

- product;
- service;
- advice;
- delivery;
- costs & price

Products

These are the physical part of an offering. This is what the customer can see and touch after it has made the purchase. An offering may include just one product, as in the case of a single piece of machinery. Alternatively, it may include many different products as in the case of a supplier of office equipment. Products are the most obvious element of an offering and are often considered by many customers and suppliers to be the most important element. *This is often wrong.* The product element may actually be relatively unimportant in solving customers' problems when compared to other elements. It is also worth emphasizing that a physical product has little intrinsic value itself, except perhaps for purposes of display. Its only real value is as part of a solution to a problem. As we have already noted: *There is no market for quarter inch drills, but there is an enormous market for quarter inch holes!*

Services

These may be a major part of the offering. This is for three reasons:

- Firstly, the product element of many offerings has little value without associated services. Common examples include the importance of help-lines to support the purchase of software, or the need for maintenance service for equipment, or training for operators. For example, Heidelberger Druckmaschinen, the maker of huge printing presses, has set up "print academies" in nine cities around the world to organize courses on printing techniques for customers and would-be customers of its equipment.[5]
- Secondly, many customers now choose to solve particular problems by purchasing a service *instead* of a product. For example, many customers lease equipment rather than buy it. Others contract-out the cleaning of their premises to service providers, rather than buying their own cleaning equipment. Similarly, many airlines do not buy engines for their aircraft, but contract with a supplier to pay for "power-by-the-hour". In this case the responsibility for the availability of the engines is the supplier's rather than the customer's.
- Offerings based on business services are rapidly increasing in importance as companies can no longer afford to retain and develop the technologies and resources that are needed to supply their offerings. These companies depend more and more on "external technologies" held by the suppliers of products and services to them.[6] For example, many companies in the automotive and fashion industries contract-out the design of their products to specialist design companies; similarly, many companies that previously designed and manufactured electronic components now use contract-manufacturers to produce components to their design; many airlines now outsource the maintenance of their aircraft and a wide range of companies now outsource much of their accounting and data processing to others.

---

[5] *Financial Times*, August 2 2001.
[6] The concept of External Technologies is fully discussed in Chapter 4.

Despite the growing importance of service in solving customers' problems, many suppliers still see service as little more than an unfortunate but unavoidable *cost* that is associated with sales of their *products*. These suppliers are much less likely to devote their efforts to developing their services than they are to developing their products. It is clear that these suppliers lack an understanding of the importance of designing and developing an integrated offering as a solution to customers' problems. Even more, these companies fail to see that customers are not interested in the supplier's own view of the "quality" or specification of its products, but only in how it will address their problems both immediately and on a continuing basis.

Delivery

Many companies approach this element of their offerings in a similar way to that in which they handle service. These companies seem to consider that delivery is just another unfortunate cost that has to be met by the supplier in order to deliver its *products* to customers. But where, when, how and in what form an offering is delivered is often critical to solving a customer's problem. *Hence delivery can often be the most vital element of an offering for customer problem-solving.* Further, we will see in Chapter 8 that actually *implementing* the delivery element of a supplier's offering is often critical in building lasting and productive customer relationships.

Delivery is particularly important when the product and service elements of an offering are undifferentiated between competitors. For example, an automotive manufacturer that buys basic components such as hoses or radiators may see little difference between the products of different suppliers. But the customer may have real problems with the cost of carrying an inventory of components or with the effects of late delivery of components on its production. In this case, it may be vital for a supplier to have an offering which is strong enough in delivery to provide "just-in-time" or "zero-inventory" deliveries to the customer's plants in several different countries.

Similarly, a producer of prepared meals for fast-food chains may face serious problems of food safety if a machine breaks down and production stops. In this case, a supplier of maintenance, repair and operations items (MRO) may operate an in-plant store of parts for the producer of food products to eliminate production disruptions caused when parts fail. The supplier may also indemnify the customer against the full costs of any breakdown caused by nonavailability of replacement parts. In this case, part of the supplier's offering is likely to be provided by a separate insurance company with which the supplier has a relationship. Similarly, a multinational oil company facing security problems at its installations in many countries may want to use a supplier that is able to deliver security services in each of those countries and is also able to work with the customer at its headquarters to deal with strategic problems. This discussion of the delivery element shows that there is no clear-cut borderline between services and delivery. We will return to this issue in Chapter 8.

Delivery is also an important part of the offerings of professional service companies such as advertising agencies, accountants, lawyers, trainers and consultants. The customers of these suppliers will often want to know that an offering can be delivered and that their problems can be addressed wherever in the world they arise. These suppliers often establish relationships with other suppliers that may normally be their competitors, in order to offer advice and service to clients in particular countries.

Advice

This fourth element of an offering concerns all the activities of a supplier, which are aimed at increasing the customer's understanding of its problems and of the supplier's offerings and abilities. The importance of advice in an offering will depend on the nature and extent of a customer's uncertainties, as follows:

- Sometimes a supplier may be able to provide sufficient advice about how its offerings can address customer problems in its brochures and websites and during sales calls. This is likely to be the case when customers have low need uncertainty and market uncertainty or when their problems are easily defined. However, advice from the supplier about its offerings is of greater importance when customers have high need and/or market uncertainty or a complex or undefined problem. In this situation the value to customers of the advice of a trusted supplier can far outweigh the price of a subsequent purchase.
- When customers have high transaction uncertainty, then a supplier will need to concentrate its advice on the specific elements of price and costs and delivery and also on the supplier's ability to actually implement the offering. We will return to the issue of implementation in more detail in Chapter 8.

The advice element in an offering is not the same as a "hard sell", in which a marketer tries to push customers into buying her offering, irrespective of the customers' problems and uncertainties. However, business marketers do need communication skills in identifying customers' problems, in linking those problems to the offering it is able or willing to supply, as we have discussed in Chapter 6. Advice is an interactive process in a business relationship. Advice from customers is important for reducing the supplier's uncertainties. Customers can advise suppliers on the nature of their problems, on the way that they would hope to use an offering and how that offering must relate to those of other suppliers and to the customer's own offering for its customers. Customers can also contribute their technologies to the interactive development of the supplier's offering.

Costs & price

Costs & price are an important element in a supplier's offering and we will devote Chapter 9 to a full analysis of these. For the purposes of understanding the elements of a supplier's offerings it is important to emphasize a number of points about customer costs, as follows:

- Firstly, the *price* that customers pay for an offering is likely to be only a small part of their overall *costs* of obtaining and using that offering. In addition to price, customers will also incur the costs of working with the supplier to develop or adapt an offering and to integrate it within their own operations. Customers will also incur the costs of using and further developing the offering throughout its life. Customers may have only poor knowledge of the real costs of the offerings of different suppliers and it may be a major part of the marketer's role to advise customers on the full costs of its own offering and those of competitors.

- Secondly, the price that a customer is prepared to pay for an offering is related to the importance of the customer's problem, the extent to which the offering may solve it and to what the customer sees as the full costs of the offering. The price that the customer is prepared to pay is not related to any intrinsic characteristics the offering might have, or the absolute "quality" of any of its elements. What is perceived by a customer to be a "fair" price is also affected by the prices of other offerings that may function as potential solutions to the problem of the customer.
- Because customers assess the price of an offering against its potential to solve their problems, the price that customers are prepared to pay is not necessarily related to the supplier's own costs of developing or implementing the offering. This means that changing or substituting different elements of the offering to reduce costs provides important profit opportunities for business marketers.

Customers will value different elements of an offering in relation to their own problems and uncertainties. For some customers, enhanced delivery will be more valuable than improvements in the specification of the product element in an offering that only fulfils a simple function for them. For others, advice may be more important than speed of delivery, while others may value a product adaptation more than a high level of service. Customers are also likely to consider the value of their relationship with a supplier when examining the price of an offering, as well as any other costs that they may incur in receiving, learning about, integrating and using the offering. Marketers must also consider the value to them of each relationship as well as their own costs, when considering prices.

Inter-relationships between the elements of offerings

The five elements of business marketers' offerings are inter-related and in some cases substitutable for each other. For example, four different suppliers that address the same customers' problems that centre on transport could have quite different offerings from each other, as follows:

- The first supplier could provide an offering built round the sale of a fleet of delivery trucks that are purchased by the customer. The customer would then be responsible for recruiting and managing drivers for the trucks, for scheduling and for using the trucks to make deliveries and for maintaining the trucks during their life.
- Another supplier could provide an offering that does not include the purchase of the trucks. Instead it could provide a *service* by hiring delivery trucks, maintained by the supplier, with guaranteed availability at a fixed mileage charge.
- A third supplier could provide a different offering by buying the customer's current fleet from it, managing the vehicles and making deliveries for the customer.
- A fourth supplier could simply provide the service of delivering the customer's goods, in the supplier's own vehicles with a guaranteed speed and reliability level and charge per item delivered.

In this example we see how suppliers with quite different offerings may compete with each other, if they provide different ways of addressing similar problems. We also see how each supplier's offering will be based on its own resources and abilities. Thus, the first supplier in this example could be a truck maker or a truck distributor. The second supplier could be a vehicle hire company. The third and fourth suppliers could be companies that offered different delivery services. We can also see in this example that the three last suppliers could also be customers of the first supplier as well as its competitors.

An example of product/service interchangeability within one company is provided in the medical area. Fresenius is the world's biggest maker of artificial kidney machines for use in hospitals. Also, through Fresenius Medical Care, they are the biggest provider of kidney dialysis services to both hospitals and the customers of hospitals, using a chain of 1,300 global clinics.[7] A further example of product/service interchangeability is provided in Box 7.1.

The characteristics of both service and product elements are inter-related with the delivery elements of offerings. For example, the ratio of the weight of the product element to the value of the offering is often critical to the logistics that can be used. Similarly, because services such as security or facilities management often have to be delivered to a wide range of locations for the same customer, then suppliers have to establish an extensive branch network to deliver their offering.[8]

Box 7.1   Product/Service Inter-relationships in the IT Industry

The Chief Executive of Hewlett Packard asserted as long ago as 1999 that the age of the "pure product" was over. As computing and communication technologies converge, the value of a product becomes closely related to other elements of an offering. So HP re-invented itself as a provider of "information-technology services and solutions". The wish to add to the service and advice elements of its offerings was the rationale behind HP's bid for the consulting business of PricewaterhouseCoopers. The same thinking could also be seen in IBM's actions to build one of the largest IT consulting operations in the world and in Compaq's take-over of Digital, mainly to acquire its consulting arm and in Cisco's $1 billion stake in consultants KPMG. Of course these moves did not take place in isolation in the network. If a consulting company becomes allied with a hardware/software producer, then that may change the consultants' relationship with its customers. These customers may doubt the independence of the consultants' advice, especially when equipment purchase is involved.[9]

Sometimes the complex offerings demanded by business customers can only be provided by a number of suppliers working together. For example, the ERP-system supplier, SAP, worked closely with its partners to develop the SAP Partner Value Net. This classifies partners into eight categories: software partners, service partners, technology partners, support partners, hosting partners, channel partners, content partners and education partners. With these partners SAP is able to offer customized solutions to individual customer's problems, using the resources of all of the companies involved.[10]

---

[7] *Financial Times*, August 2 2001.

[8] For a discussion of the interconnections between product characteristics and delivery see for example J Stock and D Lambert (2001) *Strategic Logistics Management*, New York, McGraw-Hill.

[9] *The Economist*, September 16 2000.

[10] Adapted from the SAP website: www.sap.com

The advice element is also inter-related with product, service and delivery. For example, when the product element is a commodity, then the customer may know all it needs to know about the product and product-advice may be irrelevant. However, the customer may require considerable advice about the costs and advantages of different stocking and delivery policies. A supplier may seek to simplify its products and services so as to minimize the advice that is needed and thus gain a cost advantage over its competitors that may be reflected in the price that it charges. This simplification is commonly achieved by modularizing the offering or by simplifying the choice process. Modularization and order-simplification have both been part of the strategy of Dell, whose competitors did not initially believe that customers would buy expensive computers via the internet. In general, it is the nature of the customer's problems and uncertainties that determines the role of advice, rather than the intrinsic complexity of an offering or its individual elements.

Variations in the elements of their offerings enable many business marketers to have a number of offerings to address different customer problems all at different prices, depending on variations in the other elements of the offering.

Finally, it is important to emphasize that any variations in the elements of a single supplier's offering will often have to be integrated with changes in the offerings of other suppliers in order to address a customer problem. For example, Ikea has worked closely with a number of suppliers to enable it to keep the price of its best-selling Lack table constant for over twenty years.[11] Component suppliers, machinery companies and makers of the tables have substituted materials and changed methods to lower the costs of the table. They have also worked closely with each other to reduce the weight of the tables. This has lowered the costs of delivery and made the tables an impulse purchase that customers can pick up in the store and carry home!

What Offering Focus should we Have?

Managers are frequently told to ask themselves the question, "What business are we in?" But nowadays this is a difficult question to answer because there are few easily defined businesses, industries, markets or *normal* ways to operate in them. Also, it is important for the business marketer to define her activities in terms of the problems of customers, rather than in terms of her own activities or within an industry categorization. Defining a business in terms of customer problems will enable the marketer to assess her current offerings against those problems and against other companies that address the same or related problems, *irrespective of the characteristics of their offerings.*

But designing and developing offerings requires an investment of considerable time and resources and it is unlikely that the supplier will be able to develop an entirely different offering for each of its customers.[12] Therefore the business marketer has to make

[11] E Baraldi (2003) When Information Technology Faces Resource Interaction, doctoral dissertation, Uppsala University, Department of Business Studies.

[12] Of course there are many cases, such as the Ikea example, where a supplier does develop a dedicated offering just for a single supplier. Ikea's supplier of Lack tables produces over two million of these tables annually in a dedicated factory in Poland.

an important strategic decision about the *focus* for her offerings. A company's offering focus can be of three types: a focus on a particular type of customer *problem,* a focus on a *range* of offerings based on a particular technological strength, or a focus on particular *relationships*:

- **Problem focus:** This focus involves the supplier in concentrating on a single type of problem and developing a number of offerings which solve that problem in different ways. A simple example is a business travel agent that offers train tickets, rental cars and flight tickets as solutions to the problems of business travel. However, a focus on providing a wide range of different offerings is more difficult in the case of complex problems, such as those addressed by financial services companies or producers of production machinery. This is because these companies cannot afford the range of abilities and technologies necessary to develop and fulfil a variety of offerings effectively or economically. A recent example of the difficulty of sustaining a problem focus is provided by Xerox. Xerox referred to themselves as "the document company" and aimed to produce a full range of offerings to deal with all aspects of document reproduction. However, they failed to match their successful offerings in analogue copiers with similar success in digital copiers. Many suppliers seek to get round the difficulty of sustaining a range of different offerings by acting as agents for the offerings of other suppliers and combining them with their own offerings to provide a full range. Many customers also require suppliers to bring together the development and implementation of other suppliers' offerings when they operate a so-called tiered supply-network. Another potential danger of a problem focus is that not all the customers in the same "industry", ie those customers that appear to do similar things, or all the customers in the same "market", ie those that buy the same products, will have the same problems. Hence, an overly narrow problem focus is likely to restrict a supplier's available customers to a small subset of those that buy particular products. However, a careful definition of the problems that it aims to solve will enable a company to have a clear view of the real competition that it faces rather than those companies that simply sell similar products.
- **Range focus:** This focus is based on the idea that it is likely to be more cost-effective for the business marketer to find customers that have problems that relate to their existing and expensively acquired technologies than to develop new offerings specifically for the problems of their existing customers. A range focus can take two forms.

    In the first form the company builds a range of offerings for *different* problems, based on the company's abilities and its distinctive product and/or process technologies. This focus addresses the danger of over-extending the number of different technologies that a company may need when taking a problem focus (above). A range focus seeks to maximize the company's return on its investment in a limited number of technologies. A good example is provided by Rolls-Royce. They supply a range of offerings all using its gas-turbine technologies, but suitable for powering military or civil aircraft, for propelling military ships, for pumping oil or gas, or for generating electricity. When taking a range focus, one element of all the offerings, typically the product or service element, will have only minor variation. Thus, Rolls-Royce uses the same basic designs of gas turbines, but modifies them to burn different fuels in different problem situations. This focus typically involves variation in other elements of the offering for each problem. For example, aerospace customers require Rolls-Royce to be closely involved with them over many years in joint studies of aircraft performance (advice). In contrast, naval customers take responsibility themselves for the wider aspects of ship design and performance. The offerings for pumping and power generation must provide customers with a package, bought "off-the-shelf" and delivered to any location, however remote (logistics), so that they can simply switch it on. A range focus depends on the supplier having a well-developed knowledge of the different problems of each type of customer problem and the ability to manage many different types of relationships.

The second form of range focus also involves the supplier in providing a range of offerings, all using *similar* abilities and technologies. But the difference is that these are directed to a narrower set of customers that have similar problems to each other. Examples of companies that take this form of range focus include those that supply a range of printers or drilling machines with a range of capacities and features. Many freight or security companies or those advertising service agencies that specialize in creative work or media buying also have this range focus. This form of range focus has the same advantage as the first of allowing the supplier to invest heavily in a narrow range of skills or technologies and to develop a reputation for excellence in them. This form of range focus also has the advantage when compared with the first type that it limits the number of types of problems that a supplier has to address and narrows the range of relationship management skills that it needs to have. But of course, this form of range focus restricts the supplier's ability to maximize the return on its technological assets by using them in different problem situations. Suppliers taking both forms of range focus are likely to have an offering that is highly sophisticated in one element, based on the supplier's *distinctive technology*. But these suppliers will need either to develop the other elements of the offering themselves or work closely with a cooperating company. Otherwise, customers will have to integrate the offering with those of other suppliers and use their own demand abilities to build a complete problem solution.

Suppliers that take a range focus are always vulnerable to the possibility that the technologies on which they depend may become obsolete. One illustrative example is the rise and fall of the Swedish office equipment supplier, Facit. This company developed a world-leading position in mechanical office machines (calculators, typewriters etc). Over time their products became increasingly sophisticated as they developed their mechanical technology. These advanced product features, however, were of little value when electronic office equipment was launched by other suppliers. Range-focused suppliers are also less likely to have a close relationship with customers than those taking a problem focus and this may make it more difficult for them to monitor and react to changing requirements.

- **Relationship focus:** This focus involves a supplier in seeking to capitalize on its important customer relationships and build the necessary offerings for each case. This was the approach that was successfully followed by Jack Welch during his tenure at General Electric. Rather than try to sell existing products to more customers, Welch concentrated on broadening GE's offerings for its existing customers by adding new services. Similarly, the Chief Executive of ABB, the electrical engineering company, faced the problem of a broad portfolio of offerings marketed to thousands of customers in many different ways with consequent limitations on its efficiency. For this reason ABB sought to reorientate its research and development towards a greater emphasis on its relationships with its customers, rather than simply with its own engineers, sales teams and suppliers. Atlas Copco, the supplier of pneumatic equipment for assembly operations, is an example of how a relationship focus can affect a supplier's offering. Atlas Copco had an important relationship with Ford, the car-maker. In order to sustain this relationship, Atlas Copco had to agree to Ford's request to also supply it with the products of one of its main competitors, Ingersoll Rand. Another illustration of this approach is when IBM's marketing manager was once asked why IBM was supplying Hewlett Packard's printers to some of its customers. He replied that "we'd rather give them our own, but if they want HP, my guys will go out and buy them. Customers say to us: IBM you put the whole solution together". A relationship focus is being followed by a number of large accounting companies that seek to provide profitable consulting and legal services in customer relationships that were initially based solely on auditing. For example, Pricewaterhouse-Coopers currently receives only 40% of its revenues from traditional accounting and auditing services. This approach has led to major concerns by regulatory authorities in a number of countries about the effects of complex supplier–client relationships on the traditional audit relationship. Similarly, a number of consulting companies are taking a relationship focus and building a portfolio of offerings to meet a complete set of client needs: consulting, technology, outsourcing, alliances and venture capital. Of course this approach involves the danger that the companies will be unable to support the wide range of internal technologies that are necessary. More generally, a relationship focus increases a company's dependence on a limited portfolio of relationships and restricts its ability to learn from exposure to other customers and competitive activities.

Developing the Elements of Offerings

A number of particular issues arise when we examine the development of the individual elements within a supplier's offerings. Before we move to this examination it is worth reiterating that each of the elements should not be considered in isolation. Unfortunately many business marketers devote a disproportionate share of their company's resources to one or other element of their offerings, often to the product element. Each offering needs to be developed as a totality. In doing this, marketers need to bear in mind the interrelationships between the different elements and also the possibilities for substitution of elements, as we discussed above.[13]

We can now turn to the development of the individual elements of a supplier's offerings:

- **Product:** Business marketers are often faced with a "product development procedure" in their companies. This outlines the stages that each development should go through as it

[13] For those readers familiar with consumer marketing, there is a useful parallel with the idea of the marketing mix. Irrespective of the strength of any one element of the mix, if the mix is not right as a totality, it's not right at all!

progresses from idea generation to commercialized product.[14] However, over time there has been an increasing view that these stage approaches are like a "relay race" where each department, such as research, engineering, production, does their work on a new product and then hands this over to the next one.[15] Not only is this likely to lengthen the process, but the departments do not work effectively together and are likely to "drop the baton" at each hand-over. Instead, a "rugby scrum" approach is advocated where representatives from each function within the supplier and the customer work together throughout the development process. This means that activities such as product and production design take place concurrently.[16] For this rugby scrum approach to work, business marketers cannot just simply specify a customer requirement and pass this on to a development department. Instead, they must be involved throughout the process in liaising with each department and the customer on the trade-offs between the product's performance – what it will do and the different ways of how it can be achieved and at what costs. Second, there is now greater emphasis on the process of continuous improvement. Product development is not a single one-off process to produce the product, but a continuous process of refinement. This involves business marketers in a variety of techniques, including "benchmarking" their products (or other offering elements) against those of competitors and against customer priorities and translating these into offering improvements.[17]

- **Service:** The same processes of simultaneous development and continuous improvement can be applied to the service element of an offering. But two additional issues arise for the business marketer. Firstly, each service delivery is individual and the quality of fulfilment is likely to depend heavily on the personnel involved. This means that consistency of delivery is critical to success. For this reason, business marketers need to understand the limits that staffing issues place on service design and how service can be modified to cope with those limits. Continuous improvement programmes will also require marketers to be closely in touch with those responsible for service delivery. Secondly, there is an increasing tendency for the product element in an offering to be replaced by a service as companies concentrate on fewer areas of distinctiveness and contract out major aspects of their business. This is often a difficult transition for many companies because responsibility for the successful use of an offering is often retained by the supplier. So instead of simply producing good products, the supplier must often manage a large staff to provide service provision to an agreed standard in

[14] See, for example, R Cooper (1993) *Winning at New Products: Accelerating the Process from Idea to Launch*, 2nd edition, Reading, MA, Addison-Wesley; S Wheelwright and K Clarke (1992) *Revolutionising Product Development*, New York, Free Press.

[15] Originally suggested by H Takeuchi and I Nonaka (1986) The New New Product Development Game, *Harvard Business Review*, January–February, 137–146. For recent publications see, for example, D Anderson (2004) *Design for Manufacturability and Concurrent Engineering*, Cambria, CIM Press.

[16] For recent publications see, for example, D Anderson (2004) *Design for Manufacturability and Concurrent Engineering*, Cambria, CIM Press.

[17] N Slack, S Chambers and R Johnston (2001) *Operations Management*, 3rd edition, Harlow, Pearson Education.

remote locations. Common examples where service has substituted for product include the supply of major items like railway trains and commercial aircraft. Here, many suppliers now maintain their own equipment and sell its availability, rather than selling the equipment itself. This also occurs with much more mundane items, such as when a lubricating oil supplier switches from selling cans of oil to the planned servicing of its customers' vehicles.

- **Delivery:** The development of the delivery element of a particular offering is likely to be relatively straightforward when serving customers that purchase infrequently or those that buy offerings that are not critical for their operations. But some customers may require complex and costly delivery arrangements, if these can reduce their overall costs or add to their competitiveness. Many offerings include a delivery element that is individually designed to the requirements of each customer. These individualized elements will probably involve the supplier in considerable interaction with the customer. The frequently conflicting requirements of cost reduction and high delivery performance may point to the need for the supplier to develop a range of delivery "packages" or to invest in a comprehensive distribution structure. In contrast, some other customers may prefer to avoid the close involvement with a single supplier that comes with complex delivery arrangements. These customers may prefer to use standardized offerings that entail lower immediate costs and retain the freedom associated with more arm's-length relationships.

- **Advice:** We have seen throughout this book that business relationships are based on customer problems. Very often suppliers are involved in identifying these problems as well as advising what would be a suitable solution. A supplier's advice is often as valuable to a customer as the subsequent delivery of an offering. But business marketers face two problems in managing and developing the advice element of their offerings. Firstly, advice to customers was traditionally provided by a supplier's sales force, who called on technical assistance from others as required. However, the operating costs of a business sales force have escalated and many companies have sought to standardize the advice element, increase its effectiveness and reduce their costs by providing web-based information and customer "hot-lines". Secondly, the advice element of an offering is difficult for the business marketer to control. Thus, advice on complex customer problems often leads to unplanned and uncontrolled adaptation by the supplier. The danger of incurring additional costs means that business marketers need systems to approve and monitor customer advice and the adaptations that this may lead to by assessing costs against their assessment of the overall value of each relationship.

- **Costs & Price:** The prices that a supplier charges for its offerings should not simply be the outcome of the supplier's costs of designing and implementing those offerings. On the contrary, the supplier should take the value to the customer of getting its problem solved and *the customer's overall costs* as its point of departure for pricing. A number of additional considerations will have to be borne in mind when determining price. Frequently, an offering will not solve a customer's problem completely; on other occasions the customer will have to incur further costs to integrate the offering into its operations; many times the importance of the problem and its solution to the customer will not justify the costs and hence the price that the supplier would like to charge.

Also, in many cases it is the customer that determines the price it will pay and an offering will have to be tailored to that price. We will examine the issues of costs and price for supplier and customer in Chapter 9.

Designing a Single Offering

So far we have examined the issues that business marketers face in determining the focus for all of their company's offerings together. We now turn to some of the issues involved in assessing and developing each individual offering and the elements within it. The starting point for the development of a specific offering is the problem perceived by a potential customer. The customer will evaluate the supplier's offering according to its ability to solve its problem. Value for the customer is thus related to the fit between offering and problem – and not to the features of the offering. Each of a supplier's offerings may be provided to a number of different customers that have *similar* problems. But offerings aren't automatically complete solutions, even to similar problems. We can explore the relation between offerings and problems and the ways in which they match or mismatch in the following four categories:

- Offering < Problem: This is when the offering provides only a partial solution to the customer's problem. This may be because of technological, resource or cost problems in the supplier or because of poor diagnosis of the problem by customer or supplier. Customers often have to accept the inadequacy of offerings for a long period, if more complete solutions are not available. Alternatively, they may try to find or develop a new supplier or different type of offering to address the problem more completely.
- Offering = Problem: In this case, the offering provides a solution that exactly solves the customer's problem – nothing more and nothing less. This may seem like optimal "quality". But it is similar to the situation described by Mari Sako as "contractual trust" between supplier and customer. In this situation, the supplier does only what is specified precisely in the contract and fails to demonstrate commitment to a relationship or to achieve customer satisfaction.[18]
- Offering > Problem: In this situation, the supplier's offering does more than solve the customer's original problem. This could be a good situation for the supplier if the offering also solves another problem. For example, the supplier of a production item that meets a customer specification may also provide just-in-time delivery so the item no longer has to be kept in inventory. Provided that this can be achieved within cost constraints, extra problem-solving may be an important way of demonstrating commitment and building a relationship. Marketers often refer to this as "customer delight". However, this situation could also be negative if an offering solves a problem, but also creates another one, for example, use of an offering may lead to problems of emissions or recycling.

[18] M Sako (1992) *Prices, Quality and Trust: Interfirm Relations in Britain and Japan*, Cambridge, Cambridge University Press.

- Offering <> Problem: In this situation, the offering provides a solution that exceeds the customer's problem in some aspects but fails to meet requirements in others. This situation indicates a mismatch between offering and problem, either because of over-standardization by the supplier, or because of a badly designed offering or because of poor communication between the two companies.

Each of these four situations may exist at the same time for some of a supplier's offerings supplied to different customers. This involves the business marketer in an important choice. She can continue to offer the existing offering to all her current customers and hope to live with the mismatch between offering and some problems. Alternatively, the marketer can *adapt* one or more elements of the offering for some or all of her customers in order to increase their perceived value. We will address the important issues of adaptations in the coming section.

Adapting Offerings

Each single offering of a supplier may be supplied to a number of customers, but in some cases there could be a mismatch between the offering and the problems of an individual customer. It is at this point of mismatch between offering and problem that the business marketer faces the issue of whether she should *adapt* the offering to suit the customer's particular requirements more closely. The scale of the adaptations by suppliers to suit individual customers (or by customers to suit individual suppliers) is among the most significant differences between business and consumer marketing. Adaptations are a vital but problematic issue for the business marketer.

Of course, many business marketers routinely modify one or more element of their offerings to suit each of their customers. For example, advertising agencies always develop a media campaign designed specifically for each of their clients and building contractors are likely to alter the construction materials that they use to suit each of their clients.

Thus it is important to be clear when we talk about a supplier making an adaptation that we mean that the supplier is doing something for a particular customer *that it would not normally do for other customers*. It would be an adaptation for an advertising agency if it not only designed a media campaign and bought space on behalf of its client, as normal, but also designed and managed a series of publicity events for the client. Similarly, it would be an adaptation for the construction company if it not only modified the material that it used to suit its customer, but also agreed to payment on the basis of costs plus a management fee, rather than a fixed price as normal.

By adapting one or more of the elements of their offerings to meet customer requirements, business marketers may be able to establish a new relationship or demonstrate commitment to the development of an existing one. But at the same time, marketers need to restrict the extent of these adaptations as a way of controlling their costs. Business marketers must balance these conflicting pressures of customer requirements and costs. Success in this depends on at least three factors, as follows:

- Firstly, the marketer must be able to identify real, widespread customer problems, so that it can address a worthwhile number of customers with well-designed offerings that it can supply economically. To be able to do this, the marketer must not only be skilled in customer analysis, but must also understand the product and process technologies of her company.

- Secondly, the marketer will need to develop offerings based on individual elements that can *routinely* be altered to accommodate differences in requirements. A common way to achieve this is to design one or more elements of the offering to consist of independent modules that can be assembled into different forms, easily and inexpensively. For example, Hewlett Packard uses a *modular* design for its DeskJet printers. Standard printers for the whole world are produced at a factory in Singapore. Hewlett Packard's European Distribution Centre separately purchases the power suppliers, packaging and manuals needed to customize the printers to meet the power and instructional requirements of customers in different countries. In this way, Hewlett Packard has been able to meet a range of requirements, *within their normal offerings*, and have reduced their costs of manufacturing, shipping and inventory by 25%.[19] Another way to achieve this same effect is to allow some of the elements of the offerings, such as service and product, to be substituted for each other where necessary.

- Thirdly, the marketer and her company must accept that these approaches may still not fully address all of their customers' problems. In these cases, the business marketer must assess the importance of individual customer relationships and the adaptations that are required and work with operations colleagues to determine whether adaptations should be made and how they should be implemented.

Adaptations can be made to any of the elements of an offering, but it is important to keep in mind that the different elements of an offering are inter-related so that, for example, a costly adaptation in the product element may be avoided by providing additional advice on how to use it or by changing the service element to improve the customer's processes. Adaptations to the advice element are also important in many relationships. Advice adaptations would include such things as a supplier employing special consultants for a particular customer or a supplier researching the use of its offering in a particular application so as to be able to enhance its advice to a customer.

It is important for a marketer to set the costs of an adaptation against the value of the relationship in which they were made, whilst also realizing that adaptations that are initially developed for a single customer can sometimes be applied to others. On the other hand, business marketers also need to be conscious that using scarce resources of time and money to make an adaptation for one particular relationship can also have a negative effect on others. It is important for business marketers to work closely with others in their company to translate their understanding of customer problems into offerings that can provide solutions for different customers with maximum commonality and at minimum cost. Unfortunately, business marketers often find that they have inadequate information on both the real costs of adaptations and the real costs and profitability of their relationships. We will return to this issue in Chapter 9.

---

[19] This example is drawn from R Chase, N Aquilano and R Jacobs (2001) *Operations Management for Competitive Advantage*, 9th edition, New York, McGraw-Hill Irwin.

Adaptations in relationships

A relationship may start because a supplier already has an offering that solves a customer's problem. But in many cases, that offering will have to be developed or adapted through interaction between the customer and supplier. Some or all of the elements of the offering are also likely to be adapted further as the relationship develops and the companies invest in it. This process of relationship-specific investment develops the *resource ties* and *activity links* between the companies.[20] These investments are often costly, but they work to cement the relationship between the companies. Customers may welcome this process of adaptation and investment in some cases. But in others, they may also wish to standardize the offerings they receive from different suppliers to simplify their own operations, to reduce resource ties and activity links with individual suppliers and hence to reduce their dependence on any one of them.[21]

Adaptations in different buy-cycles

In Chapter 5 we suggested that a customer is likely to look first of all within its existing relationships for solutions to its problems. We referred to this as Buy-cycle 1. In Buy-cycle 1, growth for the supplier comes from growth of the customer (the cake is growing), or growth of the supplier's share of the customer's business (its slice of the cake is growing) or new business in the relationship (new cake). Although Buy-cycle 1 implies "business as usual", it still involves the marketer in questions about adaptations: even if the relationship involves long-term exchange of a similar offering, it is still important for the supplier to develop and innovate in the implementation of that offering. This may involve investment in production or service facilities or automatic order processing, both to reduce costs and to enhance the "quality" of implementation. A customer's problems will change over time and the business marketer will have to adapt existing offerings or develop new ones for her existing relationships. We saw in Chapter 4 how important it is for suppliers to capitalize on the resources of customers and work with them on these developments.

Buy-cycle 2 occurs when either the customer or supplier seeks a new relationship. This involves both more expense and more uncertainty than Buy-cycle 1, as the companies need to invest in learning about each other as well as adapting or developing an offering. New relationships are an obvious source of growth for the business marketer. They may provide the opportunity to exploit the offerings that have been developed in existing relationships, to adapt them or to develop new technologies or offerings that cannot be developed in existing ones. When considering the potential of a new relationship, business marketers must assess the extent to which they can use the same offerings that have already been developed for existing relationships. They must also assess the extent to which the costs of any adaptation or development can be recouped in that relationship and in others.

---

[20] For a discussion of these terms, see Chapter 2.

[21] We explained in Chapter 5 that customers making this choice were deciding between a high-involvement and a low-involvement relationship.

Quality of Offerings

We have used the word quality a number of times in this chapter, always printing it "qual-ity". The inverted commas are there because quality is a word that is often used loosely by business marketers and it is important to establish clarity in its meaning. Our definition is that the quality of an offering is a measure of the extent to which it *actually* solves a particular problem for a particular customer. Thus, the quality of an offering depends on the characteristics of the offering itself as a way of addressing a customer problem *and* on how well that offering is implemented by the supplier in practice. Different customers will each have a different view of the quality of the same offering depending on their problems and uncertainties, as follows:

- Some customers faced with a particularly difficult problem will be more concerned with whether a supplier's offering has the *potential* to solve that problem. Other customers with more mundane problems may find that the offerings of many potential suppliers will be suitable for it. Therefore these companies are likely to be less concerned with the characteristics of the similar offerings of each supplier and much more concerned with which supplier will be most effective at *implementing* that offering in practice.
- Different customers will consider that different elements of an offering are more or less important to its quality, depending on their particular problems and uncertainties. For example, some customers will not be able to articulate their problem or evaluate the best way to solve it, or be able to evaluate different offerings. In this situation of high need or market uncertainty, the supplier's *advice* as to what the customer should buy may be much more important to that customer than any characteristics of the product element.
- In contrast, where the customer has little need or market uncertainty and is an experi-enced buyer, its view of the quality of an offering is more likely to be based on exactly what each of the elements of product, service and delivery do to solve its problem, rather than on the advice element of the offering.
- In other cases, it is the supplier's ability to adapt its offering to suit a particular require-ment that is critical to "quality" for these customers. We will return to the issue of implementation in Chapter 8.

Specifications

A supplier's offering may be developed against the specification of a particular customer. In this case, the customer is able to evaluate the quality of an offering against that specifica-tion. Customers are likely to develop a detailed specification when a complex offering is likely to be required, when an important or difficult problem has to be addressed. Some-times a customer will develop a *performance specification*. This is a detailed description of what the offering must do in order to solve the customer's problem. At other times the customer may develop a *conformance specification*, of the characteristics the offering must have, or of how it will solve the problem. But a customer will only be able to develop a performance specification if it has little or no need uncertainty or market uncertainty. It will only be able to develop a conformance specification if it has the product technology to design the offering that it requires and also some knowledge of the process technology that would be involved in its implementation.

Purchasing textbooks emphasize the importance for customers of clear and unambiguous specifications. But customers do not have the knowledge, abilities or resources to develop specifications for all of the thousands of offerings that they buy. There is a growing tendency for customers to express specifications in more general performance terms and to seek the involvement of suppliers in the development of the specification and a suitable offering. This tendency has been reinforced by the growing dependence of customers on external technologies in their suppliers.

Conclusions

An offering is the supplier's promise to solve a customer's problem. It consists of five elements: product, service, delivery, advice, and costs & price. Each of these offerings may be more or less important, depending on the nature of the customer's problems and uncertainties. An offering provides the link between a supplier's abilities and these customer problems.

An offering is based on the problem-solving ability of a supplier. This in turn is a function of its physical, financial and technological resources, its network of relationships with other companies and its relationship management skills. However, because a supplier's offerings are often developed and fulfilled interactively by both customer and supplier, the design of offerings also depends on the customer's demand ability. This in turn, is based on the customer's physical, technological and financial resources, on its network position and on its relationship management skills.

Both business and consumer marketers are involved in developing offerings that will satisfy the requirements of their customers and address their problems. But the business marketer faces a more challenging task:

- She must work with customers to assess their problems.
- She must develop offerings that are complex and which may have to be adapted to address the individual requirements of each customer.
- She must consider how her company's offerings relate to its overall technological position and network position and its strategy for these.

And then of course the business marketer has to implement the promise that has been made in that offering if she is to build a productive relationship with her customer. We will now turn to the issue of implementation in Chapter 8.

Further Reading

J Anderson and J Narus (2003) Selectively Pursuing More of Your Customer's Business, *MIT Sloan Management Review*, Spring, 42–49.

J Anderson and J Narus (2004) *Business Market Management: Understanding, Creating, and Delivering Value*, Upper Saddle River, NJ, Prentice Hall.

K Clark and S Wheelwright (1993) *Managing New Product and Process Development*, New York, Free Press.

A Eggert, W Ulaga and F Schultz (2006) Value Creation in the Relationship Life Cycle, *Industrial Marketing Management*, vol 35, 20–27.

J Fitzsimmons and M Fitzsimmons (2004) *Service Management*, New York, McGraw-Hill.

T Levitt (1980) Marketing Success through Differentiation – of Anything, *Harvard Business Review*, January–February, 83–91.

T Levitt (1981) Marketing Intangible Products and Product Intangibles, *Harvard Business Review*, May–June, 94–102.

V Malleret (2006) Value Creation through Service Offers, *European Management Journal*, vol 24, no 1, 106–116.

M Nevens, G Summe and B Uttal (1990) Commercializing Technology: What the Best Companies Do, *Harvard Business Review*, May–June, 154–163.

A Page (1993) Assessing New Product Development Practices and Performance: Establishing Crucial Norms, *Journal of Product Innovation Management*, vol 10, 273–290.

A Ulwick (2002) Turn Customer Input into Innovation, *Harvard Business Review*, January–February, 91–97.

P Zipkin (2001) The Limits of Mass Customization, *MIT Sloan Management Review*, Spring, 70–82.

Assignment for Chapter 7

Offerings at Airslash

In the previous assignment as Group Marketing Director for Airslash, you developed some ideas on the problems that might be addressed by Airslash with regard to a number of actual or potential customers and the type of relationship that would be needed to address these problems.

You now want to take this analysis further. For each of these actual or potential customers and the problems you have identified, examine and describe the offerings that you would propose for each customer. Although, this is a preliminary investigation, your analysis should address all the relevant issues in offering development. You may use any assumptions necessary to complete your analysis, provided that you make those assumptions explicit.

IMPLEMENTING THE OFFERING: FULFILLING THE PROMISE

8

Aims of this Chapter

- To help business marketers to understand the issues involved in developing transfer ability and in implementing offerings.
- To illustrate the processes available for implementation of product, service and delivery.
- To enable business marketers to communicate effectively with those involved in implementation and to contribute to decisions on the company's operations that affect its marketing success.
- To enable business marketers to assess whether their offerings are the promises that they should make, because they relate well to their company's problem-solving and transfer abilities, their operations, resources and technologies and their wider strategy.
- To help business marketers to assess whether their offerings are promises that their company is *able* to implement.

Introduction: Transfer Ability and Implementation

Throughout this book we have emphasized that the essence of business marketing is the development and management of customer relationships. It is within these relationships that customers can find the solutions to their problems. The solution is provided through an offering supplied by the selling company that has a number of elements: product, service, delivery, advice, and costs & price. This offering is based on the company's problem-solving ability and it amounts to a promise by the supplier of what it will provide for the customer as a way of addressing a customer's problem. But, like any promise, the offering has no real value to the customer unless the supplier can fulfil its promise and actually implement it.

It is the supplier's transfer ability that enables it to implement its offering. Hence a supplier's transfer ability is a measure of how well the supplier can actually implement *all* of the elements of its promised offering, so that the customer actually receives the anticipated solution to its problems. Implementation involves questions of time, place, performance, costs & price. The emphasis here is on conformity to the specified product, service, advice and delivery elements of the offering, consistency over time and control of cost. Successful implementation requires investment by the supplier to develop its production and service processes, its information, administrative and logistical systems, its efficiency and its relationships with those other companies that are also involved in its offering.

The supplier's transfer ability is always important for business customers for a number of reasons, as follows:

- It is important because a customer has to integrate the offerings from one supplier with those from others, so consistency of implementation is required.
- It is important because an offering may be supplied over a long period of time, so that development of the supplier's transfer ability is required.
- It is important because customers face complex problems that are not solved immediately upon an offering being delivered.

Hence, implementation does not end when an offering is first delivered. Instead, the supplier's offering is likely to be added to the offerings of other suppliers, integrated into the operations of the customer and changed through the life of the customer's and supplier's relationship with each other.

The implementation of an offering for some customers will be straightforward and will involve few operational problems. For other customers, with high transaction uncertainty, the requirements of performance, cost, consistency, timing or location will be critical and will place great demands on the supplier. It is particularly important for business marketers to understand precisely what their company's transfer abilities are and to contribute to decisions on developing them. This is because suppliers are likely to be an integral part of the operations of their customers for many transactions over a long period. Hence the implementation of the supplier's offering is likely to be critical to the customer's own operations and vital for the development of the relationship between the two.

We start this chapter by examining some of the difficulties that companies face in implementation. We then look at the management of implementation and particularly at the processes that are available for a company in order to implement its offerings and discuss in which situations different processes are appropriate. These choices of processes concern operations for products, services, delivery and cost control, as well as the task of integrating the offering into the customer's operations and thus the relationship. Finally, implementation involves the combined action of the supplier and other companies. Thus we have to examine some of the coordinating efforts required for implementation, both within the selling company and in relation to other companies involved.

Major Implementation Issues for the Business Marketer

It is vital, but increasingly difficult, for the business marketer to actually *do* what she says she will do. These difficulties in fulfilling the promises in an offering occur for a number of reasons:

- Implementation requires an increasingly complex set of resources, technologies and operations. Suppliers are more and more dependent for these on their own suppliers, distributors and development partners, and even their customers.
- A large number of different people and functions inside and outside a supplier are involved in the implementation of an offering. These include buyers, and staff in development, services, sales, operations, logistics and finance.
- Business marketing is not just about making one promise and then fulfilling it. Instead, both the offering and its implementation evolve over time. Many different individuals and functions will be involved in this evolution.

Marketers have to make sure that all those involved in implementation work towards the same aims, but they cannot *control* these other functions. Marketing people are unlikely to understand the technicalities of all of the issues involved or the strategic priorities of their colleagues. Nor can business marketers operate in isolation from these other functions. Their role is to *integrate* the work of these other functions. To do this they must be aware of the pressures under which different functions operate, as well as the specific tasks they each have to carry out. This integrative role is difficult, so that business marketers often say that selling their ideas to their colleagues inside their company is much more difficult then selling offerings to its customers outside! No doubt these colleagues find similar difficulty in communicating their thinking and their problems to marketing! It is also important to add that marketing itself is not a coherent unit. There will be a number of sub-functions within a marketing department, for example, sales, technical service, product management, marketing communication, market research, and after-sales services. Each of these will have their own particular agendas and each will have to become integrated by the marketing manager into the processes of developing and implementing offerings.

Figure 8.1 illustrates some of the links between crucial requirements of the implementation of offerings and the operational abilities in manufacturing and logistics that are needed to assist in this process.

All companies are likely to require considerable investments in the facilities and operations on which their transfer ability is based and which enable it to implement its offerings. These investments take a long time to come to fruition and must be based on a clear understanding of the ways in which customer requirements are evolving. These investments must also be based on an analysis of the company's available product and process technologies, as discussed in Chapter 4, and of its physical resources. It is vital that business marketers understand what is involved in these investments in their own company and in its principal customers and suppliers. These investments effectively determine a company's ability to implement its offerings and strongly affect the design of those offerings. Hence they impact strongly on the company's marketing strategy.

IMPLEMENTATION TASKS	OPERATIONS ABILITIES
High-performance offerings	Product design
Low defect rates	Process technology
Reliable deliveries	Logistics performance
Short delivery lead times	Logistics design
Customized offerings and variety in offering range	Process flexibility and modularized design
Developing new offerings	Innovation processes

Figure 8.1   Implementation of offerings and operations abilities.[1]

It is not enough therefore for business marketers to provide information on current or future customer requirements and leave operations decisions to others. If the wrong operations decisions are taken, they can mean that a company is unable to implement its offerings in the way that its customers require. And if marketing decisions are taken without an appreciation of operational issues, then failures in implementation are likely to occur and operational costs will rise. Operations must also evolve as customer problems change and technology moves on. Business marketers and operations managers must not only be aware of issues in each other's areas, but must be involved in them, and interact about them, on a continuing basis. Key areas for this cooperation include the design of offerings and the planning of capacity, the control of quality and cost and the management of outbound logistics for which transfer ability is crucial. Finally, a company will have to put in place its transfer abilities to implement the offerings on which its network position is based. Underpinning these abilities will be decisions that will include at least the following:

- The amount of capacity required by the organization to achieve volume targets and the need for flexibility to cope with adaptations.
- The range and locations of facilities.
- The technology investment to support process and product developments.
- The nature and structure of its supplier relationships. This is often referred to by operations people as its "extended enterprise".
- Its organizational structure and the activities it performs, to reflect its distinctive technologies, often outsourcing other activities.
- The extent and nature of alliances with competitors.
- Its relationships with distributors and subcontractors.
- The rate of new offering introduction.

[1] Adapted from S Brown (2000) *Manufacturing the Future*, London, Financial Times Books.

• The skills of its personnel to accommodate flexibility of volume, variety and other changes.

A range of operational processes are available to carry out a supplier's implementation efforts. Successful implementation will require the supplier to select processes that are appropriate in relation to the problems of specific customers.

Managing Implementation

The choices of processes through which a supplier's offerings will be implemented are major strategic decisions involving large-scale investment in physical, human and technological resources. Decisions on these resources have to be based on the current *and the anticipated future* requirements of customers. No amount of reactive, tactical measures can hope to compensate for inappropriate investment in processes that cannot adequately implement offerings to match customer requirements. These process decisions require an input from the company's marketers. We will examine these process decisions for the product, service and delivery elements of the supplier's offering. The advice element will be discussed in relation to the service element. The costs & price element is heavily dependent on the process choices for the other elements and will be handled separately in Chapter 9.

Implementation processes for products

We start by examining how implementation activities relate to the product element of an offering. Recent developments in operations such as "mass customization",[2] "lean production"[3] and "agile manufacturing"[4] have revolutionized how products are produced. Each of these innovations is concerned with two critical tasks. The first of these tasks is to optimize a company's operations for maximum efficiency in terms of standardization and economies of scale, while at the same time enabling it to fulfil offerings for diverse and changing customer requirements. The second task is to influence the company's strategic and customer direction to be in line with the company's current and evolving operational capabilities.

The first of these tasks requires a supplier to find an appropriate balance between customization and standardization. It is tempting for the marketing and selling functions of the supplier to respond positively to customer requirements for individualized offerings. But adaptations of this kind are always costly because they constrain the opportunities for economies of scale in the operations of the supplier. And what is lost in terms of efficiency has to be paid for by the customer. Therefore it is not always in the interest of the customer when suppliers agree on requests for individualization.

---

[2] See, for example, BJ Pine (1993) *Mass Customization: The New Frontier in Business Competition*, Boston, Harvard Business School Press.

[3] For example, J Womack, D Jones and D Roos (1990) *The Machine that Changed the World*, New York, Rawson Associates; and SR Lamming (1993) *Beyond Partnerships: Strategies for Innovation and Lean Supply*, London, Prentice-Hall, 1993.

[4] P Kidd (1994) *Agile Manufacturing: Forging New Frontiers*, New York, Addison-Wesley.

Moreover, in many industries the range or variety of offerings has increased enormously, for example for mobile phones, fashion, PCs and others. This increasing variety is problematic for the economies of the manufacturing operations of a company. For example, in the car industry customers are now given the opportunity to design their own cars to some extent. Even if the customers' choices are severely circumscribed, the potential number of variants of components and systems have increased dramatically. In order to handle these operations economically, cars have to be built to order because it would be a financial disaster to produce them speculatively. Building cars to customers' orders at reasonable cost and lead-time requires a modularized approach where pre-manufactured components and systems are assembled in relation to specific customer orders. This is illustrated by Figure 8.2 describing the manufacturing and distribution system of Volvo Cars in Gothenburg.[5]

Volvo Cars supply five different car models on the basis of a common platform. In spite of this joint platform the number of product variants has increased dramatically owing to Volvo's strongly stated policy to offer customers individualized cars. The five models are available in fourteen colours, and a car buyer can choose from nine engine and five transmission alternatives. A buyer can also select between left- and right-hand steering, which altogether adds up to 6,300 variants. Many other options are available, eg twenty-two types of interior trim and nine wheel variants. In the end, Volvo can offer more than one million car variants and therefore tailoring each car in accordance with individual customer demands requires a flexible and well-organized activity structure for manufacturing and distribution.

It is the individual customer order that determines the production sequence at the assembly line. So when a car body is put on the final assembly line, it has been dedicated to a specific car-buyer's order and given a unique identity. All the options chosen by this car-buyer in terms of exterior colour, engine and transmission types, interior trim, etc are linked to this identity. Variant-specific systems modules such as seats, engines etc, must therefore be available at each station on the assembly line when the specific car-body arrives.

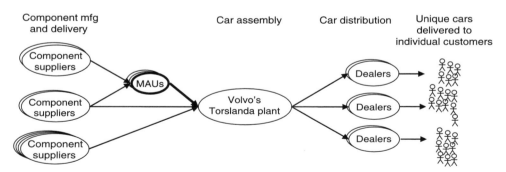

Figure 8.2   Production and distribution at Volvo.

---

[5] This example is from P Fredriksson and L-E Gadde, Flexibility and Rigidity in Customization and Build-to-Order Production, *Industrial Marketing Management*, vol 34, 695–705.

The modules have to be produced in different variants, and so there are more than 3,500 types of seats and more than 10,000 power-pack combinations possible. Most modules are physically large and represent considerable capital investment. The cost of providing buffer stock for all the potential modules would be extremely high in terms of both capital and space. Module suppliers therefore have to deliver just-in-time in pace with the assembly line of Volvo and in the same sequence as car bodies are put on the assembly line. These planning conditions imply that module suppliers have only a few hours available for their operations to assemble modules. These module suppliers have therefore located their module assembly units (MAUs) very close to Volvo's plant. Components and subsystems delivered from their large-scale manufacturing plants are assembled in these MAUs so as to be ready-to-install in cars. Fifteen MAUs supply twenty-six different modules such as seats, cockpits and exhaust systems to Volvo's assembly line.

Through this modularized process approach Volvo Cars is able to supply customers with individualized cars at reasonable cost. The key to these economies are the MAUs that function as buffers between other operations. MAUs decouple the customized operations at the assembly line from upstream operations, where components and subsystems composing the modules are manufactured in large-scale centralized supplier plants. In this way implementation of Volvo's offering in terms of component manufacturing can benefit from economies of scale in spite of the fact that offerings are highly customized.

The Volvo system illustrates one of five potential processes for implementation of the product element of an offering. What is going on in the Volvo factory follows a "line" approach. This process makes it possible to manufacture large volumes of offerings with a similar design at low cost. The line process also allows for some variety as long as it is kept within a predetermined range. This range may be extended considerably by using buffers in the form of modular assembly units as in the Volvo example.

The other four types of processes available have the following characteristics:[6]

- **Project:** This type of process can be used in implementation of highly adapted offerings. It often takes a considerable time and requires dedicated resources for each project. Examples include construction, shipbuilding, large computer installations, etc.
- **Job shop:** This process can also be used for implementation of high variety, low-volume offerings. In this case the company will produce a series of products, each of which is different, but using the same operations, such as in precision engineering or printing, etc.
- **Batch:** This process allows less variety than a job shop and uses one and the same operation until a full batch of products has been produced. Examples include the manufacture of component parts for the auto industry, most clothing, and industrial equipment manufacture.
- **Continuous:** This is an even higher-volume process, with less variety. It is used in the food industry, for chemical applications, steel making and various types of utilities.

[6] For a full discussion of the issues in process choice, see S Brown, K Blackmon, P Cousins and H Maylor (2001) *Operations Management*, Oxford, Butterworth-Heinemann, Chapter 3.

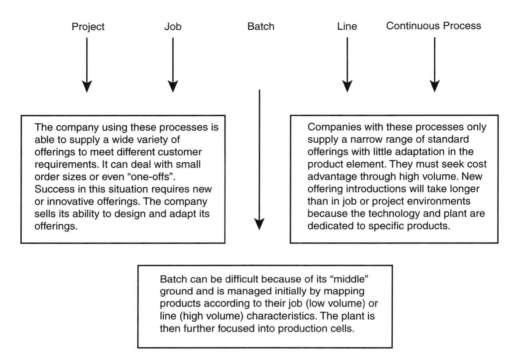

Figure 8.3   The link between process choice and marketing strategy.

Source: Steve Brown et al (2001) *Operations Management,* Oxford, Butterworth-Heinemann.

As indicated in the beginning of this section, the second critical task related to operations is to make sure that the company's strategic and market direction is in line with the company's current and evolving operational capabilities. This means that there is a close link between the process choice and the marketing strategy of the company. The choice of process effectively determines the type of offering that a company can implement and Figure 8.3 is an illustration of this connection. We will come back to the connections between marketing and other company functions at the end of the chapter.

Implementation processes for service

Two of the main characteristics of the purchase and sales processes for services are that consumption and production occur simultaneously and that the participation of the user is crucial for the outcome.[7] Thus interaction between customer and supplier is a critical factor in the implementation of the service element of an offering. When interaction is important people are important, because it is people that interact. Therefore, a useful distinction between the various processes through which the service element of an offering may be implemented can be made on the basis of the amount of personal

[7]For a discussion of this see, for example, J Blythe and A Zimmerman (2005) *Business to Business Marketing Management,* London, Thomson.

contact that is involved. Three types of service operations may then be identified, as follows:

- **High-contact service operations:** These involve the use of large numbers of highly qualified "professional" staff, such as engineering and management consultants, accountants, lawyers, systems analysts. Companies using these operations often produce offerings with little or no physical product element. Others may use them as the first stage of a complex offering involving a large-scale physical product, such as the planning studies for a mass-transit system or a new airport. This kind of service operation is often valuable for customers that have high need uncertainty.
- **Mass-service operations:** These are used by companies that have many customer transactions that require limited interpersonal contact and little customer adaptation. These operations tend to be standardized and individual personnel have little discretion in their interactions with customers in them. Examples include parcels services, airports, catalogue suppliers for maintenance or office items.
- **Service-shop operations:** This type of process falls somewhere in between the two others when it comes to interaction and personal contacts. Service-shop operations may involve high levels of contact and adaptation, but these features have to be balanced by standardization because of the lower volume of customers in comparison with mass-service operations. The discretion allowed between various staff and the customers is also varied. Examples of these types of operations include hotels, rental companies and travel companies.[8]

Marketers must be involved in decisions about the process choices that are made by their company for the service elements of their offerings, in relation to both design and implementation. Marketers are in the best position do this because of their roles as the voice of the customer. Companies that do not pay attention to this might encounter the situation described in Box 8.1.

Box 8.1   Difficulties in Service Implementation

These are the reflections of a managing director of a company that had designed and implemented various types of service offerings.[9]

"When we first introduced services we simply defined them ourselves. We did not ask our customers what their needs were or what kind of service they really wanted. We were convinced that we understood their needs well enough. This led to several service offerings. Unfortunately these were not accepted by the customers. Financially, it was a disaster. After these experiences we really understood the benefit of a more market-oriented service development process. Consequently, we increased the market orientation of our service development process by conducting workshops with lead customers. This helped us to increase our service revenues significantly."

---

[8] Adapted from N Slack, S Chambers and R Johnston (2001) *Operations Management*, 3rd edition, Harlow, Pearson Education.

[9] H Gebauer, E Fleish and T Friedli (2005) Overcoming the Service Paradox in Manufacturing Companies, *European Management Journal*, vol 23, no 1, 14–26.

A number of service management programmes can be applied to handle some of the intrinsic difficulties associated with implementing the service element of the offering. Some of the characteristics of these programmes are outlined below:

- **Service concept development programme:** This involves developing the concepts that guide the investment of resources and the activities that are to make up the service element of an offering. These concepts must be expressed in terms of the customer problems that the supplier is addressing, or "What" the service element will do (its performance specification). It is important to emphasize that the service element does not operate alone, but is combined with other offering elements. So the programme must also be concerned with how service combines with these other elements to produce a coherent offering. For example, a fire insurance company may emphasize the totality of its offering so that it not only covers the costs of damage to equipment, but also provides advice on prevention, fire control and fighting equipment (product), arranges repair and covers for business losses during those repairs (service). This supplier may need to make its offering available to its customers' locations in different countries (delivery) and may also be called on to adapt its offering to the particular requirements of companies in high-risk businesses, such as oil or chemicals.
- **Service-outcome management programme:** This involves developing the supplier's ability to achieve a required specification of service, or "How" it will solve the customer's problem. This specification is often agreed specifically with each customer. For example, the Body Shop has a close relationship with the Lane Group which is responsible for deliveries to the Body Shop's outlets. The relationship provides for 99.7% of deliveries to take place within a two-hour "delivery window". This means that the service outcome is measurable and "tangible". As a result, adherence to standards, which is part of service quality, can be measured against agreed criteria – in the same way that the implementation of a product element can be measured.
- **Customer expectations-management programme:** Customer expectations must be managed so that they relate to the offering that the supplier is able to deliver and to the offering that is justified by the potential of the relationship. Unless this is achieved, there will always be quality problems in the relationships. For example, a delivery company must make it clear that the service levels it is able to provide in most locations will be lower when those deliveries involve the use of ferries or are to remote parts of a country.
- **Internal marketing programme:** The quality of the service element of an offering is heavily dependent on the skills and orientation of those involved in its implementation. This programme aims to educate staff in the supplier's service concept and to train and motivate them to implement it. There is often an important role for marketers in this programme, both in explaining the concepts behind the company's offering and in the education task itself.
- **Physical environment and resources management programme:** The supplier's physical resources, technology, information and computing systems form the technology base for service production and the physical environment for service consumption. It is important that they are not developed solely to some internal criteria of efficiency. Instead, they must be able to support customer interaction and information and facilitate delivery of the service element to the standard required to solve customer problems.

- **Customer interaction management programme:** Of course a supplier cannot "manage" its interaction with customers completely, as any relationship is the outcome of the managerial efforts of both companies. Nevertheless, it is important for a supplier to educate customers on how they can contribute to making service interactions as productive as possible. For example, adjustments in the timing of service interactions can reduce the costs and inconvenience of queues for both customer and supplier.[10]

Many of the issues that we have discussed in these sections about customer contacts and service management programmes are clearly related to "advice" from supplier to customer. We suggested in Chapter 7 that in many cases the border between the service and advice elements is fuzzy. This is again confirmed when we deal with implementation and it emphasizes the importance for the business marketer of fully understanding the characteristics of service interactions with customers.

Finally, we mentioned in Chapter 7 that some firms are actually changing their role from being mainly a manufacturing company providing complementary services to their offerings, to a position as primarily providing a service – that is often accompanied by some product elements in their offerings. A company involved in this transformation will meet several challenges, as indicated by the example in Box 8.2. On the other hand the example also shows how a company by improving its service capabilities in design and implementation may be able to strengthen its position in relation to customers and gain a stronger foothold in their supplier portfolios.

Box 8.2   The Transformation to Becoming a Service Provider

A Managing Director expressed the challenge of becoming a service provider in the following way:

"When we first started to offer complete solutions including products, product-related services and customer support services to the customer, no customer believed that we were able to offer superior services. Most customers still thought of us as product manufacturers that do not offer services. We realized that we had to change our image from selling products to offering superior services. We started to transform our own identity to that of a service provider. After our management and service workers themselves believed that we now provide superior services, we started to promise customers superior service quality. It impacted positively on customer expectations and we built a highly reputable service provider image. Our image of a highly reputable service provider helped us convince more customers to buy complete solutions. They did not just buy more services, they started paying a fixed price covering all services over an agreed period. Furthermore, this helped us increase the average capacity utilization of our service organization."[11]

---

[10] Source: C Groonroos (2000) *Service Management and Marketing: A Customer Relationship Management Approach*, 2nd edition, Chichester, John Wiley & Sons, Ltd.

[11] H Gebauer, E Fleish and T Friedli (2005) Overcoming the Service Paradox in Manufacturing Companies, *European Management Journal*, vol 23, no 1, 14–26.

Implementation processes for delivery

Implementation of the delivery element of an offering is likely to be relatively straight-forward when serving customers that purchase infrequently or are buying offerings that are not critical for their operations. But some customers may require complex and costly delivery arrangements, if these can reduce their overall costs or add to their competitiveness. Customers will also vary in the extent to which they require delivery systems that are customized and thus adapted to their individual requirements. High levels of customization will mean that they are likely to have more interaction and involvement with their supplier. In contrast, other customers may prefer to avoid such involvement in order to be able to easily change between suppliers. They will make use of standardized deliveries that entail lower immediate costs and retain the freedom associated with more arm's-length relationships.

Therefore, when it comes to implementation of the delivery element of the offering it is important to examine the two aspects of:

- Logistics complexity.
- Customer-supplier involvement and adaptation.

Figure 8.4 shows the four types of implementation processes that can be derived from this distinction and are thus available for the supplier's choice. We will discuss the characteristics of these implementation processes and their consequences for the logistics systems of suppliers delivering sheet steel. Cell 1 is where the delivery arrangements are uncomplicated and characterized by low cost and where customers see no benefit in involvement with the supplier for adaptation and advice. Examples would include the purchase of relatively simple offerings, based on commodity products such as standard mild-steel sheets. Customers in this case are more likely to appreciate the benefits of being able to switch suppliers easily. In this case the marketer must ensure that logistics and relationship-management costs are as low as possible through efficient ordering and delivery systems. Large buyers then may be serviced by a steel producer, delivering full truckloads of standardized products, while small

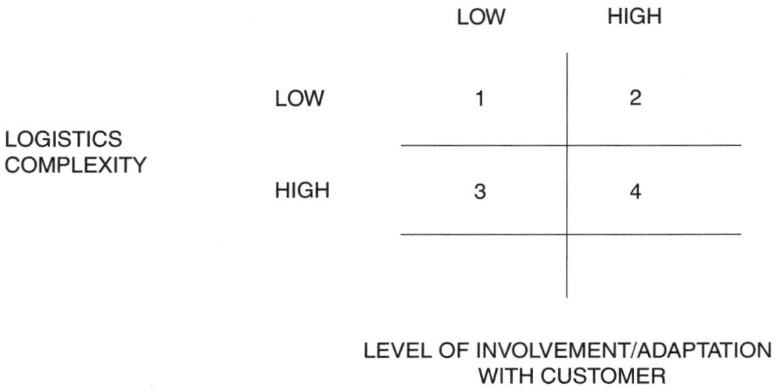

Figure 8.4 Logistics and relationship involvement.

buyers will probably buy from a distributor's warehouse. It is not only "established" companies in the steel business like manufacturers and distributors that can help users to solve their problems by operating in Cell 1. New types of companies have entered the network, such as E-steel Corp and MetalSite Corp in the USA and Steelscreen in Europe. These have relationships with producers of steel and deal with thousands of customers focusing on standardized products for customers whose main concerns are price and reducing the costs of ordering, administering and stocking. For steel producers, these new companies reduce commission costs as well as cost of sales administration. The new suppliers both compete with established suppliers and support them. For example, these new companies can make it possible for a steel producer to focus its own efforts on specialized products and use traders as a cost-efficient operator for more standardized offerings.

Cell 2 also involves customers that prefer less complex or advanced deliveries, but require adaptations to their specific supply problems. This may involve the supplier guaranteeing availability by taking responsibility for the customer's inventories (identified as "vendor-managed inventories") or providing a wider offering or customer-dedicated catalogue, with offerings from other companies, to reduce the customer's supply base. The need for technical advice is limited because of the low complexity of the delivery system. But relationships in this cell can still be important and long-term. This is because without this type of relationship companies would find that the paper-work costs of buying many items were greater than their price. When suppliers choose processes in Cell 2 they must have an ability to work closely with customers and develop and maintain a responsive relationship with them. Companies operating in Cell 2 may be producers, distributors or other firms that specialize in delivery.

Cell 3 involves complex deliveries and therefore expensive logistics systems, which are not adapted to the specific problems of individual customers. Efficient operations are provided by advanced warehousing and transport equipment in this case. For example, a steel supplier may be involved in steel-service operations such as cutting, bending or blasting. Information may be exchanged by complex systems such as EDI (electronic data interchange). In many cases customers are willing to invest and adapt their own systems to fit with the advanced systems of suppliers in this cell. Suppliers taking this route thus generally invest more in developing advanced offerings for delivery than they invest in specific relationships.

Cell 4 involves considerable adaptations made for each customer and complex delivery systems. A typical example of this is the just-in-time deliveries from component and system-suppliers to car manufacturers. In this case a supplier has to implement delivery processes that are considered valuable by the customers in spite of the huge investments they involve. For this type of integration to function well, there must be substantial integration of activities and communication in both companies. The planning and management of this investment lead to a high-involvement relationship including similar adaptations to those in Cell 2 and complex delivery systems as in Cell 3.

The implementation processes in the four cells of the matrix are very different. The variety in terms of complexity and involvement means that both the costs of delivery and the levels of skill and expertise required of the supplier will vary. A supplier trying to reach all the four types of customer problems with one and the same offering is likely to be "stuck in the middle". An "average" delivery agreement will not be able to deal with cost requirements of customers in Cell 1. This average offering will be greater than the problem perceived by the buyers in this cell (as we discussed in Chapter 7) and would therefore not be considered an adequate solution. Nor is it likely that a supplier with "average" delivery arrangements would be able to attract the demanding buyers in Cells 3 and 4. This is because the offering would not live up to the requirements of the buyer in relation to these problems. The conclusion of this analysis is that a supplier's delivery arrangements must be differentiated if they are to be valued by customers as solutions to their problems.[12]

Suppliers that aim to address this diversity of customer problems will either have to develop the resources and skills necessary for each type of delivery implementation process themselves or develop relationships with others that can provide them on their behalf. Some of these partners may contribute with low-cost arrangements, while others may provide more advanced deliveries. A supplier relying on other firms for implementing delivery will have to make sure that these processes function satisfactorily. A supplier may have to support these intermediaries and an example of what this support involves is given in Box 8.3.

Box 8.3   Business Transformation Requires Modification of Implementation Processes

In a couple of years Cisco has transformed its business from selling network-related products (switchers, routers, etc) to selling network-related offerings for leveraging voice, radio and databased applications.[13] Accomplishing this change required re-definition of its own business, as well as the business of its resellers that are important partners in implementation. Resellers had to change their roles to "providers of value-added network-based solutions". In doing so they needed to shift from "a product transaction approach to a strong consultative approach". To be able to provide value to the operations of customers, resellers have to be involved in the implementation of these network assets into the running applications of the customer. This implementation required the active support of Cisco. Cisco assists resellers by providing appropriate training, tools and support. Among other things resellers are given access to the Cisco on-line "Network Designer Product" which can be plugged into a customer information network to identify every device in the network. The Network Designer then applies a predetermined formula to help design the network. The tool produces a drawing, a bill of materials and a price quote and also enables resellers to choose, configure and purchase network products on-line. The actual implementation of this offering is then handled by the user and the reseller together.

---

[12] For a thorough discussion of differentiated delivery arrangements, see D Ford, L-E Gadde, H Håkansson and I Snehota (2003) *Managing Business Relationships*, 2nd edition, Chichester, John Wiley & Sons, Ltd, Chapter 6.

[13] T Mitchell (2001) Cisco Resellers Add Value, *Industrial Marketing Management*, vol 30, 115–118.

Many suppliers are like Cisco and use other firms to implement the delivery element of their offerings. They do so because there are normally a large number of users of their offerings and it would be very resource-demanding to interact with all of them. For example, when it comes to spare parts and MRO-items (used for maintenance, repair and operations) the product range, the number of potential buyers, and the uncertainty and variation in demand, together make supply via intermediaries a more efficient approach.

In other situations distributors or dealers may have developed strong ties to end-users. This would make it difficult and less attractive for a supplier to try to bypass these distributors that already have contact with customers. Rather than confronting the distributors, it may be a better idea to join forces with them. However, joining forces requires that the distributors would also be interested in cooperation and this is not necessarily the case. The only reason for a distributor to seriously consider a new producer relationship would be if the offering from a new source would be of help in building its own offering in relation to its customers. A producer approaching potential distributors thus must develop a "channel offering", which will need to involve the following:

- **Channel core elements:** The basic features that suppliers must contribute, such as adequate financial returns and brand equity.
- **Capability-building programmes:** For example, in terms of training programmes and information systems.
- **Incentive programmes:** To motivate improvements in distributor performance, such as growth rebates and contests for the sales force.[14]

In the same way that relationships with customers are crucial for a supplier's performance, so too can distributor relationships become valuable assets for a supplier. Caterpillar Inc. is a company that is well known for its strong distribution network involving about 200 dealers around the world. The CEO of Caterpillar has stated that "our single greatest advantage over our competition is our system of distribution and product support and the close customer relationships it fosters".[15] Box 8.4 exemplifies some of the benefits of a

---

Box 8.4   Caterpillar and its Dealers

"Local dealers who are long established members of their communities can get closer to customers than a global company can on its own; but to tap the full potential of such dealers, a company must forge extremely close ties with them and integrate them into its critical business systems. When treated in this way, dealers can serve as sources of market information and intelligence, as proxies for customers, as consultants, and as problem solvers. Indeed our dealers play a vital role in almost every aspect of our business, including product design and delivery service and field support and the management of replacement-part inventories. Dealers can be much more than a channel to customers."

---

[14] J Anderson and J Narus (2004) *Business Market Management*, Upper Saddle River, NJ, Prentice Hall, Chapter 7.

[15] D Fites (1996) Making Your Dealers Your Partners, *Harvard Business Review*, March–April, 84–95.

well-developed dealer network as expressed by the Caterpillar CEO. The box also shows the efforts that must be put into maintaining these relationships. The box also highlights the fact that dealers actually can play a role in the whole process of developing and implementing offerings.

Implementation in Relationships

Designing efficient logistics for delivery is important for any supplier in order to be able to implement its offerings. But this is only the first step in the process of implementation *at* the customers. It is vitally important to ensure that an offering becomes integrated into the customer's own operations. Offerings are ways to address problems. But problems are not solved by offerings. The problem can only be solved when the offering is integrated into the customer's operations and hence makes a contribution to the customer's own offerings. Thus, the business marketing task doesn't end with the delivery of service, product or advice. Not until the offering is fully integrated into the customer's operations is its problem solved.

This integration is such a crucial issue for suppliers delivering to an assembly line that the suppliers will often have personnel located at customers' sites to ensure integration of the offering. The benefits involved in that type of implementation are clearly illustrated in a case study of Honeywell Inc.[16] This study showed that more than a hundred supplier representatives operated in Honeywell's plants in different parts of the world. These people are responsible for the daily supply of components to the machines in the factory. Arrangements like this can improve supply conditions. This was dramatically illustrated by one supplier that was made responsible for all deliveries of cable harnesses to one of Honeywell's plants. When this system was introduced the purchasing costs of Honeywell were reduced by 10% the first year. The number of invoices decreased from 2,300 yearly to 24 and this reduced administrative costs substantially. The number of uncompleted deliveries decreased from 60 per month to an average of less than six.

These integration procedures involve customer and supplier in interaction far beyond the supply and receipt of goods. The interactions between Honeywell and these preferred suppliers are examples of the high-involvement relationships we talked about in Chapter 5. Once these relationships develop they will tend to keep customers in the repetitive Buy-cycle 1, because of the investments that have been made in the relationship. These business relationships are likely to be close, complex and long-term. Over time, it becomes difficult to draw a clear line separating the customer from the supplier. Hence, many issues like price determination, production and service development and implementation are often done jointly within the relationship. This close integration means that what is involved between the companies transcends an immediately apparent offering of products, services, advice, delivery and costs & price. Instead, the supplier's offering extends to the long-term integration of operations to make that offering work within the context of the customer.

[16] T Minahan (1996) JIT. How buyers changed it, *Purchasing*, September 5 1996, 37–38.

Integration of the offering in a customer's operations is important because it is necessary for the customer to keep its operations running, sometimes at almost all costs. This is especially the case in process-oriented industries such as chemical plants, offshore operations, telecommunication services etc. In this type of industry, customers are dependent on suppliers to take a role in ensuring continuity of operations. The same issue is also important in other types of relationships such as that between General Motors and Sandvik as illustrated in Box 8.5.

Box 8.5   Interview with Mr Lars Pettersson CEO of Sandvik[17]

Sandvik is a world leading company in "hard materials" exemplified by cemented-carbide and high-speed steel tools for metalworking applications and machinery, equipment, and tools for rock-excavation.

Question: One of your customers describes Sandvik as people in yellow overalls changing edges on the tools in the factory.

Answer: This is exactly what it is about. While we are sitting here talking there are thousands of Sandvik Coromant people that step in to factories in yellow overalls and implement new technology. They do not change edges – customers do that for themselves. But they validate that the productivity of the customer has been improved by 10% and show that to customers. At lunch-time the customer signs a statement saying that "this morning Sandvik has saved this amount for me". Then, for each customer, we can put this together per month per week, and per year. So when I met with the CEO of GM a couple of years ago I could show him exactly how much money Sandvik saved for GM the year before. And also how much we saved in GM's factories in the US, in Germany, in Brazil etc. Moreover, what I showed him was not my perception – but what his production engineers had agreed on and signed. I could also show him proposals for further improvements that GM had chosen not to implement.

This approach by Sandvik illustrates the efforts of a supplier to keep within the frame of what we identified as Buy-cycle 1 in Chapter 6: Managing Relationships with Customers. We explained there that for a number of reasons, a customer would prefer to work in a mode of "business as usual". As long as a supplier is able to show that the relationship is beneficial to it, then the customer is likely to stay with that supplier because a change in relationships would involve the customer in the costs of investments in a new relationship.

So far we have discussed principles and processes in the implementation of a supplier's offerings. These processes are likely to involve many people, both in the supplier and the customer and perhaps also in other companies and organizations. Hence, securing the implementation processes requires coordination between those involved. In the rest of

[17] Affärsvärlden (in Swedish), October 26 2005, 44–49.

this chapter we will discuss two important issues in this coordination: the first of these is coordinating implementation efforts within the supplier, and the second is coordinating implementation efforts with other companies.

Coordinating Implementation in the Supplier

The implementation activities of marketing people in a supplier company affect and are affected by those in other functions of the company, such as those in research and development, operations, finance and purchasing. Successful implementation depends on joint action with these other functions. However, sometimes these inter-functional connections are tense, particularly between marketing and the technical people. For example, marketers sometimes say that the staff in charge of designing and developing the product elements of offerings are mainly concerned with technical features and take little account of the needs of users. On the other hand, technicians often claim that marketing people make promises to customers and either don't understand or even ignore the implications of their promises for manufacturing and product development.

However, inter-functional tensions are not entirely negative and are actually necessary for successful implementation. Marketing people are the customers' representatives in the supplier and it is important that marketing transmits the voice of the customer. This voice needs to be heard when elements of the offering are developed and processes for implementation are decided. This voice is most important when customers need an adapted offering in order to address their specific problems. It is likely that other functions within a supplier will resist adaptations because they are always costly. For manufacturing, adaptations mean modification of production schedules, increased lead-times and losses in economies of scale. For purchasing, adaptations might mean that new suppliers must be introduced involving increased costs for supplier handling and reduced volumes with current suppliers.

Tensions between the different functions in a supplier actually signal that the various functions are taking their responsibilities seriously. Manufacturing, R&D and purchasing have other interests to serve than those prevailing in the marketing department. For these other functions it is important that "technical" operations and the company's suppliers are insulated from too many changes and modifications. Therefore, tensions have to exist, but they need to be handled in ways that make sure that they do not escalate into destructive conflicts which would not be in the interest of the customer.

We should also stress that there is not a unified "marketing voice" in a company. Marketing is a broad function including marketing management, product managers, the after-sales department, salespeople, technical sales, marketing communications, market research etc. These sub-functions are likely to have conflicting interests and the marketing function itself needs to be coordinated.

In Chapter 5 we discussed the "buying centre". This consists of individuals in a customer who perform various roles that affect the customer's purchase behaviour. We showed that those performing each of these roles are likely to have different opinions about what are the critical aspects of a supplier's offering in terms both of its design and implementation.

Therefore each of these people needs different information to be able to assess the features of a particular offering in relation to the problems they perceive. They are also likely to rely on different counterparts in the supplier company. This situation can lead to confusion in the customer if different representatives of the supplier with different opinions and responsibilities interact with different people in the customer. Many suppliers have established "Key-Account Managers" to cope with this "multi-interaction" and to integrate the relationship with the customer. The organizational design and location of key-account management is critical if its integrative efforts are to be successful. Most companies tend to locate key-account management within sales and marketing.[18] Some companies, however, have established key-account management as a separate line organization to avoid the tensions between marketing and other functions that may obstruct integration.

Coordinating with External Partners

A company's problem-solving abilities are based in part on the abilities of its own suppliers. In the same way, its transfer abilities are also based partly on those of others. Often, important aspects of the implementation of a company's offering are carried out by other companies such as subcontractors, transport companies, logistics providers, distributors and systems integrators. This poses particular problems for the business marketer. Not only must she be in touch with the transfer abilities and problems of her own company, but also with those of companies on which she depends. We can examine the involvement of third-parties in various aspects of the implementation of an offering, as follows:

- **Product element:** Subcontractors and suppliers may design and/or fulfil all or part of the product element of a supplier's offering. Outsourcing manufacturing operations to specialized companies and focusing on some "core competence" has been a strategic drive for most companies. For example, in 1995 IBM manufactured 100% of the printed circuit boards they used and 85% of the memory chips. Five years later both these figures were below 10%.[19] The IBM-example is representative of a general development of companies and it means that the implementation of a supplier's product element offering is increasingly dependent on third-parties when it comes to manufacturing operations. An example from another type of business is provided in Box 8.6, illustrating also that implementation of deliveries partly is conducted by other firms.

  The same approach of relying on the resources of other companies is also valid for the development of the product element of offerings. As we discussed in Chapter 4, it has become increasingly difficult for a company to be at the cutting edge of all the technologies that are important to its offerings. By relying on specialized business partners

---

[18] S Wengler, M Ehret and S Saab (2006) Implementation of Key Account Management: Who, why, and how?, *Industrial Marketing Management*, vol 35, 103–112.

[19] J Carbone (1999) Reinventing Purchasing Wins the Medal for Big Blue, *Purchasing*, September 16, 1999, 38–62.

Box 8.6   Implementation Using Other Companies

"Charlie" (name disguised) is an Indian company in the watch business that effectively exploits the technologies of other companies in the network through its position in that network and its skills in managing relationships. Charlie sells thousands of cheap watches under its own brand through hundreds of small outlets and street vendors for very low prices. The watches are assembled for it by a company in Hong Kong which uses a large number of component suppliers in China and combines them with an electronic movement produced by a major Japanese watch company.

Charlie also sources other watches from the same assembler in Hong Kong. These incorporate somewhat different components from suppliers in China, with the same electronic movement from the Japanese watch company. Charlie doesn't sell these watches under its own brand. The watches are made to the designs of a number of major watch companies. Charlie supplies the watches to these companies and they sell them under their own international brands.[20]

---

to carry out development projects for it, a company can gain access to a much wider set of technologies than it could ever develop for itself.

- **Service and advice:** The service and advice elements of a company's offering may be developed and implemented by an external contract-service organization. For example, after-sales service may be contracted-out to local service providers to make sure that service lead-times are acceptable to customers. These service providers may be specialized in different types of technologies, or different types of industries and customers. Moreover, this approach makes it possible for suppliers to overcome cultural differences which have been shown to cause problems in after-sales operations.[21] Other services that are increasingly subject to outsourcing to third-parties are telemarketing, call-centre operations and websites.
- **Delivery:** This is the element of an offering where third-party implementation is most commonly involved and we will devote the rest of this section to this element.

Business marketers commonly face choices about when they should develop and implement the delivery element of their offering themselves and when they should allow others to carry it out, either independently or on a contract basis for them. In some cases a supplier will prefer to be in direct contact with the users of its offerings. But in many cases, a supplier delivers to other companies, which in turn deal with the final user. It is not unusual for two or more intermediaries to be involved in these transfer operations. Marketers face a number of issues involved in these choices:

---

[20] This box was developed from the work of an anonymous postgraduate student.

[21] M van Birgelen, K de Ruyter, A de Jong, M Wetzels (2002) Customer Evaluations of After-Sales Contact Modes: An Empirical Analysis of National Culture's Consequences, *International Journal of Research in Marketing*, vol 19, 43–64.

- **Costs and information exchange:** A typical producer relies on both direct and indirect deliveries. SKF, the world's largest manufacturer of rolling bearings is an illustrative example. Around two-thirds of its turnover is direct sales to industrial users handled by its own sales force and subsidiaries. SKF is in direct contact with customers who buy large volumes of bearings, or where the exchange of technical information (advice) is important. Other customers buy only small volumes of bearings, usually standard types. Cost considerations mean that SKF uses distributors who have a portfolio of offerings from different suppliers to reach these. This makes sales visits and delivery economically feasible because distributors also supply customers with the offerings of other suppliers. Independent distributors account for about one-third of the total sales of SKF and an even greater proportion of its profits.
- **Market complexity:** Very often business is obtained from a large-volume customer, such as a car producer, on the basis of a promise of efficient deliveries for its after-sales customers. Distributors are important in fulfilling these promises, such as in the case of replacement bearings for cars serviced either by many thousands of repair workshops or by do-it-yourself motorists.
- **Globalization and fragmentation:** The ability of a supplier to implement the delivery element of its offering has become increasingly important as companies need to supply customers on a global basis. Moreover, the delivery element of an offering has become more important as business has fragmented with the growth of outsourcing and specialization.
- **Technical development:** This has made possible the establishment of entirely new distribution arrangements. In particular, information technology improvements have contributed to this by reducing lead times and providing increased opportunities for the coordination of material flows. In combination with efficient logistics systems these changes have considerably restructured the implementation processes for the delivery element of an offering.

The main feature of these delivery systems is that to a large extent they build on specialization in various distribution activities and on resource sharing among these specialized companies. For example, "information brokers" and "third-party logistics providers" have been able to improve delivery processes through specialization and reliance on dedicated resources. However, these resources and capabilities need to be integrated to ensure the implementation of the delivery element. Research on innovative distribution set-ups has shown that these arrangements build on networks of related companies and relationships, as illustrated by this quote:

> [Successful companies] view their distribution channels as webs of capabilities embedded in an extended enterprise. They have realized that by sharing their resources and capabilities in novel ways and new situations they can take advantage of profit-making opportunities that they could not exploit on their own.[22]

---

[22] J Narus and J Anderson (1996) Rethinking Distribution: Adaptive Channels, *Harvard Business Review*, July–August, 112–120, quote from p 112.

Thus, it is obvious that implementation efforts require the involvement of companies other than a single supplier, its customer, and the relationship between them.

Implementation in and through Networks

The traditional view of business in the marketing textbooks has been to see it from the perspective of a manufacturer, who designs and produces a product that is then transferred, more or less untouched, through a number of intermediaries to the end-customer. This view of business involves the manufacturer in designing an appropriate distribution channel for its products. However, the perspective of business marketing that we have used in this book widens this focus in three ways:

- We have widened the focus from that of a simple product to that of an offering with a number of elements.
- We have shown that the design of an offering is increasingly carried out in other companies than those that are involved in implementation. Also, the offering that is finally implemented for an end-consumer is the outcome of the efforts of many companies and of interactions between them. So business marketers have to be concerned with both design and implementation in their own company and in others in the network.
- We have transferred the focus from business marketing by a company that could be easily defined as a "manufacturer" to business marketing carried out by a wide range of different types of "suppliers" in the network.

These suppliers will have many widely differing types of offerings. They will vary in their dependence on other companies for the elements of these offerings and may or may not design or implement all of the elements of their offering themselves. Parts of their offering may be created in a number of different companies and merged in others. They may then be inventoried in a separate company and installed by another. Sometimes separate companies are involved in transportation or after-sales service. Very often the companies in the network may be distributors who seek to design the offerings of their suppliers and also influence how those offerings are implemented. For example, they may wish to control the deliveries from their suppliers as well as to their customers. This means that some or all of the elements of a supplier's offering may actually be designed or implemented by either the company itself, or a customer, or a third-party.

The importance of the network means that the business marketer will have to examine the design and implementation of her offering within this wider focus. Marketers cannot restrict their role to finding out what customers want and then communicating these requirements to designers and to operations staff and then assume that an offering will be designed and implementation will take place. Instead, business marketers must work closely with operations to relate customer requirements to the company's technologies and resources and to its existing and emerging operations capabilities.

Marketers also have to accept that the successful development and implementation of their offerings must relate to the current and evolving problem-solving and transfer abilities of many different companies in the network. All of these will have a stake in the fulfilment of the supplier's promise and a view of their respective roles in it.

Relationships and the network in which they embedded are crucial also for the adaptation of offerings. The Swedish steel producer SSAB has modified its strategy from a reliance on standardized steel offerings towards customized offerings based on high-strength steel.[23] However, the first phases in the manufacturing of these steels have to be standardized in order to gain economies of scale in the operations. Adaptations are then required in order to customize these steels to the various user contexts. Buyers use the steels in their own production systems. But changing to this new quality will require that the offering is adapted to fit in with the customer's other production inputs. Implementation in the operations of the potential customers is a considerable task. Firstly, customers have to be convinced of the benefits of this new offering in comparison with what they already use; secondly, integration into the customers' operations requires adaptations of various kinds involving a large number of other companies.

Figure 8.5 describes the various companies and business units involved in the adaptation of the high-strength steel that was to be used by Johnson Controls in the manufacturing

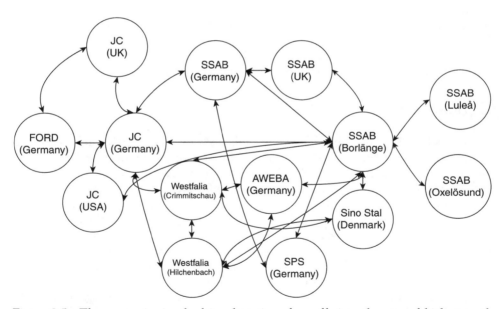

Figure 8.5   The companies involved in adaptation of an offering: the case of high-strength steel.

[23] This example is derived from F Skarp (2006) Adaptation of Products to Customers' Use Contexts, doctoral dissertation, Chalmers University of Technology, Industrial Marketing.

of car seats for Ford of Germany. The German toolmaker Aweba was also involved in the design of the part that was to be manufactured in high-strength steel. The figure shows that not only were Johnson Control's German operations involved in the implementation of the new offering but also their business units in the UK and the USA. In the same way SSAB's sales subsidiaries in Germany and the UK played important roles in the adaptations, as did the production facility in Borlänge and the internal suppliers of raw steel in Luleå and Oxelösund. Westfalia is a subcontractor of Johnson Controls, operating two plants that manufacture the part of the seat where the new steel was applied. To implement the new offering in the production operations of Westfalia, both supplier and user made considerable adaptations. Westfalia needed to make changes in their pressing line and pressing tools, while SSAB modified the features of the product element of its offering by switching from one of its raw steel sources to the other. The successful implementation of the new offering required input from other firms as well. In order to adapt the offering to the user's operations the Danish steel service centre Sino Stal was involved in slitting the steel produced in Sweden before delivery to Westfalia. To avoid some problems in the pressing operations of the user the slitting programme at Sino Stal was modified. Later, some of the slitting operations were moved to SSP Germany in order to better match the user's requirements.

This example shows that adaptations can be crucial for the implementation of an offering. These adaptations can be undertaken unilaterally by the supplier, or by the customer. In many situations it is joint adaptations efforts within the relationship that are the most important. This case also demonstrates that third-parties sometimes are crucial for adapting an offering in a way that ensures successful implementation.

Conclusions

In this book we have described how the boundaries between companies in business networks have become blurred as they jointly develop offerings and merge their technologies, operations and information. We have also shown that companies themselves can no longer be separated into neat categories of manufacturer, wholesaler or retailer so that now we simply see a great diversity of "suppliers". Both this and the previous chapter have shown that it is not just companies that cannot be isolated from each other. The staff in these companies cannot work in isolated functional areas, or "silos", such as marketing, purchasing or production. Instead, all staff have to be aware of how their expertise is integrated into the totality of the company's work and each member of staff has to contribute to decision-making in other areas in addition to their own.

Operations management and the implementation of a company's offerings at customers involve issues that are not normally considered part of the responsibilities of a business marketer. But operations have a number of impacts on business marketers as follows:

- A company's transfer ability is based on its operational capability. The actual implementation of an offering is carried out by staff other than those in marketing. So marketing must understand the operational issues in their companies, the problems that operations staff face and the broader technological and operational strategy within which they are working.

- Marketing must be involved in the inevitable trade-offs and compromises between current customer requirements, the potential of different relationships and the existing and developing capabilities of the supplier.

- Business relationships involve a continuing cycle of offering and implementation and inadequate quality in either of these can ruin relationships. Marketing must be involved in avoiding failures and in building capabilities. It is not enough for them to simply apologize to customers and blame operations when things go wrong!

- A supplier's offering must evolve over time as customers face different problems and as the supplier's own operations evolve. Business marketing must be involved in planning the direction of that evolution and be aware of the constraints and opportunities it represents for the company's offering and its implementation.

- The development of a supplier's operations may lead to cost savings and more effective problem-solving for customers. On the other hand, the design of an offering and the promises that a marketer makes may severely hamper current and future operations. Business marketing is about working with colleagues in all functional areas to bring the company's operational skills to bear to promise a solution to a customer's problem and to fulfil that promise. This cannot be achieved if marketers are figuratively and literally outside the company and its operations.

Further Reading

C Abecassis-Moedas (2006) Integrating Design and Retail in the Clothing Value Chain, *International Journal of Operations and Production Management*, vol 26, no 4, 412–428.

U Alvarado and H Kotzab (2001) Supply Chain Management. The Integration of Logistics in Marketing, *Industrial Marketing Management*, vol 30, 183–198.

RB Chase and DA Garvin (1989) The Service Factory, *Harvard Business Review*, July–August, 61–69.

L-E Gadde (2004) Activity Coordination and Resource Combining in Distribution Networks, *Journal of Marketing Management*, vol 20, 157–184.

S Garcia-Dastugue and D Lambert (2003) Internet-enabled Coordination in the Supply Chain, *Industrial Marketing Management*, vol 32, 251–263.

YP Gupta, SC Lonial and WG Mangold (1991) An Examination of the Relationship between Manufacturing Strategy and Marketing Operations, *International Journal of Operations and Production Management*, vol 11, no 10, 33–44.

A Gustafsson and M Johnson (2003) *Competing in a Service Economy*, San Francisco, Jossey-Bass.

TJ Hill (2000) *Manufacturing Strategy: Text and Cases*, Burr Ridge, IL, Irwin/McGraw-Hill.

R Schmenner and M Tatikonda (2005) Manufacturing Process Flexibility Revisited, *International Journal of Operations and Production Management*, vol 25, no 12, 1183–1199.

T Skjoett-Larsen (2000) Third Party Logistics – from an Inter-organizational Point of View, *International Journal of Physical Distribution and Logistics Management*, vol 30, no 2, 112–127.

Assignment for Chapter 8

Implementation at Airslash

In previous assignments as Group Marketing Director for Airslash, you developed some ideas on the problems that might be addressed by Airslash in a number of actual or potential customers and the type of relationship that would be needed to address these problems.

You have also examined and described the offerings that you would propose for each customer.

It is now time to take the exercise a stage further. Prepare a briefing document for a discussion with the operations department on what you see as operational requirements in order to implement these offerings in each case. You should bear in mind that you will have to talk to managers at different levels from the Chief Operating Officer downwards and that these managers will face different issues. You are conscious that unless the cooperation of operations can be achieved and unless operational arrangements can be put in place then no marketing development can take place. You may use any assumptions necessary to complete your analysis, provided that you make those assumptions explicit.

COSTS, PRICE AND VALUE 9

Aims of this Chapter

- To explain the different elements of cost for both customer and supplier and to show how these affect the development of customer relationships.
- To provide a structure for the business marketer to develop an approach to pricing based on the analysis of business relationships and on the costs of customer and supplier.
- To explain the concept of value for the business marketer.

Introduction

Costs, price and value are important but complex issues for the business marketer. If the business marketer doesn't understand the costs for the customer of developing, receiving and using an offering over time then his relationship with that customer is unlikely to develop. If the business marketer does not fully understand his own costs of developing and implementing offerings within relationships then he is unlikely to achieve profit. If all other aspects of marketing strategy and implementation are sound, but pricing policy is flawed, then the marketer's company may fail. Many pricing decisions are made without thinking through all the issues involved, or they are based on a hunch, an estimate of costs, a target profit or the price of a competitor or on whatever emerges from a bargaining session with a customer. Many pricing decisions are based on an inadequate understanding of both supplier's costs and customers' costs. There have been many attempts to provide guidance on pricing for the business marketer but marketers find that many of these guides are of little help because conditions seem to vary so widely.

Because of the complexity of the pricing task and the importance of relating closely to particular conditions, this chapter does not attempt to provide a procedure or a set of steps that will lead to the "best price". Instead the chapter aims to highlight some of the important issues and considerations that the marketer must bear in mind when taking pricing decisions. The chapter starts by analysing the costs of customer and supplier and how these costs underpin the marketer's pricing decisions. Following this, the chapter explains the relations between price and customer problems and uncertainties. We then examine issues related to the value of offerings and of relationships and how questions of relationships and network position affect pricing. Finally, the main part of the chapter is devoted to the pricing of an offering. Here we show that the price that a customer is prepared to pay may involve tradeoffs between different elements of the offering. We also raise issues about the control of price and pricing of new and established offerings.

Business pricing must be firmly based on the costs of the customer and the supplier. But price and costs are also part of the marketer's offering. Therefore, business pricing is a *creative* task for the marketer and the price of his offering has to be "bought" by the customer in exactly the same way as the other elements of the offering.

Pricing Issues for the Business Marketer

Pricing decisions are difficult enough in consumer markets, but the business marketer also faces a number of extra issues that further complicate the matter. For example:

- Some business marketers charge the same price to all of their customers, while others negotiate individually with each one. These individual prices arise because the marketer supplies a different or an adapted offering to each customer or has to negotiate with each one separately. These different prices multiply the number of pricing decisions that the marketer has to take, the number of cost and profit analyses that he has to make and his problems of price control. The extent of price negotiations means that business price decisions are rarely taken unilaterally by the supplier and are often an important element of the interaction between customer and supplier. Business marketers must have full information on their costs and the value to them of business with each customer to form the basis of those negotiations.
- Some business marketers have to work to a fixed specification of requirements from a customer that includes what the price must be. This is often referred to as target pricing or costing. These marketers must then manage their costs within this limit. Other business marketers have to evaluate the cost and benefits of variations within the different elements of their offering in order to be able to provide a choice of offering and price for their customers.
- Some business marketers have to operate under long-term contracts with particular customers that specify that the price paid will reduce each year of the contract. In this situation the business marketer has to work with colleagues in other functional areas to develop offerings and reduce their costs within the company to meet these requirements.
- Some business marketers have to work with inadequate information on the costs that their company will actually incur when it supplies an offering. This is either because the information is not available in their company, or because a new offering must be developed and it is difficult to forecast what this will cost.

- Business marketers have to calculate their own costs of supplying an offering. They also have to work out the full costs that the customer will have to incur in addition to the price it pays, to gain the benefits of the supplier's offering.
- Business sales and purchases take place within a relationship. The business marketer must also evaluate the costs for himself and for the customer of maintaining or developing that relationship. He must be able to relate these costs to the value of the relationship to his own company and to the customer and relate this to the price that he charges.

Costs

The costs of the business marketer's own company and of his customer underlie all of these pricing problems and any approach to business pricing must be based on a full understanding of these cost issues. The costs of a customer or a supplier do not end with the delivery of an offering. Both customer and supplier are also likely to incur further costs in integrating the offering into the customer's operations. Full revenue for the supplier from the offering may only occur after this integration has been achieved. Revenue for the customer from the use of the offering may also occur long after delivery. Other deliveries, further development, costs and revenue for customer and supplier may continue for many years. There will also be secondary effects from the offering on the costs and revenues of the customer's own customers, and on the suppliers of both companies.

We have noted earlier in this book that it is often difficult to separate the activities of customer and supplier in the process of developing an offering. This difficulty of separation also carries over to the costs of a customer and supplier that are associated with an offering or a relationship. These costs will always show up in the accounts of one or other of the companies, but not necessarily the one in which they were incurred!

The challenge for the business marketer is to incorporate his costs and those of his customer in his pricing in each of their transactions and throughout the two companies' relationship. Some aspects of costs can be easily quantified. Others will depend on the marketer's judgement and his ideas for the future development of a relationship.

The marketer needs to examine his own company's costs and also consider how the customer is likely to evaluate its own costs. The customer is also likely to make an evaluation of the supplier's costs and of how these relate to its offerings, its prices and to its other customers. Business marketers are often involved in helping customers to make a more realistic assessment of their costs and customers are also likely to attempt to do this for the supplier!

For the customer, the most easily recognizable cost is the price it pays to the supplier. For the supplier, the most obvious costs are the direct costs of implementing an offering: the costs of labour, materials, advice, adaptation and delivery. However, both a supplier and a customer are also likely to incur additional costs, as follows.

Indirect costs

Business marketers incur two types of indirect costs that must be paid for through the prices of its offerings irrespective of the volume of business. The first type of indirect costs is represented by the general overhead costs of running the entire business. These are incurred almost irrespective of the overall *level* of business. These include the rental of its premises, the maintenance of its operations and its accounting and general management costs. Also included in these indirect costs are the costs of operating the marketing function and the costs of developing the company's technologies, offerings and operations. The second type of indirect costs are those that are specific to a particular relationship and these are of two kinds:

- **The initial costs of a relationship:** These are incurred before any transactions have taken place. They include the costs for both companies of finding out about each other and communicating, influencing and negotiating about the offering and its suitability for the customer's problem. These initial costs may also include the costs of developing a new offering or of adapting an existing offering or operations. Some companies, such as those supplying the aerospace industry, often have to develop a completely new offering, based on existing or new technologies, for each new aircraft, before they can expect any orders. Often the supplier has to bear the risks of these developments and it will only be able to recover them if the customer is able to sell its aircraft.

    These initial costs are investments by the companies based on their assessment of the initial potential of a relationship.

- **Recurrent costs:** These costs are incurred regularly throughout a relationship. For example, both companies incur the costs of developing and managing their relationship with each other; the supplier and the customer both may have to continuously develop or adapt the offering; the customer and supplier may also incur costs of changing their operations to accommodate the offering; the supplier may also have the costs of providing maintenance and service to ensure that the offering continues to address the customer's problem.

    These costs are investments in the continuing potential of the relationships. Without them, transactions may not continue.

The customer and supplier will have other relationships, other offerings and other problems. Devoting resources and attention to this offering and this relationship may mean that they have to give up some of the benefits, with their associated costs from these others.

Recovering costs in relationships

Some companies have large general overheads, such as the costs of operating a major factory. Professional services companies, such as accountants, lawyers or consultants, often have the high-fixed costs of employing large numbers of expensive personnel. These costs can only be reduced through expensive redundancy schemes. These indirect costs must be recovered by all the company's relationships as a whole.

Other companies have relatively low general overheads and most of their indirect costs are specific to each single relationship. This situation is common in many service-dominated businesses, such as advertising. Many advertising agencies often employ account management and creative staff to work solely on one of their major accounts. If an account is lost, then the staff involved will have to leave the agency. Similarly, major retail chains often have a continuing relationship with a particular firm of architects. These architects are also likely to invest in staff members solely for this relationship.

If a supplier does not recover all its indirect costs, at least in the long term, then the company's survival is at risk. On the other hand, if too much of the company's general indirect costs are allocated to particular relationships or transactions, then this can lead to over-recovery of the company's indirect costs and unrealistic price quotations and a failure to get business. Companies must also be flexible. For example, if a company has high indirect costs either for the company as a whole or for each relationship, then it is important to cover these when pricing individual transactions. However, once these indirect costs have been recovered, the supplier can then consider further business, or build new relationships with prices based only on the direct costs of each one. On the other hand, marketers must keep in mind the costs of their investment in a relationship. They cannot make an investment and then supply offerings at prices that do not reflect costs on the basis of some vague promise of future revenue. All relationship investments and individual transactions must take place on the basis of full cost analysis and must relate to the strategy for that relationship and the potential of that relationship for future revenue, profit or any other benefit.[1]

Direct costs

Direct costs are the actual costs of implementing the offering in *a particular transaction*. They include the costs of labour and materials in implementing the product and service elements, in providing any advice and in delivering the offering. It is normally important for a supplier to cover these direct costs. This is particularly so when the company has relatively low indirect costs, both general and relationship-specific, but high direct costs. For example, many construction companies have very few permanent staff or amounts of equipment. They also work on large projects for customers that buy new offices or plants very infrequently and so there is no continuing relationship with them. These contractors have high direct costs which include paying for their subcontractors and renting equipment for each project they undertake.

Assessing costs

In all cases it is important that the marketer has good information on his overall cost structure and the specific costs of each relationship and transaction. Marketers also need to be able to allocate direct and indirect costs to each of their offerings, relationships and the transactions within them. However, many companies do not know the real costs of each of their transactions or relationships. Many accounts departments provide cost and revenue information about *products* and *operating units* and not about the other elements supplied to a customer or the adaptations or investments made in particular relationships.

---

[1] This is often referred to as the "myth of the follow-on order", in which a customer asks for a special deal on a small order on the basis that a big one is to follow. He repeats this a few times and then the big order does come, but for a competitor, leaving the first supplier to count his losses!

So-called Customer Relationship Management (CRM) software may well provide good information on the price that has been achieved from each customer and on some or all of the direct costs of a relationship, but it is unlikely to provide the necessary data on the important indirect costs of the company's investment in each of its relationships. Thus many companies continue to sell to some customers at prices that do not reflect either their real direct or indirect costs or the potential of a relationship. On the other hand, suppliers can sometimes incur the costs of development in one relationship and then use this development in others, without further investment. The marketer must consider this when thinking about price for the new relationship. For example, the marketer may decide to charge the new customer a lower price, based only on the direct costs of an initial transaction, as a way of building the new relationship, or charge a higher price to take short-term advantage of the situation. In some cases a supplier will be prepared to make at least some transactions even below their direct cost, if these losses can be outweighed by the potential value to the supplier of a continuing or developing relationship.

We have already noted that the costs of customers and suppliers do not end with the delivery of an offering. Some of these additional costs are easy to observe and frequently measured. Others are much more difficult to determine and are often ignored. Figure 9.1 shows an analysis of a customer's costs of buying from three different suppliers. All three suppliers had to be assessed by the customer before they received their first orders. But the customer was also involved in the costs of revising its specification for purchases from Supplier A. The customer incurred the same costs for inspection of the incoming offerings from each

	Supplier		
Cost of defect prevention $'s	*A*	*B*	*C*
Qualifying visits	250	250	250
Laboratory tests	200	200	200
Specification revision	300	–	–
Cost of defect detection			
Incoming inspection	600	600	600
Processing inspection reports	1,200	1,200	1,200
Cost of defect correction			
Manufacturing losses	1,590	150	200
Handling and packing rejects	1,500	280	600
Cost of complaints and lost sales	13,200	–	2,043
Total	18,840	2,680	5,093
Total value of purchases	63,820	67,947	84,896
Ratio of additional costs (%)	29.5	3.9	5.9

Figure 9.1 **Comparison of a customer's costs of buying from three suppliers.**

Source: David Ford (1985) *The Handbook of Purchasing Management*, Aldershot, Gower.

supplier. But again, the customer incurred significantly more costs in buying from Supplier A for manufacturing losses and for returning faulty deliveries to the supplier. Finally and most importantly, the customer incurred major costs in the cost of complaints and lost sales incorporating Supplier A's offering. These additional costs amounted to nearly 30% of the total value of purchases from Supplier A. The figure shows how differences in quality of implementing their offering dramatically affect the relative competitiveness of the three companies. The figure emphasizes how important it is for marketers to understand customers' full costs when comparing themselves with competitors and when considering their prices. The figure also shows how important it is for the business marketer to be involved in the implementation of their company's offering, as we discussed in Chapter 8.

Price and Customer Problems

Now that we have examined some of the complexities of cost for suppliers and customers we can turn to the question of price determination for the business marketer. As in all other aspects of business marketing, our starting point should be the problems of the business customer.

Business marketing is about making a profit by providing a solution for a customer to one or more of its problems at a price that exceeds the supplier's costs. However, the problems that customers face vary enormously and this variation will affect the price that can be charged by a supplier. This variation in problems means that there is no price that is right for a particular offering under all circumstances. Nor is there a single objective value for any offering.

We can outline some of the ways that customer problems influence suppliers' prices, as follows:

- It may be very important for some customers to solve a particular problem. So the value of a solution to them will be high and they will be prepared to pay a much higher price than other customers for whom the problem is less important. For example, keeping a factory clean is much more important for a customer in the food industry than it is for one in engineering.
- Some problems are intrinsically more difficult for both customer and supplier to solve than are others and their costs of providing a suitable offering or obtaining a solution may vary accordingly. But customers may not understand either the difficulty of the problem, or the supplier's costs. Hence they may be unwilling to pay a price that reflects those costs. Also, minor changes in a supplier's offering to meet a customer's particular requirements may have a dramatic effect on that supplier's costs.
- The difficulty of solving a customer's problem will vary depending on the experience, skills and resources of that customer. The supplier's costs will vary depending on the capabilities of the customer, but it may be hard for the business marketer to explain this to a customer or to pass on any increased costs to that customer.
- Some customers may have relationships with many suppliers, each of which offers a suitable solution for a particular problem. These customers may value some of these

relationships differently from others and this will affect the price that they are prepared to pay to them. Other customers find that when a particular problem arises, they do not have a relationship with a suitable supplier.

- Customers often do not know how effective a particular offering will be in addressing a problem, or which offering is the best of a number of alternatives. Hence they sometimes find it hard to decide how much they should be prepared to pay for each of the offerings.
- Customers are often quite clear about some of the problems they face and about what would be the best solution for them. In this situation, customers are likely to be very concerned to obtain the best deal for a particular offering and to pay the lowest possible price.

Box 9.1   The Price that a Customer is Prepared to Pay for a Supplier's Offering will Depend on:

- The importance of its problem to the customer.
- The uncertainties that the customer faces in addressing this problem: the extent to which the customer believes that a particular offering provides the best solution to its problem and the extent to which it believes that offering can be implemented by the supplier.
- The value to the customer of its relationship with the supplier as a source of future solutions.
- The number and characteristics of alternative suppliers and offerings that are available to the customer.
- The total costs that the customer must incur in order to obtain the solution – as well as the price, these costs may also include:
  —the costs of adapting its own operations to accommodate the offering;
  —the costs that will be incurred in using the offering throughout its life;
  —the effects of buying an offering from one supplier on the customer's relationships with its other suppliers.

Price and Customer Uncertainties

A customer's uncertainties when seeking to address its problems will also affect its attitude to price. We will now examine the effects of different uncertainties in turn, as follows.

Transaction uncertainty

A customer may have *transaction uncertainty* for a wide range of problems, both simple and complex. For example, a customer may require the delivery of packages to a range of addresses by a certain time, or of sheet steel to a certain specification. The customer may have relationships with a number of suppliers, each with a suitable offering, so the customer has no *market uncertainty*. In these cases the customer's transaction uncertainty requires a supplier whose *transfer abilities* enable it to provide a standard offering quickly, cheaply, reliably and with no additional costs. If a supplier accepts this situation, then success for that supplier will depend on achieving lower costs than its competitors in both the development and implementation of its offering. If the supplier takes this low-cost/low-price approach then it will probably mean that neither the supplier nor the customer will invest significantly in their relationship and it will remain one of *low-involvement*.

But a supplier may not accept this situation and may choose not to compete by supplying a simple offering at low price. The supplier may realize that in many cases the total cost for the customer of making a purchase is often far greater than the price of what is bought. For example, many companies acknowledge that the average administrative costs of placing and receiving an order can exceed $100. Hence, in this situation the supplier could apply its *problem-solving abilities* to diagnose that the customer's *real* problem is not about the price or "quality" of each item required. Instead, its problem is one of how to choose, order and receive a range of reliable individual offerings with minimum trouble, evaluation, time, disruption or managerial involvement. To address this redefined problem, the supplier could offer a credit card service for the customer to issue to each of its staff involved in buying. This would simplify and reduce the costs of placing and paying for orders. Alternatively, a supplier could offer a wide range of product and service items from a single catalogue, pre-approved by the customer, thus reducing the customer's costs of searching and ordering. This is often done for so-called MRO (maintenance, repair and operating) items.

But of course, transaction uncertainty for a customer isn't just limited to questions of price and delivery for simple offerings and problems. In some cases, a customer may have transaction uncertainty because of its concern about the complex *implementation* of an offering and its long-term financial consequences. The supplier's transfer ability is also crucial in these situations. For example, a newspaper publisher or a producer of fresh flowers is likely to be very concerned with a carrier's reliability of delivery of their offerings against schedule. A solution to this problem may involve the supplier and/or the customer investing heavily in equipment and operations in a high-involvement relationship with considerable impact on cost and price.[2]

Need and market uncertainty

Sometimes it is difficult for a customer to make sense of a complex problem or identify the right type of solution to address that problem. In other words, the customer has *need uncertainty*. Sometimes the customer faces a wide choice of potential offerings or a situation where the technologies involved are changing rapidly. In other words, the customer has *market uncertainty*.

In both of these situations it may be difficult for a potential supplier to quickly assess the customer's requirements or to immediately provide a suitable offering or guarantee

---

[2] We have discussed these "relationship-specific investments" in terms of "actor bonds", "resource ties" and "activity links". See Chapter 2.

efficient implementation of the offering. Some potential solutions may also require both the customer and supplier to make adaptations in their operations or in their offerings. Both customer and potential supplier may also find it difficult to identify the costs of solving the problem or to assess a price in advance.

A solution for a customer with need and/or market uncertainty is only likely to be obtained within a developed or a *high-involvement* relationship between customer and supplier.[3] If there is no relationship, then the supplier will have to develop one if it is to solve the customer's problem. The supplier will need to include the costs of building this relationship and of the adaptations it has made in its pricing calculations. The supplier will also have to evaluate the risks involved in making substantial initial investments against the likely future revenue after the initial problem-solving.

If there is already an established relationship, then the supplier must audit that relationship to assess its potential and determine whether it wants to solve the problem for the customer: Does it want the work? Factors affecting this decision for the supplier are likely to include:

- The costs and problems of developing and fulfilling an offering to solve the problem and the likely revenue from doing so.
- The financial effects of solving the problem on this and on the supplier's other relationships (see below).
- The economic consequences on the relationship of not agreeing to solve it, or of trying and failing to solve it. The customer may view the relationship as an important way of solving difficult problems. If the supplier declines to do this, then it will affect the customer's perceptions of the value of the relationship.

When a customer has need and/or market uncertainty, it is a supplier's *problem-solving ability* that is likely to be critical to correctly identify the appropriate solution for a customer's problem and to develop an offering that will meet its requirements. The value of this ability to the customer should be reflected in the supplier's price to that customer. The supplier may also assess that when a customer has high need or market uncertainty, it will often accept inadequacies in the supplier's transfer ability and hence in the actual implementation of its offering. For example, a large retailer may have a complex problem in using data on its customers' purchase habits. The retailer may accept some hassles over delays in delivery of the necessary software or minor glitches in its operation, as long as the software has the ability to ultimately solve its problem at reasonable cost.

Hence, it is important for the business marketer, when considering price, to identify the real problems and uncertainties of each customer. This is instead of simply working on the basis of either the customer's initial view of what it wants, its immediately apparent competitors or even its current offerings. Customers pay a price because of the value to them of their relationship with a supplier and the value to them of the solution to their problem that they receive, not because of any intrinsic value of the offering or its cost to the supplier.

---

[3] We discussed the issues of high- and low-involvement relationships, and when a customer may choose each type, in Chapter 5.

High- and low-involvement relationships and pricing

The difference between high- and low-involvement relationships, or between complex and simple-problem solving has important strategic implications for the business marketer. If the supplier (or customer) chooses those low-involvement relationships based on only limited problem-solving, then the supplier will require a tightly controlled cost structure and operations and its pricing will have to reflect this. If the supplier (or customer) chooses to develop a high-involvement relationship based on its ability to solve complex problems, whether based on its problem-solving or its transfer abilities, then the supplier and probably also the customer will have to make long-term investments in its technologies, its operations and in each relationship. The costs of these investments will have to be reflected in the supplier's pricing policy. These costs will also restrict the supplier's relationship portfolio to those customers that are prepared to pay for these expensively acquired skills.

A customer faced with a complex problem is likely to look to existing relationships first because of its previous experience of problem-solving and the investment that it has made in the relationship. We referred to this situation in Chapter 5 as Buy-cycle 1. Also that supplier is likely to command a higher price than a new supplier, even though some of the costs of its investment have already been recovered. This is unless the customer insists on taking into account that this investment has been previously made and recouped!

Box 9.2 Examples of Pricing for Customers' Problems[4]

One large distributor of many small, low-value products knows that its customers have problems when they urgently need items to cope with breakdowns or for new developments and they are unable to stock all of these parts. It solves the customers' problems by providing speedy, reliable deliveries of guaranteed products either by courier, from trade counters, or by next-day surface mail or, in an emergency, by helicopter. Customers are prepared to pay a price for these problems to be solved which is much more than the "normal" price for each item from conventional distributors. Hence this supplier is able to have a pricing policy expressed (internally!) as "Never knowingly oversold"!

The Canadian aerospace company, Bombardier, discovered that many small companies might benefit from private business travel, but could not afford to buy an aircraft at current prices. It launched a fractional-ownership programme with American Airlines. This allows companies to buy as little as one-eighth of an aircraft, thus dramatically lowering the price of entry into business-jet aviation. The offering also gives security and convenience by providing pilots trained by American Airlines and planes that are maintained by the original maker. Over 75% of the customers for this offering have never owned a business jet before.

---

[4] *Source*: The Growth Philosophy of Bombardier, *The McKinsey Quarterly*, 1997, no 2, 4–29.

Price and Value

A customer pays a price to receive value and it can receive value in two ways:

- **The value of the offering:** This is a measure of the extent to which the offering solves a problem for the customer. This value depends on the quality of both the offering itself and of its implementation, as we discussed in Chapters 7 and 8. The value of an offering also depends on how important the problem is for the customer to solve. The marketer must make a careful assessment of this value. Sometimes the value can be calculated in monetary terms: for example, a customer may currently do all its own testing of the instruments that it uses in its production but it may consider buying a testing service from an outside supplier. A potential supplier will need to estimate the current costs to the customer of employing staff to do the work for itself and also its costs of replacing any outdated equipment to continue to do so. The supplier should also try to assess the current costs to the customer of any disruption in its current operations and complaints from its own customers that these may lead to. The supplier can then compare these costs with its own costs of providing the service. The price that it then decides on must be low enough to give a significant saving to the customer, when compared to current costs, but be above the supplier's costs. The actual level within this range will depend on the importance to the supplier of the order and the potential value of its relationship with this customer.
- **The value of the relationship:** A relationship itself has value for a customer in two ways. Firstly, the relationship will have a *current* value. This is because the customer and supplier will have learned about each other's operations and so the interactions between them will be more predictable and reassuring. The adaptations that have occurred to suit each other's operations mean that the supplier's current offering may be enhanced or be more efficiently implemented. Secondly, the relationship will have a *potential* value. This is because the learning and adaptation in a relationship may provide the potential for new solutions to evolve to address future problems.

A relationship also has present and future value for the supplier. These values need to be assessed by the marketer through a relationship audit and communicated to the customer. If the marketer does not consider relationship value when setting prices, then he may set a price that is too high and harm the relationship. If this happens, he will lose the benefits of previous investments in the relationship and fail to gain the advantages of future benefits.

Sources of relationship value

There are three aspects of a relationship that provide value for both customer and supplier, as follows:

- **Activity links:** These coordinate the activities of the two companies, such as in the case of a just-in-time production system.
- **Resource ties:** These adapt the resources of each company to the requirements of both of them. For example, both companies might provide a joint development team to work on a new security system for remote sites.

- **Actor bonds:** These provide the basis of the social exchange between individuals for mutual learning and joint problem-solving.

Together, these three aspects of a relationship can provide value to customer and supplier in a number of ways, including the following:

- A relationship can lower operational costs because the supplier and/or customer have modified their offering so that it "fits" more easily with that of the counterpart.
- A relationship can reduce development expenses for both companies based on information from each of them about their capabilities or the use of the offering.
- A relationship can improve material flow for both companies brought about by reduced inventories due to changes in delivery frequency and lot sizes.
- A relationship can lead to quicker and cheaper problem-solving through familiarity with each other's ways of working and through trust in each other.
- A relationship can reduce administration costs through more integrated information systems and because of experience of each other's ways of working.
- Both customer and supplier in a relationship may be able to apply what they have learned in any one relationship to their other relationships.
- The companies may be able to gain access to other parts of a network through their relationship with particular customers and suppliers.

Each of these ways of reducing costs and increasing value requires investment that must be recovered by one or both of the companies through the prices they charge. The supplier must assess the value of these investments to the customer and hence to itself as a source of future profit. The price the supplier charges must then relate to its current direct and indirect costs, the wider costs that the customer incurs and the future value of the relationship to the customer and to the supplier as well as to the current value of the offering to the customer.

Price and Relationships

We have seen above that many of the pricing issues facing the business marketer centre on his relationships as both a vehicle in which to provide value to customers and as a value themselves. A relationship may involve a supplier in addressing many different problems for the customer. This multiple problem-solving causes two pricing problems for the marketer. Firstly, it is often difficult for the marketer to separate out the different problems that are being solved in a relationship and the value to the customer of each single offering or solution. Secondly, because there may be many episodes in a relationship it is difficult for the marketer to record or to control what is being done for the customer and the costs, revenue, profit, prices and value that are involved. Therefore it is helpful to separate the issues of pricing for individual transactions from those of pricing for a relationship, as follows.

Pricing for transactions

The marketer has to fix the price charged for each transaction within each of his relationships. But in many cases it will not be practicable to review price on every occasion. In this case the marketer will have to develop a list price for all customers or negotiate a standard price for each unit of the offering as a whole that is delivered, or for each element individually. For example, some companies will provide a certain number of days of advice after a sale and then charge separately for each one after this. But this approach may not be flexible enough to cope with individual requirements or to face local competition. So the marketer may have to provide flexibility, either by giving discounts for volume or prompt payment or by allowing salespeople to have some discretion over the price to be charged. These methods can easily get out of hand and the marketer must then face the issue of how to control the price that is actually achieved in individual transactions, as opposed to the notional or list price. We will turn to this issue of price control shortly.

Pricing in a relationship

Pricing for the business marketer is not simply about making a profit on each transaction with its customers. Because the marketing company's relationships with its customers are its prime assets, the pricing task is to maximize the rate of return on each relationship over its life. This is often referred to as the "lifetime value" of the customer. Marketers invest in their relationships and their transactions are the way in which they generate a return on those investments. However, in seeking a return on their investment it is equally important that they do not jeopardize the long-term value of the relationship to themselves and to the customer.

Like any investment in tangible assets there will be a pay-back period in which to recoup a relationship investment. This is illustrated in Figure 9.2. In the early days of a relationship the supplier is likely to incur considerable costs in building the relationship. Some of these costs will be the indirect costs of operating its sales-force, or of marketing

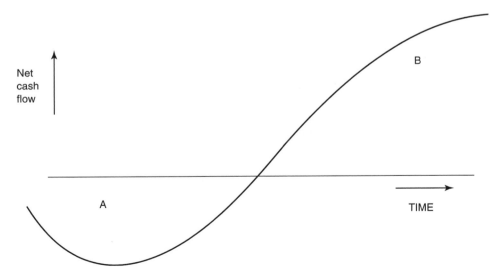

Figure 9.2 Cash flow through the life of a relationship.

communication that must be spread across all relationships and are often referred to as "customer-acquisition costs". There may be other costs of developing or adapting an offering for a customer. These will result in a negative cash flow from the relationship in its early stages. The costs of managing a relationship are likely to be lower after the supplier starts to fulfil the offering. These costs are often referred to as "customer-retention costs". It is also likely that the revenue from the relationship will increase and at some point will become positive. However, the relationship is still not profitable at this time. Profitability will only be achieved when the total positive cash flow exceeds the negative cash flow. This is when the area under the positive side of the curve "B" is greater than that on the negative side "A". The time to achieve profit from the start of a relationship is likely to be quite long, even in professional service companies that charge for the time of their staff on a daily basis. For example, one IT consulting company only charges at half its normal daily rate for its consultants when they are working on a new account. Therefore it does not generate the normal rate of profit on its staff time in the early stages of a relationship. This company also calculates that many of the nonchargeable days of its consultants are actually spent developing ideas for new customers and so the costs of these days delay the time by which the relationship becomes profitable. Another professional services company calculates that on average it is 18 months before it starts to make a profit on its relationships. This is because of all of the extra tasks of adaptation and sorting out difficulties for which it is unable to fully charge the customer.

The pricing decisions of a business marketer must reflect the fact that the costs of keeping a customer are far less than gaining a new one. This has a number of aspects, as follows:

- The supplier must be careful not to take its long-term relationships for granted. It must continue to invest in them at a level that relates to their potential and resist the temptation to "milk" them for short-term profit.
- The supplier must also adjust its prices to give its customer a share of the benefits of its lower costs. This is especially because the relationship may have already solved some of the customer's most difficult problems and therefore the customer is likely to be less "excited" by the marketer's offering.
- On the other hand, the marketer must also bear in mind when pricing that a customer will also have lower costs of relationship management in established relationships and would have to incur "switching costs" in developing a relationship with a new supplier.

One way of managing price in established relationships is through so-called "open book" agreements where the supplier agrees to disclose its costs of supply and to price at an agreed margin on top of these. This transparency provides the customer with reassurance that the marketer is trying to achieve cost improvements, but not taking advantage of the customer. Many marketers are apprehensive about these agreements but they do provide the supplier with an opportunity to be open about a relationship and its value to them and to demonstrate commitment to its future.

Very often business (and consumer) marketers will seek new or additional orders by lowering their prices. However, it is important for the marketer to realize that the customers who are likely to respond to a low-price offering from one company may equally respond to price reductions from other suppliers. These customers are likely to have little loyalty to any supplier. Instead they may be customers that are mainly concerned with low initial price and less concerned with building a relationship which would provide them with long-term value.

Price and the relationship portfolio

Some relationships may have the potential for growth in sales; some may be an important source of learning; some may provide access to different parts of the network; but others may only be considered as a source of current revenue, with no longer-term potential. Those relationships with high potential will require investment to realize that potential, while others will not justify it. A marketer may use some of the revenue generated from one low-potential relationship to invest in others with a greater potential, so as to maximize the return on the portfolio as a whole.

The interrelationships between costs and revenues in a relationship portfolio mean that a business marketer cannot fix prices or assess the value of a relationship in isolation. Instead, he must bear in mind its contribution to the portfolio. Examples of portfolio pricing may include the following:

- Charging a high price to maximize revenue from a relationship with a low potential.
- Charging a lower price to encourage a customer to develop the relationship. The marketer would then be pricing on the basis of the potential of the relationship, not its current value or immediate costs.
- Assessing the wider portfolio benefits of a relationship, such as the access it provided to other parts of the network, or the learning from the relationship that could then be applied elsewhere. The marketer may then set a price in the relationship that generates a lower margin, but that could be set against value in other relationships.

Common pricing

Ideally, a business marketer should develop an individual offering, including the price that is charged that relates to the problems of each customer. But many companies have a large number of relationships and it may not be possible to find out the precise requirements or the price that can be charged in each one.[5] Companies can reduce their costs and complexity by seeking to standardize their offerings, including their prices, across their current portfolio as far as possible, and seeking new relationships with similar requirements to their existing ones. Sometimes companies can achieve the benefits of both standardization and adaptation by providing a modular offering that each customer can choose from at fixed prices.

Price and the network

Business marketing takes place in a complex network of many companies of different sorts. Hence it is important for the marketer to be aware of the way that the surrounding network affects pricing decisions. There are a number of aspects to this, including the following:

---

[5] There may also be legal difficulties for the supplier if it discriminates against some customers without justification by charging a different price for the same offering in similar volumes.

- The marketer must not just consider the problems and volume of demand from his immediate customers. The nature of these problems and the level of demand for its offerings will be derived from the demand of the final end-user in the network. Demand for the business marketer's offering will not increase or decrease by the same amount as this final demand and there will often be significant multipliers, both positive and negative. For example, if a producer of consumer durables finds that demand from its consumers has declined slightly, then it may postpone many of its purchases of production equipment.

- When setting price, it is important for the marketer to appreciate that a sale has not really been finalised until the final end-user in the network has made a purchase and received the offering. The revenue from the price paid by this customer is shared between all those in the network who have contributed to the offering. The actions of any of the companies in the network can affect that sale and the viability of all of the companies involved. This joint responsibility means that the business marketer's efforts cannot be restricted to simply "selling-in" to its immediate customer without considering how that and subsequent customers will be able to "sell-out" based in part on the price that he has charged. Similarly, the business marketer must also appreciate that if he cuts the price of its offering to a final customer he will automatically devalue the inventory of any intermediate distributor of that offering.

- It is important for the marketer to examine the different ways that prices are set across the network, rather than simply consider how his current competitors set their prices for similar offerings to the same customers. If new companies enter the business, they may apply technologies that either are new or have not previously been used in particular applications, or they may price on an entirely different basis. For example, a new supplier may charge as a whole for different elements of an offering that are currently priced separately by some suppliers.

- In some networks one company will be the price leader. In this case, other suppliers and customers will compare prices and offerings with those of the leader. The price leader may be the company with the highest sales volume, or it may be the technology leader. Because of its position, the leader is likely to act to preserve stability in the network. Price leaders are therefore only likely to be an important influence during periods of relative technological stability in a network.

- A supplier must realize that its own network position and the network position of its customers will affect their view of their problems, their knowledge of alternatives and the prices that they believe are appropriate for a particular offering. A supplier must assess the relative importance of its offering and the problem that it solves when compared to a customer's other suppliers. A customer's network position is likely to be more important as a determinant of the price that it is prepared to pay than the marketer's costs of producing the offering.

- As well as its relationship with its customer, the marketer may have a relationship with the customer's customer or with other connected companies. These may influence the customer's attitude to the supplier, its freedom to choose others and hence the price that it is prepared to pay.

- A price decision by one company may lead others to make changes, elsewhere in the network, whether they are customers, suppliers or competitors. These changes could

[226]

CHAPTER **9**

precipitate a price war between companies. This means that the marketer must examine his pricing decisions on the basis of whether he wishes to achieve network change or stability.

Costs, Price and the Offering

Costs & price together form the fifth element of the supplier's offering that may be bought by a customer. In this final section of the chapter we discuss a number of issues that centre on this vital element. The price that a supplier charges a customer for an offering should be based on the value to that customer of the solution provided by all the other elements of an offering: product, service, advice and delivery, and by any adaptations to these. Price should not be *determined* by the direct costs of providing these elements or the indirect costs of the supplier's investments in its abilities or relationships. However, price must reflect the fact that those costs have to be recovered and it is these costs that have made an offering possible and that have provided benefits to the customer.

We will firstly examine the impact on price of the tradeoffs between the different elements of an offering and the variations in value that this may lead to. We will then deal with the influence on the price of an offering from the prices of competing offerings and then examine some of the particular issues faced by business marketers seeking to control their prices. Finally we will discuss some principles for pricing of new offerings and re-pricing of existing offerings, before we end the section by relating price to the quality of offerings.

Variations and tradeoffs in offerings

A range of different customer problems can often be solved by different combinations of the elements in an offering. For example, a supplier could offer a standardized product element, with minimal service, at a low price. Alternatively, it could offer a product element that was more closely adapted to the customer's specific requirements with advice on integrating it into the customer's operations, but at a much higher price. Because each supplier's offering is a unique combination of elements, customers have to compare a wide range of different offerings at different prices and this may lead to market uncertainty for them. The marketer must be sensitive to this and be able to explain the actual value to a customer of different offerings for a specific problem, when compared to other offerings. He must also be able to analyse precisely what are the price and other costs that each competing offering involves. It is also important to reiterate that, when solving complex customer problems, the marketer must choose a combination of product and service specification, advice, delivery, price and adaptations that is not only acceptable to the customer, but that also relates to his own overall cost structure, his operations, his ability to implement the offering and his strategy for each relationship.

A marketer must be able to find out how customers would trade-off variations in the elements of an offering. A methodology to do this is outlined in Box 9.3.

Box 9.3 Tradeoff Analysis

Suppose that a company is considering an offering based on the following differences in specification for each of the five elements:

- Product:
  —a microchip with the speed of either a 386 or 486 version 1
  —or 486 version 2

- Service:
  —service calls provided on the day of request
  —or the following day

- Advice:
  —provided through a help-line
  —or a call-out service

- Delivery:
  —next day
  —or same-day delivery

- The supplier is also considering the following adaptations for particular customers:
  —no adaptation
  —adaptation to the product or the service elements only
  —adaptation to both product and service

If customers are asked to indicate their preferences between these different levels, a clear picture can emerge of the value that they place on the different elements and their levels. A hypothetical example of tradeoff analysis is given in Figure 9.3.[6] The analysis indicates that product speed (44% of total importance) and the level of adaptation offered (25% of total importance) are clearly the two most significant elements of the total offering.

More importantly, conjoint analysis also indicates the tradeoffs that buyers will make between different product offerings, based on the utility values of the different attribute levels. In this case, for example, the analysis shows that customers definitely want a product based on a 486 version 2 chip, given its high utility value (4.3) over the version 1 chip (−0.3).

Conjoint analysis also enables a business marketer to analyse the value to customers of different combinations of elements of an offering. For example, one question is whether customers would prefer this offering to include help-line advice, next-day delivery and possible adaptation to both product and service, or whether they would prefer call-out advice, same-day delivery, and only service adaptation.

[6] The methodology of this approach is explained in P Green and G Wind (1974) New Way to Measure Consumer's Judgments, *Harvard Business Review*, 53 (July–August), 107–117, and P Naude and F Buttle (2001) Assessing Relationship Quality, in D Ford (ed), *Understanding Business Marketing and Purchasing*, London, International Thomson.

We can see from Figure 9.3 that the second offering is the most preferred, given the various utility levels, as below:

- Help-line advice, next day delivery and possible adaptation to both product and service: $-1.4 - 1.4 + 2.8 = 0.0$.
- Call-out advice, same day delivery, and only service adaptation: $1.4 + 1.4 + 0.8 = 3.6$.

Through this analysis a marketer can determine which offering provides the greatest value and charge a price for that accordingly.

Pricing and competitive offerings

Price is an important, but dangerous competitive weapon for the business marketer. It must be managed with regard to the value of an offering to customers, the overall competition that the company faces and the competitive situation in specific relationships. The price that a supplier is able to charge in a customer relationship will depend on its position in that customer's portfolio of suppliers. Late entrants to the portfolio will often have to "buy" into a relationship with a combination of price and/or other elements of an enhanced offering. They may have to charge a low price because the total costs to the customer of using a current supplier are low, perhaps because it has already incurred the costs of adapting to that supplier. A new supplier is unlikely to be able to replace a current supplier by setting a marginally lower price. This is because the customer will not only compare prices between offerings, but will also take into account the value of its existing relationship, the "switching costs" of building a new one and the uncertainties that it will face.

The current supplier in a relationship may lower its own price to fight off competitors that offer lower prices. However, there can be dangers in this. If a current supplier dramatically reduces price to counter a new offering, then the customer may well ask why, if it is able to charge such a low price now, it charged a higher price before! Customers are likely to have different expectations of the suppliers in their portfolio. It may see one as the supplier of standardized offerings at a low price, another as a provider of solutions to difficult problems, but at a high price, and another as an emergency provider, again at a high price. Relationship strategy involves working within these customer perceptions, but attempting to change them over time.

Although price is an important element of strategy for the business marketer, it is customer problem-solving that must remain at the core of strategy. There are dangers for the marketer if it relies too much on low prices to gain business, because there will be little else to sustain its relationship with customers other than that price. It is much easier for a customer to compare suppliers' prices than other elements of their offerings and a price-oriented supplier is vulnerable to any other offering at a lower price. Price reductions can be implemented quickly and so marketers often use them instead of investing in their offerings and their relationships. But competitors can easily follow a price reduction and this may lead to a damaging downward spiral.[7]

[7] A Diamantopoulos (1999) Pricing, in Mike Baker (ed), *The Marketing Book*, 4th edition, Oxford, Heinemann, 337–352.

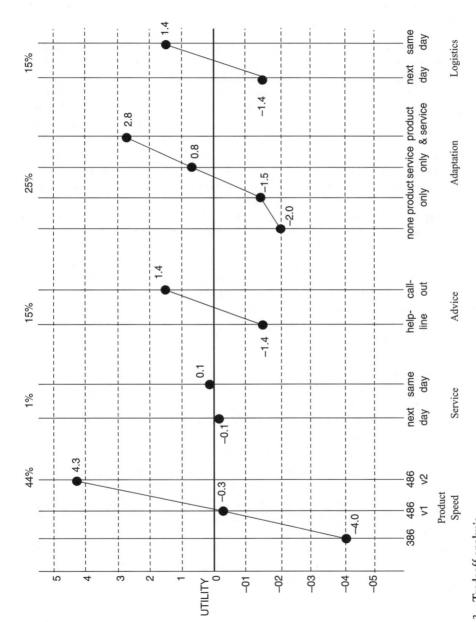

Figure 9.3 Tradeoff analysis.

Controlling the price of an offering

It is important for a supplier to control the actual price to a customer in each transaction and relationship. Price control has a number of dimensions, as follows:

- **Controlling adaptations:** Business marketing often involves continuous adaptations to an offering to suit a customer's specific requirements. All adaptations involve costs. If these costs are not passed on to the customer, then profits will decline. If they are passed on, then the company may become uncompetitive, despite the "quality" of the offering as a problem solution. The marketer, in conjunction with the customer, must balance the costs of improving an offering against the extra value to the customer and the customer's willingness to pay for that improvement. Real customer orientation sometimes means *not* giving customers what they ask for, but instead suggesting a more "standardized" offering that can be delivered at an overall lower cost. This again points to the value to a supplier of building relationships with customers with similar requirements and spreading costs over different relationships.

- **Price control and the sales-force:** Price control is often reduced when a sales-force is given discretion to negotiate a price in a specific relationship. For example, if a company has a profit margin of 20% on its list price and a salesperson negotiates a price reduction of "only" 5% then the company is giving away 25% of its profit. Sales people often do not appreciate the real effects of price erosion on profits and this is made worse because they are often rewarded for achieving sales volume, rather than profit.

- **Quoted price and achieved price:** The discounts and price reductions negotiated by the sales-force are only some of the ways that the price that a supplier actually achieves can be eroded. It is common for business marketers to give discounts for many things, for example:

  —for early payment (which are often taken by customers even if they pay late!);
  —for volume (which customers often try to insist on even for a small order because, "a big order is following");
  —retrospectively for all orders given over a previous year;
  —for the customer's costs of provided transport for an offering;
  —as a contribution towards the customer's advertising to its customers.

Often marketers do not fully understand what their "achieved price" for each customer actually is. This is simply because their accounting systems do not provide accurate price information. A number of items must be deducted from the notional price that is charged to a customer in order to arrive at a figure for achieved price. These deductions include special payment terms, customer-specific rebates, extra packaging, order handling costs, dedicated stockholding costs, freight costs and the costs of unusable material left over after production. Often a full calculation of these costs will highlight that the company is making a negative real profit on many orders.[8]

---

[8] For a full discussion of this issue see, Johan Ahlberg, William E Hoover, Hanne de Mora and Tomas Naucler (1995) Pricing Commodities: What You See is not What You Get, *The McKinsey Quarterly*, no 3, 67–77.

Prices are also often poorly controlled over a portfolio of relationships. In one study, Marn and Rosiello showed that one marketer had an average achieved price of $20 per unit, but that only 16% of its customers actually paid this price. The prices actually charged to different customers varied between $14 and $26, ie by plus or minus 25%. The lower prices were often given irrespective of the importance of the relationship to "old favourite" accounts who knew who to call in the supplier to get an extra discount.[9] This research clearly emphasizes that price control can only be achieved on the basis of a clear relationship and portfolio strategy and reliable accounting information.

Pricing a new offering

When a new offering is introduced into a number of existing or potential relationships the supplier will not have recovered any of the costs of developing the offering and both customer and supplier will have little experience of using the offering. It is also likely that the offering is still being developed at this time and the supplier may need help from the customers to achieve this.

The common approaches to pricing of new products refer to the choice between a "skimming" and a "penetration" approach. The business marketer can use these approaches as a starting point, but will need to modify them to cope with the realities of complex business networks:

- **Skimming pricing:** This is when the supplier charges a high initial price. It may be appropriate when the new offering gives the supplier a technological advantage over other suppliers, or where it has well-developed relationships with the customers. Skimming pricing may help the supplier to recoup the costs of developing the offering within a relatively small number of relationships. Skimming pricing involves taking advantage of a technological opportunity and the supplier must be quite sure of the extent of his technological advantage and take a view of how long it is likely to last. This analysis is particularly important in the pharmaceutical industry, where suppliers seek to maximize their profits on new drugs by skimming within the period of patent-protection. Business marketers should also be aware that skimming may be resented by a customer, particularly if that customer believes that it had a role in identifying a problem or developing a solution, or if the marketer needs its help for further development.
- **Penetration pricing:** This refers to low initial pricing for a new type of offering. Penetration pricing may be appropriate in a number of situations – such as when the supplier has few technological or relationship advantages; or where the offering has wide application in a number of relationships; or where there is a need to generate high sales to recoup development costs; or where close interaction with the customer is not needed to explain the offering or to integrate it into the customer's operations. Penetration pricing may also mean that the marketer shares the benefits of the new offering more fully with customers and this may assist the development of the company's relationships.

[9] Michael Marn and Robert Rosiello (1992) Managing Price, Gaining Profit, *Harvard Business Review*, September–October, 84–94.

Re-pricing existing offerings

The business marketer will need to consider re-pricing an offering when the offering is further developed, or if the company wishes to change its relationship with a customer, or if the relative value of the offering changes for the customer. The customer may want to pay a lower price if the relationship is based on a problem that has become less important to it, or if newer offerings are available that provide a better solution. The supplier will have to respond to this situation either by changing the basis of the relationship to extend the problems it deals with, or lower its relationship management costs and its price, or end the relationship. The supplier's costs are also likely to decrease with experience and the customer is likely to expect a supplier to pass on some of the benefits of this. It will be important for the business marketer to anticipate and plan for these changes through regular audits, rather than to assume that its offerings and its relationships will continue in the same way indefinitely.

Price and the quality of an offering

We have emphasized that it only makes sense to apply the word "quality" to an offering in relation to a specific problem of a specific customer. So marketers must be very careful when making generalized statements about the quality or value of their offerings. But customers do form ideas of the quality of offerings and it is important for marketers to be clear about them in both their own pricing deliberations and in discussions with customers.

We have already seen that for each customer, "quality" has two aspects. The first is the customer's evaluation of the extent to which the supplier's offering is a solution to its problem. This is the quality of the offering. And the second aspect is their assessment of the likely or actual quality of the implementation of the offering. Obviously, a marketer must relate the price of what he provides to a particular customer to this "quality", when compared with other potential suppliers.

Each aspect of quality will vary in importance depending on the customer's problem, as follows:

- Some customers with a complex or difficult problem or with high need uncertainty about different solutions will be more concerned with the quality of the offering, or its "promise". Quality for these customers will be about the relevance of the supplier's offering to its problem. They will be mainly concerned with the supplier's problem-solving skills and may be prepared to, or may have to, accept lower "quality" in the actual implementation of the offering, or the fulfilment of the supplier's promise. In this case the supplier may be able to charge a high price for a "high-quality" offering, even when its implementation is of lower "quality". Conversely, even if the supplier's implementation was superb, it would only be able to command a lower price if its offering was of low quality.
- On other occasions, a customer may be solving a simpler problem, or buying a simpler or more easily specified offering, or one for which implementation was critical. In this case, the more important aspect of quality will be how effectively a supplier fulfils its promise.

In this case the supplier may not be able to charge a high price even if the quality of its offering is excellent, if its implementation was of lower quality. Conversely, the supplier may be able to charge a high price, even for an offering that was not of particularly "high quality", if its implementation was "high quality".

- In other cases, both offering and implementation are important. However, some customers may not understand that the implementation performance of different suppliers varies, even if their offering is of similar quality. It is then important for the marketer to explain the value of high-quality implementation to the customer and that other, cheaper offerings may subsequently cause problems for the customer.

Conclusions

This chapter has not produced a list of the steps that a business marketer should follow in order to arrive at the "right price". There is no right price for an offering in all situations, and, if there were, it would soon need to be changed as the situation evolved! Instead, the chapter has outlined some of the factors that the marketer needs to bear in mind when considering prices. Through all of these, there are some fundamental considerations. Price is but one of the costs that a customer incurs when it seeks to solve a problem by buying an offering. Some of these costs relate to the acquisition and use of the offering and some concern its wider relationship with the supplier. Both the offering and the relationship in which it is acquired have value to the customer. The marketer must consider this wider cost and value structure for the customer when considering individual transactions. Similarly, the revenue from its sales is not the limit of the value of a transaction to the supplier. Nor are the supplier's costs limited to those of producing and implementing its offering. Business marketers need to relate the costs of the development and fulfilment of their offering to the revenue that it receives, the costs of developing and managing their customer relationships and to the wider benefits they receive through those relationships.[10]

Marketers are responsible for maximizing a supplier's long-term rate of return on its investments in a portfolio of relationships. A strategic approach to pricing is essential for this. But pricing in business markets produces both accounting and administrative problems:

- A marketer cannot manage prices properly unless he has accurate and timely information on costs and revenue. Cost information must include the indirect costs of investing in a relationship as well as the cost of managing that relationship and the

---

[10] The debate between customer and supplier about the supplier's costs and difficulties is often difficult for the business marketer. The debate often centres on whose responsibility the costs are and who should cope with them. An interesting example of this was provided when Boeing was developing the 777 airliner. United Airlines was the lead customer and was involved in the development process. At one meeting between the senior management of the two companies the Boeing representative announced that they had suffered some cost increases. To this, the response from United was reported as being brief and to the point: "Tough".

costs and achieved price of transactions in it. All too frequently, however, business marketers attempt to manage their relationships without a clear idea of their real profitability.

- A marketer cannot manage prices properly if he cannot control the discretion given to individuals to negotiate price or the effects of complex discount structures on the actually achieved prices.

Both of these are problems of information. They mean that marketers must work closely with financial staff to help them appreciate what information they need and why they need it.

Business pricing shares many features with consumer pricing. But the business marketer is less able to set price for the whole of a market or segment. Instead the business marketer must deal with much greater complexity. The marketer must be able to tailor price to wide variations in customers' views of their problems and the value to them of potential solutions. At the same time he must seek the administrative convenience of price standardization wherever possible. He must also balance short-term revenue against the long-term value of relationships and relate the price he charges in an individual relationship to the wider portfolio and the network in which he operates.

Further Reading

M Christopher and J Gattorna (2005) Supply Chain Cost Management and Value-based Pricing, *Industrial Marketing Management*, vol 34, 115–121.

R Cooper and R Kaplan (1991) Profit Priorities from Activity Based Costing, *Harvard Business Review*, May–June, 130–137.

S Dutta, M Bergen, D Levy, M Ritson and M Zbaraki (2002) Pricing as a Strategic Capability, *Sloan Management Review*, Spring, 61–66.

A Hinterhuber (2004) Towards Value-based Pricing – an Integrative Framework for Decision Making, *Industrial Marketing Management*, vol 33, 17–22.

GD Kortge and PA Okonkwo (1993) Perceived Value Approach to Pricing, *Industrial Marketing Management*, May, 133–140.

R Lancioni, H Jensen Schau and M Smith (2005) Intraorganizational Influences on Business-to-business Pricing Strategies: A Political Economy Perspective, *Industrial Marketing Management*, vol 34, 123–131.

A Marshall (1979) *More Profitable Pricing*, London, McGraw-Hill.

KB Monroe (1990) *Pricing, Making Profitable Decisions*, 3rd edition, New York, McGraw-Hill.

M H Morris and G Morris (1990) *Market Oriented Pricing: Strategies for Management*, New York, Quorum.

T Nagel and R Holden (2000) *The Strategy and Tactics of Pricing: A Guide to Profitable Decision Making*, Englewood Cliffs, NJ, Prentice Hall.

H Simon (1992) Pricing Opportunities and How to Exploit Them, *Sloan Management Review*, Winter, 55–65.

M Voeth and U Herbst (2006) Supply-chain Pricing – A New Perspective on Pricing in Industrial Markets, *Industrial Marketing Management*, vol 35, 83–90.

Assignment for Chapter 9

Price decisions at Wallace

Wallace is a supplier of equipment for producing plastic components. Most of its customers use the equipment to produce small components that are minor parts for their own products and which are not critical to the performance of these products. They represent only a small proportion of the total cost of items that they buy. Wallace's business with these customers consists of replacing worn out or life-expired equipment. Wallace finds that these customers are very price sensitive and it finds it difficult to interest them in the advantages of its machines or in further development. Sales to these customers are static, but they still represent around 60% of its revenue.

Wallace also has a smaller number of other customers with very different requirements. These customers produce higher-value and performance-critical items such as the cases for mobile phone handsets and other electronic equipment. These companies have to change over their machines quickly to make new shapes with different "feel", colour and strength. These customers face significant problems in designing their components for ease and speed of production and often turn to suppliers for help. Unfortunately Wallace is not the major supplier to most of these customers and its recently appointed marketing manager says:

> We have been working with some of these customers for quite a time, but we are often just scratching round for the crumbs that fall from the table of our competitors.

At the same time, the poor profit performance of Wallace in the past means that the company board is unwilling to allow marketing to "buy business" by lowering its prices or to "speculatively" develop a whole new range of equipment specifically for these customers. The Marketing Manager's relations with the Board are not good and the Board "wants results, not talk".

Recently, the marketing management has been working with his development and financial colleagues to simplify the company's model range and to introduce a pricing policy that he believes more closely reflects the real costs of producing each machine. One outcome for this is that it appears that many of its long-established standard machines, bought mostly by its older customers, have much lower production costs than were previously attributed to them. This is because there has been no significant development expenditure on them. In contrast, Wallace appears to be losing money on many of the machines it sells to its newer customers who pay higher prices but require major adaptations to the machines that they buy.

Question

Produce a report for the Marketing Manager that could be given to the company's Board of Directors. The report should present the following:

- An outline of the pricing issues that face the Marketing Manager at Wallace.
- A pricing approach to the company's established customers.

- A recommendation of whether or not the company should continue to seek business with the new "development" customers and a recommended pricing approach to these customers. The report should explain the justification for any alternative approach that you recommend.

Finally, the report should explain the contribution that would be required from different functional areas and cover any wider issues in the approaches to pricing that you recommend.

DEVELOPING MARKETING STRATEGY

10

Aims of this Chapter

- To explore the concept of strategy and to translate the concept into the context of business networks.
- To provide an insight into the complex issues of strategy development and, in particular, into how marketing strategies in business networks develop over time.
- To offer a realistic perspective of the role of management in developing marketing strategy.

A Framework for Strategy Management

We start this chapter by briefly reviewing the conceptual framework of strategy management as it emerges in current management literature. In particular, we are concerned here with the concept of strategy itself, the idea of strategy options and the strategy development process. Having established a basis for examining strategy management in general, we will move on to explore the key issues in developing strategy in the particular context of business networks.

The concept of strategy

Managers, academics, business journalists and the public use the notion of "strategy" in the context of management and marketing both freely and frequently. The term is used with many different and shifting meanings. But the popularity of the notion of strategy appears to be based on the belief that taking a wide-angled and long-term view on an issue can help to distinguish what is trivial from what matters most in addressing an issue and can also assist in achieving desired goals, under particular circumstances. There is a widespread conviction that taking a "strategic view" will help managers to operate more effectively and will provide valuable guidance for how to act under different circumstances. The underlying logic of this approach is appealing, especially in a complex context, such as a business network and few would actually question the logic and thus the value of "strategic thinking".

Because the meaning given to the notion of strategy varies and shifts we need to clarify how we will use the term here. One of the clearest divergences in the meaning of strategy in a management context is that, to some, strategy means *the ideas or plans that a company has*, while to others, strategy is *what a company actually does.*

To use the notion of strategy to describe ideas and plans about a future course of action is problematic. One problem is that the ideas and plans of particular individuals in a company tend to differ and it is by no means obvious whose ideas and whose plans should be considered as the strategy of the company. The question that arises is: should one consider the plans of the board or those of top management, or those of some other members of the management team, and disregard the ideas and plans of others? A further problem is that, as the saying goes, there tends to be a chasm between what is said and what is done!

We will, in this chapter, refer to marketing strategy as what a company is *actually* doing, rather than as the plans or ideas of its managers. The reason for that is that results are achieved and can best be explained from what is being done with respect to the company's customers. This does not mean, however, that there are no problems with this way of using the notion of strategy and to define a company's strategy as its actual conduct does not resolve the ambivalence of the notion of strategy.

This is because strategy implies intent and change in what is being done and it always has a time dimension. Strategy is future-oriented. Hence, ideas and plans are still important because they have the power to shape what is done and what will be done. The conduct of a company towards its customers reflects the ideas and interpretations of the individuals in the company. Any description of what is being done rests upon a perspective, a way to make sense of it and is thus linked to ideas.

Defining strategy as *pattern* in the actual conduct of the company also has some consequences that may appear startling.[1] It implies that every company *has* a strategy in the sense it has its own approach to business. It also implies that the strategy pursued by a company can be the outcome of unintended, unconscious and uncontrolled behaviors.[2] But this way to define strategy offers some important advantages. The main one is that it permits us to distinguish analytically the content of strategy, *what* is being done, from the *process by which strategy is formed*. Consequently, this view of strategy also allows us to assess and evaluate different strategies and the ways in which they are implemented as managed or unconscious, effective or ineffective, good or bad.

The content of strategy and strategy options

The idea of strategy implies that we can distinguish what are the important and less important things that can be done in order to achieve desired results and goals. In business

---

[1] L Araujo and G Easton (1996) Strategy: Where is the Pattern?, *Organisation*, vol 3, no 3, 361–383.
[2] H Mintzberg (1985) Of Strategies, Deliberate and Emergent, *Strategic Management Journal*, vol 6, no 3, 257–272. H Mintzberg (1987) Crafting Strategy, *Harvard Business Review*, July–August, 66–75.

COST   REVENUES

                                                        WHO?

                                                        The set of

HOW?   customers

Organizational and   served

technical solutions

implemented

                                                        WHAT?

                                                        The value to the customer

                                                        provided by the supplier and

                                                        its offering

Figure 10.1   Strategy choices.

this means that we have to answer the question, "What actions make a difference for the performance of a company?". That, of course is not a simple question to answer, and is probably impossible to answer in absolute terms once and for all. Yet, if a company is to manage its strategy, then the question cannot be avoided. Tentative answers or assumptions that reflect the company's current understanding of its context and of its way to operate will have to be provided.[3]

In principle, business strategy is about achieving desired economic and financial performance. In turn, this depends on the revenues a company receives from what it does and the costs entailed in its operations. The critical question then becomes, "What choices about the company's operations impact most on the amount of revenues generated and costs incurred?" This way to approach the problem is common to most of the thinking on business strategy. Broadly taken, it assumes that the strategy of the company can be characterized in terms of a set of "*strategic choices*".

This way to conceptualize strategy is illustrated in Figure 10.1, which builds on the ideas of customer portfolios, offerings and implementation that we have developed in earlier chapters. Starting from the profit and loss statement of a company it suggests that the current and future revenues of a company depend on two broad variables:

- The first is the set of customers it serves, or aims to serve (the "Who" in Figure 10.1).
- The second is the value provided to the targeted customers: in other words the differential features of the broad offering to these customers (the "What" in Figure 10.1).

It is also suggested in Figure 10.1 that costs depend on the actual organizational, technological and managerial solutions that are implemented by the business in reaching and serving its customers (the "How" in the figure).

[3] P Drucker (1974) *Management: Tasks, Responsibilities, Practices*, New York, Harper & Row.

It is generally assumed that companies can exercise some degree of choice, even if limited, about the portfolio of customers that they serve and the nature of their offerings to these. All other things being equal, broadening the actual customer base leads to increased revenues while reducing the customer base leads to decreased revenues. The *structure* of the customer *base*, or the differences between its customers has a bearing on how attractive a company's offering will be to them. Both the set of customers that a company serves and its offerings to them will change over time and differ from those of other companies. The tendency in how customers and offerings change for a company is the most important descriptor of that company's strategy profile. The company's current and future revenues depend on whether the company is maintaining, acquiring or losing customers, and at what rate. Traditionally, the scope of a customer base is referred to in marketing as the "market served" and the link between the change in the market served and the company's revenue is relatively straightforward: the broader the market scope, the greater the potential revenues. But in the context of business marketing the scope of a customer base is likely to be more appropriately expressed in terms of particular customers.[4]

The link between *what* the company offers to its various customers and the economic and financial performance of the company is more complex. Current marketing thinking concentrates on the differences perceived by customers in the offerings from different suppliers and refers to that as "market differential". The choice of the supplier, ie the purchase, falls on the offering perceived by the customer as offering a greater value. The argument is that what matters for a single customer is not simply the content of an offering in terms of the elements of product, service, delivery, advice, cost & price, but how that offering compares with competing alternatives from other suppliers. This differential in offering explains whether and how much the customer buys from a supplier and therefore impacts on the company's performance. The perceived "value" of an offering is the difference between the expected benefits and the expected costs of a supplier. When this difference is greater than that of the alternatives that a customer takes into the consideration, then a sale can be realized and revenues are generated. Current marketing literature alleges that there are, in principle, two options in order to generate "value for the customer": the first is to act on the benefit content of the offering (differentiating the elements of the offering); the second is to act on the costs that the customer has to sustain. This dimension of strategy is made complex because the "value for the customer" and the existence of the differential is subjective, individual and relative to the characteristics and needs of each specific customer. In other words the differential is only partly dependent on the actual content of the offering. The presence and extent of a differential are explained by the features and contexts of the customer.

---

[4] As we are exploring the idea of strategy in a general business context in the early part of this chapter we will refer to "markets" and "market" strategy for the sake of simplicity. We will then turn our attention to the particular problems and characteristics of strategy for companies operating in business *networks*.

The costs of a company depend on *how* the company goes about its business: how it organizes and what solutions it adopts in order to approach customers and to fulfil its offerings for those customers. A single "quality" of offering and implementation for a particular customer can be achieved through several different organizational and technological approaches that require different resources and different activity patterns and therefore entail different costs. Both the amount and structure of these costs follow from the operational solutions that the company adopts. Some solutions are obviously more cost efficient than others. Some require investments that render the cost structure less flexible. The basic options when it comes to organizational and technological solutions are less clearcut in current strategy thinking. There is an increasing tendency to distinguish "internal" from "external" solutions. This involves consideration of whether to bring in-house or to outsource more or less important parts of the operations of the company. Outsourcing sales, R & D, production or other parts of the operations are options that are increasingly debated, as we discussed in Chapter 4.

The broad conceptual framework of thinking about strategy options is based on the view that the economic and financial performance of a company reflects the thrust of its operations in the three dimensions:

- the scope of its customer base;
- the differential of its offerings;
- the technical and organizational solutions adopted.

Choices that a company makes on the three dimensions and, in particular, how these are to change, produce actual results for the company. Companies adopt different strategies in terms of their choices with respect to scope, differential and approaches and there is not one strategy profile that can be singled out as more effective than others. Whether a certain strategy will be effective depends on circumstances, the reactions of customers and the reactions of others who compete for these. The strategy profile of any company evolves over time.

Therefore, in order to explore a company's strategy profile it is necessary to examine the directions in which these choices are changing. We must emphasize at this point that it is difficult to draw a clear distinction between marketing and overall business strategy because they are so closely interwoven. However, marketing strategy is the central element of the overall strategy of any business.

The strategy development process

Considerations of the options and content of strategy are only part of the standard current conceptual framework of strategy management. The second important part of the conceptual framework concerns the strategy development process. This is the process by which the choices that shape the content of strategy are actually made. Considerations of process involve the following questions: How are decisions about the content of strategy taken? How should they be taken? Who should take them? What are effective and ineffective ways to decide what to do?

Concerns about the strategy development process stem from the evident need to adjust the strategy of a business over time to changing circumstances. Strategies, in the sense of choices with respect to the customer scope, differential and solutions may work effectively for a company at a certain point in time. But they are not likely to remain effective indefinitely because of changes in the context in which the business operates. This context will change as new actors enter and incumbents leave; as customers' needs and what they demand change over time; as available technological and organizational approaches evolve. These changes continuously transform the business context and tend to make the strategies that once worked become less and less effective. Change in the context is continuous for most businesses today and results in the need for often radical redirecting of strategy choices. Hence there is a need to *manage* strategy: that is to review, revise and adjust the strategy that was hitherto pursued by the company.

Current thinking on strategy highlights three features that characterize the strategy development process and have a bearing on the task of strategy management, as follows:

- The actual content of marketing strategy is not the result of a few major decisions taken from time to time. Instead, the content of marketing strategy emerges over time in a series of decisions taken by the management as it attempts to cope with problems as they arise in the operations of the company. Management acts and reacts all the time to more or less confined problems. How managers choose to react adds up to their broad strategic choices.

- Marketing-related decisions are taken under time constraints and consequently with only a limited search for information and for possible alternative solutions. Moreover, strategies are future-orientated and their effectiveness depends on what the future context will be. This is clearly impossible to foresee. There are always limits to what management does know, or can know, at any one time. Therefore the decisions that shape strategies are always taken with some and often wide margins of uncertainty, which cannot be resolved.

- The strategy development process involves, and should involve, all those who have relevant knowledge and information of circumstances and possible solutions in order to make informed decisions. Those who have such information and knowledge in a company are most often the middle management.

Given these features of the strategy development process, actual strategy appears to result from a *flow* of decisions taken by various managers in different parts of the company, rather than being the outcome of single discrete decisions taken by the top management and implemented throughout the company's organization.

These characteristics of the strategy development process have consequences for the role of top management in managing strategy. Top management's role is not a simple one and is not that of making the decisions about the content of strategy. But top management is obviously accountable for the performance of a company and for developing effective marketing strategies. This means that the role of top management can be translated as the responsibility to manage the *process* of strategy development. This task is clearly broader than that of making decisions. It has been observed that the task consists primarily of creating and maintaining the conditions necessary for effective changes in the content of strategy to occur. This broad view of the role of the top management in developing effective, organization-wide strategies emphasizes three areas where the top management has unique responsibility:[5]

- The first is to provide sense and purpose for the company's activities that can orient the individual managers' behaviours.
- The second is to create and maintain the conditions for middle management to take sensible decisions. This amounts to building systems and structures that support informed action in the company.
- Finally, top management has the responsibility to foster and promote the development of the competence and skills of those in the company so that it can produce more effective responses.

The emphasis on strategic planning as the tool of strategy management that has dominated the strategy thinking in the past is clearly giving way to a broader notion of strategic management that aims to ensure a timely response to events inside and outside the company. The conventional wisdom on how strategy should be managed was previously that companies should carefully monitor or analyse what is happening in the surrounding market and take the necessary measures in order to adapt to these changing conditions. More recently, thinking on strategy appears to embrace the idea that companies can exercise some influence over the dynamics of markets. The contemporary, so-called, resource-based view of strategy management makes a strong point that companies, rather than adapting to what happens in the market, should exploit unique resource combinations in the market wherever possible. The argument is based on the idea that, in order to be effective, a strategy must fit the market but also fit the set of resources that any company is composed of. On this point, strategy thinking has moved from:

"Structure needs to follow strategy" or that formulating strategy is a function of market opportunities and adaptation by the company

to a view that is more like:

"Strategy follows the structure" or that formulating strategy is about finding a space in the market where the current resources and capabilities of the company can be effectively exploited.

Strategy in Business Networks

Throughout this book we have been considering the peculiarities of marketing when the customers are businesses and other organizations. We have explored how the features of these business "markets" affect the conventional wisdom on the task of marketing. The

[5] CA Bartlet and S Goshal (1989) *Managing across Borders: The Transnational Solution*, Boston, Harvard Business School Press.

prevalence of interactive exchange, interdependencies and complex business relationships have led us to think of the world in which business companies operate as *networks* rather than markets. The particular dynamics of relationships and networks affect the core issues of strategy and the task of management. These dynamics lessen the importance of some of the issues emphasized in current strategic thinking on the content of strategy and on the strategy development process, whilst they bring others to the foreground.

Regardless of the angle from which we try to capture the nature of business networks, we always come back to the specific interdependencies that exist between customers and suppliers and which account for the particular "heaviness" of business networks.[6] A business network is characterized by continuity. Any company in the network is part of a complex whole in which the company builds on the resources and activities of others and in turn, provides a building block for the activities of those others. Such a context offers only limited freedom for companies that need to find a structural hole to fill in the network. Every company in the network has to take into account and build on the existing structures of the network. There is inertia in the network that is built on the investments made by companies and which contributes to the notable rigidities in business networks.

This inertia is only one facet of a business network. The other facet is that a network can be considered as a task that is never accomplished. The technologies and traditions that underlie business networks are in continuous evolution. There are continuous changes to activities and resources and a search for solutions to solve problems of many kinds: technological, commercial, organizational and inter-organizational. This never-ending search, whether apparent or invisible to others takes place at a huge variety of positions within the network. This perpetual motion lightens the heaviness of the network.

We will now look further at the "What", "Who" and "How" of strategy in the particular situation of business networks.

The offering – the "What" of strategy

This dimension is at the core of a company's strategy since it represents the rationale for a customer to patronize a certain supplier. Customers patronize suppliers for a wide range of reasons, depending on the nature of their problems and uncertainties. The overriding criterion of business customers (as we discussed in Chapter 5) is "economy" in the broadest sense. That is the expected economic consequences of working with a supplier for the costs and revenues of the customer's own operations. Customers' perceptions and awareness of these expected economic consequences vary: some will focus on short-term financial consequences; others will be more concerned with long-term impact on their economic performance. These different foci will depend on the context of the customers' business and the interpretation that the customer makes of it. A customer's perceptions are individual and subjective and invariably change over time with changes in the circumstances under which it operates. Unfortunately, customers themselves often find it difficult to spell out their reasons for using one supplier rather than another. This is why the

[6] The idea of the "substance" of business relationships and the "heaviness" of their content is fully explored in Håkan Håkansson and Ivan Snehota (eds) (1995) *Developing Relationships in Business Networks*, London, Routledge.

assessment of the actual offering differential is complex and the identification of generic options for the supplier is uncertain. This complexity is further added because business offerings are supplied within a relationship, which also has value for both customer and supplier. Assessing the value and costs of a relationship, from the customer and supplier's perspective, is a useful analytical exercise even if it cannot be precisely quantified. It has to be done because, without a workable assumption of this value, a supplier (or customer) lacks any guidance for its conduct.

A peculiar aspect of the value of an offering to a customer in a business network is that it is a moving target. The value of working with a supplier is linked to the search for solutions to problems that arise in the customer's operations. But companies may ignore or cope with some problems while others may disappear, arise unexpectedly or increase in urgency. It is common to consider that the cost–benefit consequences for a customer depend on the various elements of a composite offering: product, service, advice, delivery and costs & price. But we have argued throughout this book that customers actually "buy" suppliers themselves and their skills and resources, rather than any single offering that they may produce. From the perspective of business customers, the economic consequences of purchases appear clearly to originate in different facets of its relationship with the supplier as a whole, as follows:

- the fit of their resources (offerings, operations and administrative systems, etc);
- the coordination of their activities (implementation, scheduling, logistics etc);
- the interaction between them (knowledge transfer, willingness to serve, trust, reliability etc).

It is essential to take the customer's point of view when assessing an offering differential so as to explore what is bought and the value that is received, rather than simply what is sold. A differential in performance for business customers has two aspects, as follows:

- Firstly, it is based on the superior economics of current solutions to customer problems, based on the current features of the supplier's offering and its ability to implement this offering.
- Secondly, it is based on the expected superior ability of the supplier to solve problems that might arise and its expected potential to propose novel solutions: that is, its capacity to innovate the offering.

Strategy in terms of what is and what might be done in a relationship with customers is more a matter of formulating the nature of the *interface* with customers than of deciding on the elements of the offering. Value for a customer depends on the nature of this interface that allows the supplier to develop and implement offerings that will be valued as solutions to problems that arise. In this way, the "what" of strategy in business networks shifts toward the question of "how" relationships with customers should work, rather than what they should contain. This approach is neatly expressed in Amcor's promise in Box 10.1.

Assessing the effects for a customer of its interface with a supplier requires an understanding of the customer's perception of the supplier's offering, but also of the customer's internal operations and its position in the surrounding network. A framework for such an assessment is illustrated in Figure 10.2 that draws on the ideas on costs, price and value

---

Box 10.1   The Promise of Amcor

Amcor is a leading company in packaging. It is present in 40 countries, has 30,000 employees and 240 plants and supplies Coca-Cola, Nestle, Cadbury, Unilever, Heinz, Danone and many others. It provides a broad range of offerings, but formulates its value proposition in terms of promise, as follows:
   "Amcor's Product Leadership and Innovation process provides customers with:

–a more structured approach to identifying their packaging needs;
–broader opportunities for involvement in packaging development;
–means to create product differentiation;
–ways to improve speed to market."

---

developed in Chapter 9. This figure provides a framework for reviewing the main options for the configuration of the customer interface and makes the important separation between the value to the customer of the supplier's offering and the value of the customer's relationship with the supplier. The figure uses the separation between the customer's indirect and direct costs that we used in Chapter 9. The customer's direct costs include the price paid for an offering and the costs of receiving and using it. The customer's indirect costs are the costs of managing and sustaining its relationship with the supplier and the general costs of its operations that will be allocated to this particular relationship. This

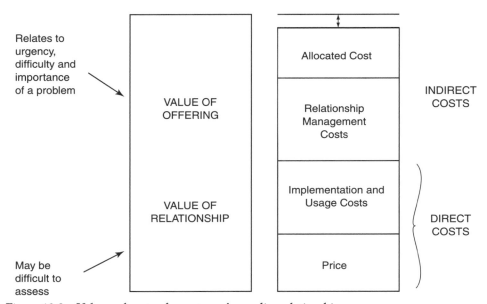

Figure 10.2   **Value and costs of a customer's supplier relationship.**

assessment clarifies the economic consequence of the configuration of the customer–supplier interface. This assessment is a necessary basis for orienting interaction with the customer and for allocating the supplier's resources, and it also provides a background for communication with the customer.

A final consideration of the "What" of strategy in business networks concerns the autonomy of the supplier in configuring the interface with the customer. Business customers are not passive, especially when their need for a problem solution is urgent or critical. Business customers may be as active as the supplier in devising various aspects of the relationship: activity links, actor bonds and resource ties. Consequently, supplier and customer tend to configure the interface between supplier and customer and the "What" of strategy *interactively*. This interactivity has implications for the second dimension of strategy: the choices regarding the customer base.

Customer base – the "Who" of strategy

Every company at a particular point in time is characterized by the set of customers it serves, by the offerings that it provides for them and by how the two are changing. Many business companies have a large number of customers, but it is common for a relatively few of their customer relationships to account for a major portion of total sales. Research shows that ten major customers often account for more than two-thirds of the sales and that for many companies 80% of sales are often made to no more than 20–30 major customers. Of course exceptions do exist, depending on the size of the company and how its customers are defined, but a business company's customer base is typically rather concentrated. Examples of customer concentration include suppliers to the automotive and aerospace industries and to retailers, in advertising agencies, accounting companies, steel producers, consultants and electronics suppliers.

Few business marketing companies constantly renew their customer base or sell to new customers all the time. Most companies serve relatively few customers on a continuous basis and only a minor portion of their sales in any one year is to customers with which they have never done business before. Again, research shows that for established companies new customers seldom represent more than 5–10% of the total business at any one time.

This concentration and continuity cause each company in a business network to be unique in the set of customers it serves and the suppliers it uses, as we observed in Chapter 2. It also means that the possibility of freely choosing customers is rather limited. Customer choice or change involves the acquisition of new customers that currently belong within the portfolios of others and this involves considerable effort. But in another sense, the choice of target customers available to a company in a business network is also rich. This is because it is often possible for a business company to provide very different offerings and relationships and to target customers operating in many different ways at various positions in the network. A typical example of this varying set of customers occurs when a company supplies a number of original equipment makers (OEMs) as well as resellers and distributors.

Hence the customer base for most businesses tends to be heterogeneous. It often consists of companies with greatly different characteristics, varying from large to small, old to new,

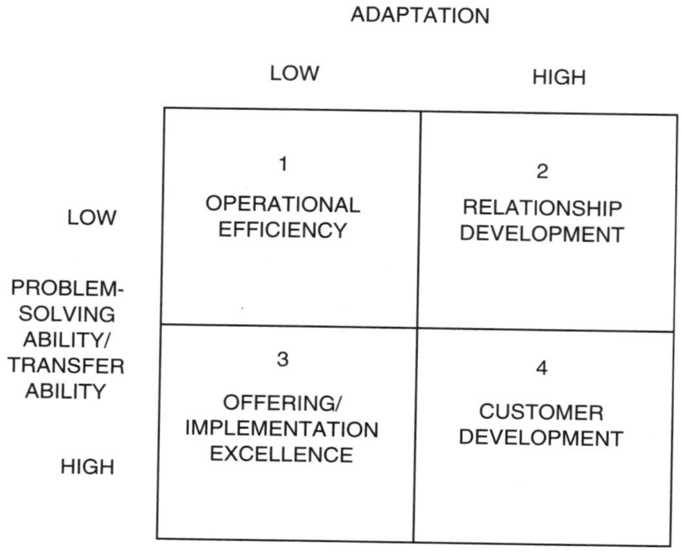

ADAPTATION

	LOW	HIGH
LOW	1 OPERATIONAL EFFICIENCY	2 RELATIONSHIP DEVELOPMENT
PROBLEM- SOLVING ABILITY/ TRANSFER ABILITY		
HIGH	3 OFFERING/ IMPLEMENTATION EXCELLENCE	4 CUSTOMER DEVELOPMENT

Figure 10.3 Customer requirements and supplier strategies.

innovative to conservative, and also ranging widely in their profitability, management style and growth potential. These heterogeneous customers will have very different requirements from suppliers and different relationships with them. Also, because of the active role of customers in shaping the interface with suppliers and the features of the offering, the heterogeneity of the customer base is dynamic. This dynamism leads to a situation in which a company tends to cope with variations in customers by making adaptations to its offerings and to their relationship. This differentiation between customers is an important competitive weapon in business networks. But cost issues mean that it is equally important for marketers to control and confine these adaptations.

The framework in Figure 10.3 can be used to assess the variety in customer requirements and to explore the options available to a company. The figure relates to the discussion of the content of customer relationships in Chapter 3. The figure suggests that the requirements that customers have of their suppliers typically vary on two dimensions in business networks: the problem-solving and transfer abilities of the supplier and the customer-specific adaptations that they require. As we have seen in earlier chapters, some customers require levels of problem-solving ability that are standard and common to most suppliers while others may need problem-solving ability that is much higher and not mastered by all suppliers. Similarly, the requirements of customers for the transfer ability of suppliers can vary from the high to low or the simple to complex. Some customers are satisfied with a standardized offering or implementation, or one that is within the supplier's normal range; others require specific implementation adapted to their particular requirements. These differences reflect the nature and the context of the customer's business. They follow from differences in customers' use of an offering, their network position and their strategic posture. Adapting in order to be the "ideal" supplier for every kind of customer can strain the costs of the supplier company because quite different organizational and technological resources are likely to be required. Therefore an important choice facing a supplier is to clarify what adaptations it will and will not make and specify the limits to which it will stretch its resources. There are two aspects to this choice: the first is the obvious one of limiting the costs that differentiation involves; the second and less obvious aspect is that prioritizing particular customer requirements accumulates experience and develops capabilities on which the future configuration of the customer interface can be built.

Figure 10.3 suggests four different avenues for developing the offering differential of a company, as follows:

- **Cell 1 Operational efficiency:** A supplier operating in this cell does not have strength in either of problem-solving ability and transfer ability, nor does it have skills in adaptation. In this situation its strategy must be based on achieving *efficiency* in what it does. This may give it a competitive position based on low price with customers whose requirements are low on both dimensions.
- **Cell 2 Relationship development:** A supplier operating in this cell is following a strategy based on skills in adapting to the specific requirements of customers. This is likely to depend on its strong relationship-management skills, but its flexibility in operations will also be important. This strategy will appeal to customers that place emphasis on the value of their relationships and suppliers' adaptations within them.
- **Cell 3 Offering/implementation excellence:** Suppliers in this cell are strong in problem-solving ability and transfer ability, but do not have a strong capability to adapt. This strategy of providing excellence in a standardized offering and/or implementation will be appropriate for customers who do not require adaptation in a relationship, but who place value on a supplier's offering.
- **Cell 4 Customer development:** Suppliers in this cell have the resources to be excellent in both problem-solving and transfer ability and also are able to adapt strongly. This strategy is likely to involve the supplier in high costs. It is appropriate for those customers with the most demanding and particular requirements.

The amount of resources available to a company for its adaptations is always limited and not all customers' requests can be met. Business companies have to balance the requirements of their relationships and the pressure to adapt within them against cost-efficiency in their operations and a focus on resource and technological development. This means that suppliers have to decide on which customers to prioritize: that is to manage their relationship portfolio. The importance of portfolio decisions reflects the fact that a company's relationships in a business network are valuable assets. As with any assets, the problem for the company is how to allocate its available resources to optimize its returns. Even if a company denies it, the company's different customers will receive different treatment as it is impossible to satisfy the requests of all of them. Giving priority to some customers is part of the process of "investing" in those relationships rather than in others. The strategic intent of a company involves maximizing the return from its customer portfolio as a whole.

The rationale for giving some customers priority is often hard to see because the various concessions and adaptations are arrived at through interaction with customers. These

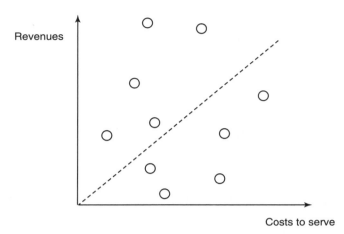

Revenues

Costs to serve

Figure 10.4   Customer portfolio matrix - revenues vs costs to serve.

adaptations are even harder to monitor and keep track of. The task for management is to monitor how the customer base and customer relationships develop and to make explicit the criteria for attributing priorities to some and not to other customer relationships. Assessment of the structure and change of a relationship portfolio offers a basis for developing a consistent and effective marketing strategy and provides guidance on how to allocate efforts, investments and adaptations. The customer relationships of a company will vary in their volume of business, profitability, rate of growth and strength of the relationship, and also in how they can be leveraged for other purposes such as technical development or more general business development. The first reaction of a manager, when asked which of these purposes should be taken as a criterion by which to prioritize relationships, is likely to be the claim that it should be profitability. Yet research shows that profitability always varies greatly across the customer relationships of a company and over time. One way to assess this issue of relationship profitability is to analyse customer relationships for their relative cost-to-serve and revenue, by constructing a matrix such as that in Figure 10.4.

A snapshot picture of the different relationships in a portfolio plotted as in Figure 10.4 provides only one of the elements needed in order to make choices regarding the future customer scope of a company. But it can be used both to assess the current portfolio situation and to track changes over time. This can provide a useful starting point for formulating strategy with respect to the customer base. An analysis of the customer portfolio will always show differences in profitability of single relationships. The persistence of some "unprofitable" customers in a portfolio is common and not a bad sign in itself. Some of the less profitable, or nonprofitable, customers may be valuable for other reasons; they may be the growing customers with future potential or customers that are a good source of technical or commercial know-how. Also, a single customer relationship cannot be evaluated in isolation and the existing interdependencies between relationships have to be taken into account. So, for example, an offering developed in one relationship may subsequently be

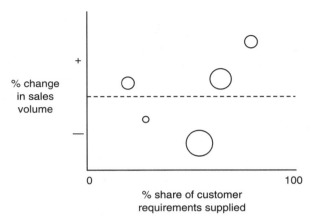

Figure 10.5 Customer portfolio change matrix.

profitably employed in others. Just as in financial portfolio management, the principle is to manage the customer base for *overall* profitability at a company-wide level, to which different relationships contribute in different ways.

Another element in deciding on options with respect to the customer base is to monitor relationship development over time. This can be achieved by tracking the development of a customer portfolio as suggested in Figure 10.5. This brings together changes in the sales volume in particular relationships and the share of a customer's requirements supplied by the company. It has to be kept in mind, however, that the overall analysis of a customer portfolio with respect to profitability and change in the content of relationships cannot substitute for the need for single account analysis and the individual management of the company's main customer relationships, as we discussed in Chapter 6.

When evaluating their options with respect to their customer base, most companies have the ambition of acquiring new customers. This may be a viable option but it does involve developing new relationships and, as a rule, breaking into the active, existing supplier relationships of a customer. In many mature, global businesses this is an option that may not be easy to pursue. Another option in these cases is for a company to concentrate on trying to more fully exploit its existing customer relationships by broadening its offerings and capitalizing on its intimacy with the problems and possible solutions of existing customers. The rationale for focusing on existing relationships lies in the typical pattern of profitability of customer relationships over time. Customer relationships are costly to develop, especially in the initial phase, because of the costs of developing offerings and of mutual learning. Relationships tend to become more profitable at a later stage, as these initial investments in offerings and management efforts bear fruit.[7]

---

[7] Håkansson and Ford have also suggested that it may be difficult to build relationships with different characteristics from those which a company is used to. Hence a company may be forced back to relying on its existing relationships or building new and similar ones. Håkan Håkansson and David Ford (2002) How Should Companies Interact, *Journal of Business Research*, vol 55, no 2, 133.

Again it is the presence and strength of interdependencies in a business network that makes the issues of "who" rather peculiar. The issue appears less that of the company's choice of target customers and more that of its current and future status and role in the network. This implies that strategy for a company in a business network involves manoeuvring for an overall position or status within the network rather than simply choosing customers. In this manoeuvring for position, it is difficult to isolate the customer side of a company from its supply side and this linkage affects the next traditional issue of strategy: that of technological and organizational solutions.

Technical and organizational solutions – the "How" of strategy

Most, if not all companies struggle continuously with technical and organizational issues. Companies update their product and process technologies, commercial arrangements, organizational structure and support systems. This continuous process of organizing and renewing is imposed by the need to continue being a potential provider of innovative, unforeseeable solutions. This pressure to be considered by customers as a business partner for future as well as current challenges shapes this third dimension of the marketing strategy of companies in business networks: the "How" or the company's technological and organizational arrangements.

Any options for a supplier in the "What" of its customer interface and its offering and the "Who" of its customer base involve a specific combination of resources and capabilities. This required combination of resources and capabilities determines how the company will organize itself and what technologies it will need in order to develop and implement its offering and manage its relationships. Decisions to extend the current customer base, for example to acquire new customers or to give priority to adaptation or to excellence in offering or implementation will entail a series of these operational decisions with long-term effects and important cost consequences.

Different combinations of resources and capabilities can be used in order to achieve the performance required. As with the two previous dimensions, there is no one right or best organizational and technical solution. But there are at least three criteria on which to assess the impact on economic performance of alternative organizational and technical solutions underlying a certain strategy, as follows:

- **The cost criterion:** This is a rather obvious criterion, but it must not be limited to a concern for short-term cost efficiency. Different technical and organizational solutions will involve different cost levels and also different cost structures. Typically the choice will be between solutions that are cost-efficient but incur high indirect costs and solutions that are less cost-efficient, have higher direct costs but result in greater flexibility.
- **The commitment criterion:** Some technical or organizational approaches may tie the company into a particular set of relationships, operations, technologies or offerings for a long time and preclude other possibilities of offering or serving other customer categories. Technical and organizational solutions have thus to be evaluated in the light of the strategic flexibility they allow.

- **The development criterion:** Different organizational and technical solutions, once adopted, tend to lead the attention of management in a particular direction and limit the range of alternative options that will be identified. Also, organizational and technical solutions vary widely in the extent to which they allow renewal and innovation.

The combination of resources and capabilities required in order to execute an intended strategy invariably involves a set of resources and capabilities that are partly internal and partly within other companies such as its suppliers, development partners and customers. We have emphasized throughout this book that external resources and capabilities are a growing part of the total set that are needed to provide the solutions on which strategy is based. We also observed that the ease with which these external resources can be accessed and mobilized depends on the relationships the company has developed.

The extent to which the company chooses to rely on internal or external resources and capabilities is an important dimension of choice in their strategies. Some companies choose to exercise the direct ownership control of a larger portion of the resources and capabilities they need than others. For instance the electronics and computer industries offer examples of how such strategies can vary.[8] The option to rely more on external resources and capabilities is often motivated by a requirement for greater strategic flexibility and developmental potential. On the other hand, external resources tend to limit the autonomy of a company. They also impose a requirement to manage "collective strategy" on those on whom access to and mobilization of external resources and capabilities depend.

Organizational and technological solutions in business networks always have components of external as well as internal elements that need to be connected. Strategic choice in developing offerings and relationships requires reconfiguring and reconnecting the set of internal and external elements.

Hence the "What", "Who" and "How" of strategy in business networks are closely interlinked.[9]

Strategy Development in Business Networks

We have seen in the previous section that the peculiar features and dynamics of business networks impact on the task of strategy management and make some choices stand out as less critical and others as more so. In this section we will examine how the task of strategy in business networks impacts on the traditional concept of the *process* of strategy choice and strategy development.

There is a tradition about strategic choice in business education, consulting and practice that builds on the logic of "think before you leap", and better still, "think hard, before you

---

[8] For a comparison of business models of Dell vs Compaq, see M Kaplan (2002) *Acquisition of Electronic Commerce Capability: The Cases of Compaq and Dell in Sweden*, Stockholm, The Economic Research Institute of the Stockholm School of Economics.

[9] Gary Hamel (2000) *Leading the Revolution*, Boston, Harvard Business School Press.

leap". In practice, this means that if a company is faced with a major choice it should approach it by making a careful analysis and evaluation of the problem and of the available alternatives; decide which alternative is the most promising one by referring to explicit criteria and then implement its decision. This logic that we might call the "rationalistic" approach to choice consists of three distinct steps: analysis, decision and implementation. At first sight it is appealing and under certain circumstances it has proven rather effective. It works when gathering and interpreting data diminishes the decision-maker's uncertainty about the consequences of various alternative courses of action. This is typically the case when the context of the decision is relatively structured and stable.

Unfortunately, for companies that operate in business networks this is seldom the case. The strategy choices that we have identified have to be taken in a context characterized by what theorists call "genuine uncertainty". Genuine uncertainty means that many of the factors that have a critical effect on the outcomes of strategy are not only unknown; they are unknowable. They are unknowable for at least two reasons. The first is the complexity of factors that underlie the dynamics of business networks. This complexity makes these critical factors difficult to map. This difficulty is compounded by the even more important second reason: the effectiveness of a strategic choice has a clear time dimension and the outcomes of a chosen course of action will depend on the future courses of action of others. For example, the future reactions of competitors and customers to new technologies and ways of doing business can never be known in advance; they are unknown for these actors themselves. These actors also face a similar predicament themselves. The plans of all the different companies in the network are continuously "in-process". How they will unfold is genuinely unknowable.

We have emphasized that interdependencies impact strongly on the strategy development process. Any strategic choice entails a series of activities, investments and different individuals, functions and companies and these cannot be disconnected from each other. This makes it difficult both to define precisely, at a given time, what decisions are actually strategic and what are all the existing alternatives that have to be taken into account.

Interdependencies mean that the choices of companies are interactive. This is because no company can deploy its own resources and capabilities except in conjunction with those of others. So managers in practice must choose and adopt alternatives depending on the expected reactions of others. Once these reactions become known, they tend to adjust their choices and adapt them to the changed situation. Whatever choice any one actor adopts reflects the choices of a counterpart. Coping with problems in a business relationship leads to solving problems jointly, in interaction. This produces continuous adaptations to the actions and reactions of others. As we repeatedly observe, these actions and reactions occur under time constraints and with incomplete information. They involve continuous reading and interpreting of a situation and adapting to and influencing each other.

Interdependence between companies means that in reality the strategy process is interactive, evolutionary and responsive, even if those involved believe themselves to be masters of their own destiny. "Strategy deals not just with the unpredictable, but the unknowable. No analyst could predict the precise ways in which all impinging forces could

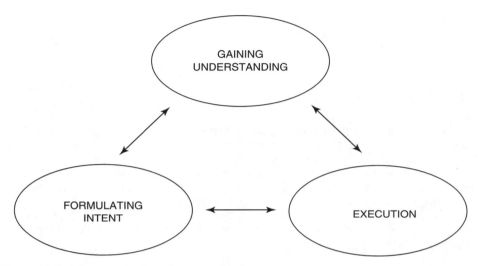

Figure 10.6   The organic view of strategy development.

interact with each other, be distorted by nature or human emotions, or be modified by the imaginations and purposeful counteractions of intelligent opponents."[10]

These features that are typical of business networks make the rationalistic approach to strategic choices problematic. This is because no amount of analysis is likely to resolve the inherent uncertainty. There are no given moments in the flow of choices that are intrinsically strategic and insistence on implementing a predetermined course of action would preclude the possibility of adapting to changing circumstances. The rationalistic logic does not represent the reality of the strategy management process in business networks.

Instead, the strategy management process in business networks appears to follow what we might term an "organic logic" illustrated in Figure 10.6. The choices underlying strategy, the "What", "Who" and "How", emerge in the continuous interplay between three types of processes in the company that occur in parallel. These are as follows:

- **Gaining understanding:** Companies have to engage in continuous interpretation of the context in which they operate. This process is based on information and data and its purpose is to gain an understanding of how the context is actually working. The primary purpose of analysis in business markets is to arrive at a set of workable assumptions about how the network operates, how it develops and how companies react in it. In these circumstances, being able to recognize patterns of behaviour offers guidance for how a company should act and react. Gaining understanding involves formulating assumptions about how companies react, what they value, what needs to be done to develop problem-solving and transfer abilities and how it can be done. This task is

[10] JB Quinn (1988) Strategies for Change, in JB Quinn and H Mintzberg, *The Strategy Process*, New York, Prentice-Hall.

continuous and not linked to particular moments in which decisions are taken. The process of gaining understanding is not a picture but a plot. This approach is nicely illustrated in Box 10.2.

Box 10.2 Japanese Success[11]

"Their success, as any Japanese automotive executive will tell, did not result from a bold insight by a few big brains at the top. On the contrary, success was achieved by senior managers humble enough not to take their initial strategic positions too seriously. What saved Japan's near failures was the cumulative impact of 'little brains' in the form of salesmen and dealers and production workers, all contributing incrementally to the quality and market position these companies enjoy today. Middle and upper management saw their primary tasks as guiding and orchestrating this input from below rather than steering the organization from above along a predetermined strategic course."

- **Formulating intent:** It is important to spell out in which direction the strategy of a company should develop along the three dimensions of content: "Who", "What" and "How". Without intent a company lacks the basic criteria for allocating and coordinating resources and activities of the operations. Making intent explicit, even if by necessity it is based on assumptions about the future, provides guidance as to how to react to events, such as to changes in the demands or requirements of customers. Formulating intent identifies a preferred future state, rather than the most likely future. This preferred state cannot be fully decided or specified. At the same time, formulating intent is more than setting quantitative goals or targets, or extrapolations from a current situation. To serve the purpose of coordination and criteria for taking decisions, a formulation of intent has to convey meaning, be understood throughout the organization, to be "what everybody knows".[12] Companies attempt to achieve this through vision or mission statements. These statements are only effective if they relate closely to the reality that the company faces. They must also express an intent that is achievable, is communicated and understood throughout the company, and is followed through by action.
- **Execution:** Acting in business networks, which consists of *interacting* in relationships, entails purposeful and planned acts. But also, and most importantly, it involves reacting to the signals from and requirements of customers. Behaviours, actions and reactions are the substance that makes things happen and produces results. Executing activities is

---

[11] *Source*: RT Pascale (1994) Perspectives on Strategy: the Real Story behind Honda's success, *California Management Review*, vol xxvi.

[12] I Nonaka (1991) The Knowledge Creating Company, *Harvard Business Review*, November–December, 96–104.

a necessary condition of achieving effect and possibly desirable outcomes. Consistency in behaviour is important in relationships because it impacts on outcomes and makes that behaviour intelligible to others. The uncertain and interactive nature of business relationships means that the way that the individuals involved in them react reflects how they frame, assess and interpret a situation. Their reactions are based to a large extent on convictions rooted in their past experiences that have been translated into their own rules of behaviour. Execution is thus dependent on generating action.

It is important in the organic logic of the strategy development process in business networks that the three processes of gaining understanding, formulating intent and execution are parallel and mutually interdependent. Gaining understanding is linked to executing action but execution, in particular in reaction, cannot wait for understanding. In most situations, it is one of the consequences of interaction in business relationships that companies must decide and act on partial and incomplete information. The set of actionable assumptions about how others will behave and about the consequences of that behaviour is the only guidance available to managers. This understanding often follows action that has been executed by a company and its experience of the outcomes from it. Gaining understanding involves continuous evaluation of the outcomes of actions against a purpose or intent. This process amounts to "learning-by-doing", or trying different approaches and then being ready to correct them when needed. Acting in this way may lead to new goals as well as to new ways of reaching them. Recurrent evaluation and interpretation of experience are critical for understanding how the business network works.

Formulating intent is based on the partial understanding that comes from the execution. Intent focuses the learning and hence influences the understanding that will be gained. Companies in business networks face a complex set of choices underlying marketing strategy and no-one in the company will have a full picture of what is or will be needed. What appears as a strategic decision is but an indication of an intended direction to be tried out. Intent allows for adjustments and reformulation. A formulation of the content of a desired strategy is at best an expression of intent about direction of change. Execution cannot be reduced to prescription or control of behaviours. It is not taken care of by taking strategic decisions or by attempts to implement a formulaic programme. Instead, execution is the outcome of the organizational culture of those who interact in business relationships and of criteria that stem from strategic intent and from ideas that have emerged from previous actions. "A strategy is the pattern or plan that integrates an organization's major goals, policies, and action sequences into a cohesive whole. A well formulated strategy helps to marshal and allocate an organization's resources into a unique and viable posture based on its relative internal competencies and shortcomings, anticipated changes in the environment and contingent moves by intelligent opponents".[13]

---

[13] JB Quinn, Strategies for Change (1988) in JB Quinn and H Mintzberg, *The Strategy Process*, New York, Prentice Hall.

An example of this is provided by Honda, after it was overtaken by Yamaha as Japan's number one motorcycle producer. Honda responded with the formulation of intent:

Yamaha so tsubu su!

We will crush, squash and slaughter Yamaha!

Honda implemented this by launching 81 new products in 18 months. This massive effort nearly bankrupted the company, but it did regain market leadership.[14]

The organic logic of the strategy development process in business networks affects the nature of the task of strategy management and the role of top management. It means changing focus away from discrete strategic decisions and it points to the interplay of the three processes through which the choices with respect to strategy content emerge.

Management's Role in Strategy Development

The task of managing strategy is properly that of senior management and it involves responsibility for the three processes we have outlined in the organic model, above. In this view, the role of senior management is less about making the decisions about the choices involved in strategy. Instead, it is more about ensuring that the choices being made by middle management produce the desired performance and add up to an effective strategy. The critical role for senior management is thus to support the three processes and to ensure consistent conditions for those making the operative choices.

The behaviour of individuals in a company is guided by how the situations they meet are framed and interpreted. These individual interpretations can be inconsistent and conflicting. Directing the behaviour of individuals involves working towards consistency in the way that the context and the situations that arise in a business network are framed. Much of the responsibility of managing marketing strategy is organizational, in the sense of directing attention and action through various tools of organizing. Management studies have identified several "tools" that management can use to direct attention and interpretation of the context. These ultimately represent ways to manage strategy. A common framework is the one illustrated in Figure 10.7, as follows:

- Formulating a desired *strategy* offers criteria against which to evaluate the alternatives met in operations.
- Organizational *structure* specifies accountability and directs attention of different roles.
- Management control and support *systems* impact on what is measured, believed and thus taken into account in making choices.
- The individual *skills* and abilities of those in the company affect the way to frame situations and devise solutions.

[14] Steve Brown, Kate Blackmon, Paul Cousins and Harvey Maylor (2001) *Operations Management*, Oxford, Butterworth-Heinemann, p 41.

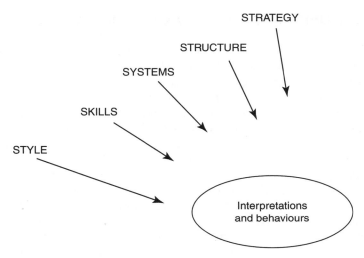

Figure 10.7   Tools of management.

Source: TJ Peters and R H Waterman (1982) *In Search of Excellence: Lessons from America's Best Run Companies*, New York, Harper & Row.

- The *style* of management or management culture offers norms and values that especially in an uncertain context offer guidance on how to act.

The role of strategic *planning* is also affected by the features of the strategy development process. Strategic planning has an important role to play in strategy development but it has to be consistent with the organic logic of the process. Strategic planning is important beyond the plans it produces. Plans have two functions: first, they are a way to express and to communicate the company's strategic intent, more or less explicitly; second, they serve as a coordinating mechanism. Quantifiable plans are needed in order to coordinate the activities of different parts of the company, such as marketing and sales with production, research and development, purchasing and human resource management, etc. Plans are thus a base on which to coordinate various activities throughout the company but are not a road-map to desired performance. They cannot be a blueprint for strategy. The dynamics of business networks will make any blueprint obsolete in a short time and subject to adaptations and change. The value of strategic market planning lies primarily in learning about how the context works and outlining alternative solutions for coping with it. Planning serves two purposes: the first purpose is learning, ie gaining understanding in a more systematic way. The second purpose is attention arousal and diffusion of understanding throughout the company's organization. Planning helps a company to focus on issues that cannot be solved for the moment but that need to be monitored and dealt with in the future. What is often overlooked is that one of the main outcomes of planning is the listing of unresolved problems for which effective solutions are not in place.

Final Considerations: Strategy Content and Process

The characteristics of business networks bring to the foreground the interdependence of the process and content of strategy. Ready-made opportunities do not exist in business networks. But opportunities can be created if ideas are developed alongside the capabilities to construct and exploit them. Consequently, effective strategy in business networks originates in the capacity of a company to sense and understand the network in which it operates and to work for and through its various actors: customers, suppliers and others. The development of an effective marketing strategy involves finding and enacting new and more effective ways to organize the company's own and others' activities and resources. In that sense, strategy in business networks has a collective dimension.

The content of a strategy will be effective if it represents a novel or improved solution to customers' problems. But no successful strategy content remains a novel solution for long. This is not necessarily because of competitive action, but because no solution is ever the ultimate one and also because the problem for which it was developed will change or disappear. Thus, effective strategy content is a moving target. It requires the relentless search for further development and this is linked to the effectiveness of the strategy process itself. In this way, the content of strategy follows the process of its development.

Marketing strategies in business networks will always be an outcome of how a company organizes itself to monitor and induce change and to innovate in relation to its customers. This is why we have emphasized in this chapter that the primary purpose of strategic management is not to outline a blueprint for strategy, but to ensure continuous monitoring of possibilities and formulation of ideas to be developed. The critical issue is the configuration of the company's interface with its customers and the specification of internal and external resources that need to converge to produce the desired effects for it. Business marketers must manage the processes of individual and collective learning, beyond that of simply gathering and distributing information. The models suggested in this chapter are one way for a company to "read" the network around it. Top management must ensure that this process of reading is systematic and involves all those who can contribute to its interpretation and to consequent action.

Elsewhere, we have argued that the strategy development process in business networks needs to take into account three *paradoxes*[15] of those networks, as follows:

- **Firstly:** A company's relationships are at the same time both assets and liabilities. They are the basis of its current activities and future possibilities but at the same time they restrict the range of those possibilities. This means that in developing its strategy a company has to manage the choice of *conforming* to some of these restrictions and *confronting* others in order to achieve change.
- **Secondly:** A company's relationships are the outcome of purposive action taken by the company. But at the same time, a company is the outcome of its relationships. Therefore in developing its strategy a company has to balance the *conservation* of its current

---

[15] ID Ford, L-E Gadde, H Håkansson and I Snehota (2003) *Managing Business Relationships*, 2nd edition, Chichester: John Wiley & Sons, Ltd, pp 200–201.

position in the network in which it is involved and of the *creation* of a new position within a changed network of relationships.

- **Finally:** All companies strive to achieve some degree of influence and control over the network of which they are a part. But achieving that control generates friction and confrontation and restricts initiative by others in the network. Complete control by any one company would eliminate initiative by others. Therefore, in developing its strategy a company has to balance the extent to which it will seek to *coerce* others in the direction of its choice or to *concede* to their aims, abilities and understanding.

Finding the right balance in these three dimensions will affect the scope and content of a company's strategy in the network and the norms and values that inspire its approach to the strategy development process.

Further Reading

J Dyer and H Singh (1998) The Relational View: Cooperative Strategy and Sources of Inter-Organisational Competitive Advantage, *Academy of Management Review*, vol 23, no 4, 660–679.

L-E Gadde, L Huemer and H Håkansson (2003) Strategising in Industrial Networks, *Industrial Marketing Management*, vol 32, no 5, 357–364.

R Gulati, N Nohria and A Zaheer (2000) Strategic Networks, *Strategy Management Journal*, vol 21, no 4, 203–215.

Gary Hamel (2000) *Leading the Revolution*, Boston, Harvard Business School Press.

W Chan Kim and Renee Mauborgne (2005) *Blue Ocean Strategy*, Boston, Harvard Business School Press.

Henry Mintzberg (1996) Five P's for Strategy, in Henry Mintzberg and James Brian Quinn (eds), *The Strategy Process*, 3rd edition, New York, Prentice-Hall.

Henry Mintzberg (1998) Generic Strategies: Toward a Comprehensive Framework, *Advances in Strategic Management*, vol 5, Greenwich, CT, JAI Press, pp 1–67.

Kenichi Ohmae (1989) The Global Logic of Strategic Alliances, *Harvard Business Review*, March–April, 143–154.

RT Pascale (1994) Perspectives on Strategy: The Real Story behind Honda's Success, *California Management Review*, vol XXVI, 47–72.

Michael Porter (1996) What is Strategy?, *Harvard Business Review*, November–December, 61–78.

James Brian Quinn (1980) *Strategies for Change: Logical Incrementalism*, New York, Irwin.

Assignment for Chapter 10

Marketing strategy at Airslash

As the newly appointed Group Marketing Director for Airslash you have been carrying out an exercise to help you learn about the company and its operations and to try to apply some creative thinking. You have investigated a number of actual and potential customers and examined the problems that Airslash could perhaps solve for them. You have also tried to think through what type of relationship and offering would be needed for these customers, and you have also investigated some of the operational issues in implementing an offering.

You now have to prepare for the Chief Executive's "Strategy Retreat" which has just been announced for the coming weekend! Because the Chief Executive wants the company to be "marketing-led", she wants you to start the meeting with your views on strategy for the company.

Prepare a paper that you will use as a basis for your speech. You should use the experience that you have gained in examining problems, offerings and implementation to highlight some broad strategic issues for the company. In particular you should examine issues surrounding the range of customers, relationships and offerings in the company and the operational issues that it faces. You may use any assumptions necessary to complete your analysis, provided that you make those assumptions explicit.[15]

[15] Note: The Airslash assignments were developed from an original idea of Professor David Gillingham's of Coventry University. Many thanks.

INDEX

Note: Page references in *italics* refer to figures.